Action Learning

for Developing Leaders and Organizations

Action Learning

for Developing Leaders and Organizations

PRINCIPLES, STRATEGIES, and CASES

Michael J. Marquardt, H. Skipton Leonard,
Arthur M. Freedman, and Claudia C. Hill

AMERICAN PSYCHOLOGICAL ASSOCIATION
WASHINGTON, DC

Published by
American Psychological Association
750 First Street, NE
Washington, DC 20002
www.apa.org

To order
APA Order Department
P.O. Box 92984
Washington, DC 20090-2984
Tel: (800) 374-2721; Direct: (202) 336-5510
Fax: (202) 336-5502; TDD/TTY: (202) 336-6123
Online: www.apa.org/books/
E-mail: order@apa.org

In the U.K., Europe, Africa, and the Middle East, copies may be ordered from
American Psychological Association
3 Henrietta Street
Covent Garden, London
WC2E 8LU England

Typeset in Meridien by Circle Graphics, Columbia, MD

Printer: United Book Press, Baltimore, MD
Cover Designer: Berg Design, Albany, NY
Technical/Production Editor: Kathryn Funk

The opinions and statements published are the responsibility of the authors, and such opinions and statements do not necessarily represent the policies of the American Psychological Association.

Library of Congress Cataloging-in-Publication Data

Action learning for developing leaders and organizations : principles, strategies, and cases / Michael J. Marquardt . . . [et al.]. — 1st ed.
        p. cm.
  Includes bibliographical references and index.
  ISBN-13: 978-1-4338-0435-9
  ISBN-10: 1-4338-0435-2
  1. Organizational learning 2. Active learning. 3. Organizational learning—Case studies. 4. Active learning—Case studies. I. Marquardt, Michael J.

  HD58.82.A327 2009
  658.3'124—dc22
                                        2008040491

British Library Cataloguing-in-Publication Data
A CIP record is available from the British Library.

Printed in the United States of America
First Edition

Contents

III

Preface

The four coauthors of this book discovered Action Learning at different times and in different places over the past 14 years. Yet, each of us quickly recognized the immense power and potential of this amazing tool. We saw Action Learning not only as a great driver for organizational, group, and individual change but also as a tool that used a process that was respectful, humane, and caring. We saw that great results could be achieved with great compassion. We also quickly witnessed how this tool could effectively work in every culture and in every type of organization.

Over the past 14 years, we have had opportunities to share our passion for Action Learning with hundreds of organizations and thousands of people in every part of the world—Africa, Asia, Europe, Australia, and the Americas. Action Learning never becomes unexciting to us because it is so vibrant, so powerful, so helpful.

Being academics and practitioners, we have been able to continually test, improve, and increase the speed and power of Action Learning. We have created the World Institute for Action Learning and, together with affiliates around the world, seek to share our learnings and experiences with others via forums, research, publications, and training.

Writing this book has been both a labor of love as well as a learning experience. We have searched through the literature and the stories of Action Learning, we have challenged each other, and we have asked challenging questions so that we could paint the picture of Action Learning that we have witnessed.

We owe a debt of gratitude to many people who have helped us along this Action Learning journey, beginning with Reg Revans, the father of Action Learning, who inspired us with his stories and insights. Other Action Learning giants on whose shoulders we have stood in our quest to understand and apply Action Learning include Lex Dilworth, Michael Pedler, Victoria Marsick, Joe Raelin, Katy Cashera, Karen Cowan, Richard Swanson, Marc Sokol, Bill Clover, Judy O'Neill, Yuri Boscyk, Rob Kramer, and Alan Mumford. A special thanks is given to Rob Kaiser, who offered invaluable counsel and suggestions with respect to the chapter on evidence for Action Learning.

We wish to acknowledge Action Learning leaders around the world who have helped build the World Institute for Action Learning— Chuck Appleby, Bea Carson, Ng Choon Seng, Fumiyo Seimiya, Garry Luxmoore, Herman van Niekerk, Florence Ho, Taebok Lee, Myoung Sook Choi, and Antony Hii.

Writing a book is like having a temporary family member living with you who requires lots of time and attention. We would like to express our thanks to our families, especially Eveline Marquardt, Faith Leonard, and Doug Hill, for their patience and support and to ask for their forgiveness for any neglect while we worked on this project.

Finally, we wish to thank our readers for granting us the opportunity to share our story, our dreams, and our love for Action Learning. May it assist, guide, and inspire you to take this tool to develop yourselves and your organizations.

Michael J. Marquardt
George Washington University &
World Institute for Action
Learning

H. Skipton Leonard
Carey School of Business,
Johns Hopkins University &
World Institute for Action
Learning

Arthur M. Freedman
Carey School of Business,
Johns Hopkins University &
World Institute for Action
Learning

Claudia C. Hill
Personnel Decisions International
University of Minnesota

Introduction

Although Action Learning (AL) as a methodology has been around for more than half a century (and traces its roots back several millennia, at least to Socrates), its popularity has dramatically increased in the last 10 years. Today, most leadership development programs for "high potentials" in the United States and in global corporations include an AL component. Many countries in Asia have enthusiastically embraced AL, including Korea, where almost every major corporation is using AL. A major American business magazine, *Business Week*, identified AL as "the latest and fastest growing organizational tool for leadership development" (Byrnes, 2005, p. 71).

One reason why AL is gaining such traction as a leadership development strategy is that it is so effective in developing the kinds of leadership skills that are most needed in contemporary organizations. For instance, although leadership development programs typically stress the need to develop the ability to work collaboratively with team organizational members, they struggle to find ways to help participants actually develop, practice, gain feedback, and refine these skills. AL develops the ability to collaborate, partner, share, and follow as well as lead naturally through the process of solving real and complex organizational issues. In addition to learning how to collaborate, participants experience firsthand the value of being better team and organizational partners. AL, as a leadership development strategy, is unique in its capability to improve performance and competency in virtually all leadership skill areas. Most leadership development programs teach or demonstrate the value and importance of the various leadership skills. In AL, participants are required to use and develop these skills to improve individual, team, and organizational performance.

Strong communities of AL practice have begun to grow in North America and South America, throughout Europe and Australia, and in the Middle East. Recently, we have received a number of requests from organizations in Africa to use AL to solve the enormous and pressing problems in that continent.

Although the hard research evidence to support the efficacy of AL is encouraging and growing (see chap. 10, this volume), a primary reason why AL is experiencing such large growth is because the results from AL projects have been so dramatic and tangible. The universal appeal of AL stems from the dual outputs of the process: Organizations get innovative solutions to pressing problems at the same time that AL dramatically improves the capabilities of individuals, teams, and organizations to solve problems for which there is no known solution or the current solutions are unacceptable.

Action Learning Core Principles and Goals for This Book

> There can be no action without learning, and no learning without action. (Revans, 1998, p. 14)

The central premise that forms the basis for AL is that people learn much more rapidly when they are put into action solving problems. Most of us recognize this simple reality because of our life experiences. Although "book learning" (including audio and video tapes, Webinars, and many, if not most, training programs/seminars) is certainly useful and sometimes necessary for solving problems, these sorts of "programmed learning" approaches often result in limited and temporary learning. On the other hand, "thoughtless" action generally results in an overreliance on habit and routine that limits creativity and encourages the application of older, "tried-and-true" solutions when a more innovative approach is necessary to address problems and situations never encountered before.

So, although programmed learning and action are necessary conditions for rapid learning and the development of creative and innovative solutions, they are not sufficient. People need to reflect on what they are doing and, in particular, assess the impact of their actions; they need to examine what is working, what actions can be improved, and what they will do differently in the future. Reg Revans (1992), the acknowledged creator of AL, believed that active questioning was a necessary ingredient in all learning. Ask yourself, can you think of any learning that you gained to an important problem that wasn't preceded by a question or series of questions (other than learning not to touch a hot stove again!—this kind of learning is addressed in chap. 3)?

A number of authors (Marquardt, 1999; Pedlar, 1996; Yorks, O'Neil, & Marsick, 2002) have extended Revans's (1992) model to provide the following paradigm for facilitating rapid and efficient learning:

$$L(\text{learning}) = P(\text{programmed knowledge}) + Q(\text{questions}) + R(\text{reflection})$$

This relationship can be seen as the basis for the process and success of AL. This book provides the current state of the art for operationalizing AL. In this book, you will learn

- why AL is so appropriate for developing leaders for the organizations of today and tomorrow;
- how to structure learning in small teams with simple ground rules and a trained coach;
- how to effectively coach AL teams;
- how to develop great questions that are appropriate to the stage of problem solving and team development;
- how to effectively manage an AL program and embed the process within the larger organization and larger developmental programming;
- how to use the principles of AL in other developmental and problem-solving settings;
- the key theoretical underpinnings of AL as a tool for personal, team, and organizational learning; and
- how research evidence supports AL as an effective method for building leaders and organizations.

Here is a brief case example that demonstrates both the value of and potential for using AL to solve important and complex problems.

The Pizza Man Delivers Fresh Questions Worth $35 Million
An engineering consulting firm was commissioned to develop an innovative, cost-cutting process for a government department and quickly established a task force to work on the problem. The team leader (Bill) introduced the group to AL and encouraged the engineers and scientists to use this approach. Progress, however, was slow and new breakthrough ideas were not emerging. And the final project was due within a week.

One day, as group members were working late into the evening, they decided to order out for pizza so they could continue wrestling with the project for a couple more hours. When the pizza man arrived, Bill made a startling request. Noting that his group was composed only of internal engineers who had similar experiences and viewpoints, he decided that some different outside fresh perspective was needed. "How about joining us for the next hour and earn a big tip?" he asked the pizza man. "We will check with your boss and get his approval. All you need to do is listen to what we are doing. If there is anything that you do not understand or if you see wall charts that don't make sense to you, all you have to do is ask questions." This sounded good to the pizza man, although one can imagine the surprise and frustration felt by Bill's colleagues, who probably muttered, "We have only a couple more days to work on this project, and now we are going to waste an hour with a pizza man!?"

The pizza man sat down. After several minutes of listening and observing, he decided he would have to earn his tip. He noticed a chart on the wall and asked why an arrow went from point A to F. A disgruntled group member gave a reason, but then another member said "no, here is another better reason." A third member chimed in, "Well, if the second reason is okay, why don't we simply go from point A to point D?" The group realized that the pizza man's "dumb" question had caused them to examine some unchallenged statements and assumptions they all had been making.

After the pizza man left, the group began with clear sheets of paper and a determination to look outside the box. Over the next couple days, they incorporated many new ideas that emerged from the "fresh" questions of the pizza man. Their breakthrough project was submitted to the government, which resulted in a $35 million savings over the life of the contract. Thanks to the pizza man! (Marquardt, 2004, p. 57)

Why Another Book on Action Learning?

There are many fine texts available on the process of AL coaching. In fact, several of us have previously authored books that describe the process of AL in some detail (Hill, Leonard, & Sokol, 2006; Marquardt, 1999, 2004). In addition to describing the latest methodology in AL coaching practice, this book fills several glaring needs in the AL literature. First, along with describing in great detail how to conduct AL sessions, we have tried to educate the reader with respect to how and why AL works. Examining the process through the lens of the disciplines of psychology, education, organization development, and management makes it clear why the process works so well. The AL practice that we advocate in this book is consistently aligned with the best practice principles that have been developed through decades of research in the areas of brain physiology, learning theory, education, social psychology and sociology, organizational psychology and organization development, and management science.

We do not claim that AL was developed through reasoned application of all these disciplines. Rather, the methodology described and advocated in this book was developed empirically by asking the simple yet profound questions that any person trying to improve performance asks (or should ask)—what is working, what can be improved, and, on the basis of this analysis, what will we do differently in the future? As social scientists and educators, we have tried to use accepted principles from the disciplines above to explain and understand why this powerful process works. We find many explanations for the power of AL that are consistent with what we know about how people, teams, and organizations learn. This is gratifying. Ultimately, however, disciplined research involving the development and testing of hypotheses needs to be conducted to confirm the causal links between the various theoretical principles and the success of AL.

The need for further research in this field points to a second gap that this book addresses. In chapter 10, we present the evidence that is currently available on the efficacy of AL as well as the various mechanisms and principles that determine the success or failure of an AL process. Although the research in this area is somewhat of a "tough read," we have resisted the urge to treat it in a superficial or simplistic manner. Much of the research is based on doctoral dissertations that possess more rigor than readability. We trust that readers who commit to "plowing through" this literature will find it very useful in their efforts to discuss, explain, and promote AL authoritatively. To our knowledge, this is the first major book to provide a comprehensive review of the AL literature.

A third gap that we address is the lack of a rigorous discussion of AL as an organizational intervention. Anyone who has conducted an AL program understands that the process is a systemic organizational intervention. Successful AL programming requires practitioners to look at the process through the lens of organization development and consultation practice. We devote several chapters to describing the organization development aspects of AL and proposing best practices in embedding the program in the organizational process. This involves working and consulting with senior management and project sponsors as well as asking the kinds of great questions of AL teams that will encourage them to reflect upon larger, systemic aspects of work and solutions.

This book addresses some important gaps in our understanding of why questions that promote reflection have such power. In chapter 3, we note the potential that AL has to make critical reflection a way of working, thereby increasing both the quality and quantity of learning. How does this occur? When reflection is associated with action, the link between emotion, cognition, and the human spirit is forged. In that forging, a special type of energy is released. That energy fuels the curiosity required to break away from "tried and failed" practices and fans the courage required to explore the untried. It engages a learner in an experience that is so unlike the day-to-day entropy of organizational life that a new freedom emerges, the freedom to ask questions that do not have ready answers. This freedom to explore the unknown underlies the core competence of an effective life-long and self-directed learner. In a number of chapters, we explore the role of reflective dialogue and the power of questions. Ultimately, the enduring legacy of an AL experience is seen in the improved capacity of its participants to learn, and learning begins when a question is asked.

Finally, we discuss AL within a broader set of management and developmental activities. We describe how AL can be integrated with other leadership development programming and strategies as well as how the principles and strategies of AL can be applied to many other organizational settings, such as individual coaching, team meetings, strategic planning sessions, supervision meetings, team facilitation, and so on. We hold that the basic $L = P + Q + R$ model can be successfully applied to many other settings that have the goal of performance improvement. As we make clear in chapter 2, although the principles undergirding AL can be applied to a great many team or interpersonal problems, AL as a rigorous methodology should be limited to situations in which it is appropriate.

Who Will Find This Book Valuable?

We have written this book to appeal to a number of audiences. Practicing AL coaches, of course, will find this book useful in increasing their understanding of the process as well as improving their skill in asking great questions that are aligned with the stage of problem solving or the particular group dynamic (see chap. 5, this volume) that is involving the team. Experienced coaches will also appreciate the extensive discussion of organizational issues (see chap. 7) that are facing or will face them in the AL coaching programs.

Professionals who are or will be managing AL programs will find the discussion of how to embed their programs in the organizational fabric (see chap. 7) invaluable. Training and development professionals who are responsible for larger leadership development programs will appreciate the discussion of how to integrate AL into larger leadership development programs (chap. 8). Managers and leaders who have a general understanding of AL but need to understand "what goes on under the hood" before investing money, time, and resources in an AL program will find this book to be very useful as a resource.

The depth of discussion and the extensive treatment of theory and research make this an ideal book to use as a main text in university courses that cover AL as well as leadership development. This would be an excellent text for the many colleges and universities around the world that are including AL in their curricula. College and university professors will find the treatment of these topics appropriate at the graduate level as well as for advanced undergraduate students. Students looking for resources and ideas for their theses and dissertations will be attracted to this book.

Because of the rapid growth of AL in organizations around the world, organizational consultants who need to demonstrate their comprehensive and in-depth understanding and skill in AL in order to earn credibility with clients will want to have thoroughly read this book and have it on their shelves for reference. Executive coaches who extend their practice to team coaching will find that the techniques and methods presented in this volume will mesh nicely with the approach and methods they use in their individual practices (chap. 9). Many executive coaches have remarked to us that the concepts, values, and practices in AL augment and improve their one-on-one coaching effectiveness. After all, the practices and principles that work in improving performance in teams will also work with individuals.

Road Map for the Book

This text is logically organized into three parts: Part I: Foundations of Action Learning; Part II: Implementing Action Learning; and Part III: Best Practices From the Present to the Future.

PART I: FOUNDATIONS OF ACTION LEARNING

This section presents the theoretical underpinning of AL as well as the principles and methods of practice that we believe are most effective for improving performance and facilitating learning at the individual, team, and organizational levels.

Chapter 1 demonstrates the need for leaders to become better learners and for organizations to become truly learning organizations. Further, the chapter makes the case for AL as the best and most powerful option for developing leaders and organizations.

Chapter 2 presents the six necessary and sufficient elements for effective AL as well as simple yet profound ground rules that give AL such flexibility and power. The chapter also examines the role of questioning, reflection, and active dialogue in AL.

Chapter 3 examines the process of learning in AL and discusses how the theories and principles developed in the disciplines of psychology, education, organization development, and management support and explain the power of the AL process. Using paradigms that have been useful in organizational and personal change disciplines, chapter 3 also examines the change process that occurs in AL.

Chapter 4 explores the power of AL to develop leaders and leadership skills. This chapter demonstrates how AL can be effective in developing all of the leadership competencies generally targeted in leadership development programs.

Because the art of asking great questions to promote reflection and learning is so central to the process of AL, chapter 5 examines in considerable depth how coaches can ask questions that are aligned with and tailored to stages of problem solving or team development. The material in this chapter will be invaluable to coaches in diagnosing the issues that bedevil teams so that they can intervene with questions that get the team process unstuck and on the road to improved performance.

PART II: IMPLEMENTING ACTION LEARNING

This section addresses many of the issues that are overlooked and ignored by coaches but that are critical to the success of AL programs. Many of these factors are related to the process of successfully embedding the program in the organization so that it is not a stand-alone and isolated process. Other chapters look at the way AL can be integrated into larger leadership development programs and how the principles of AL can be extended to other management, leadership, or developmental activities.

Chapter 6 examines the other major focus of this book—the power of AL as an organizational change intervention. The reader is introduced to relevant theory and practices from the discipline of organizational development and consultation and is shown how an understanding of organizational change can be useful in enhancing the power of AL as an organizational intervention.

Chapter 7 guides the reader through the process of embedding AL in the organization, which includes selling AL to senior leadership, identifying appropriate problems, structuring and populating AL teams, identifying and training sponsors, and ensuring and maintaining organizational support for the program. This chapter also addresses alternative program structure and coaching models as well as the increasingly frequent use of "virtual" teaming using technology to span distance and time zones.

AL is often just one component of a larger leadership development process. Chapter 8 addresses how AL can be used successfully to complement and augment other leadership development strategies commonly used by organizations. Several interesting case studies are supplied to demonstrate how this integration has been successfully implemented.

Chapter 9 discusses how the principles and values that are used successfully in AL can be applied to positive effect in other leadership, management, and developmental activities, such as executive and individual coaching, team meetings, team facilitation, strategic planning sessions, one-on-one discussions and supervisory feedback meetings, and individual problem solving.

PART III: BEST PRACTICES FROM THE PRESENT TO THE FUTURE

This section begins by addressing what is currently known about AL from research evidence to best practices. The final chapter represents a vision from a number of perspectives regarding the future for AL.

Chapter 10 discusses research related to AL within the evidence-based practice model. This chapter not only discusses evidence for whether AL is an effective strategy for solving problems and developing leaders and organizations but also presents data, mostly exploratory in nature, on the "active ingredients" or mediating variables that determine whether the AL process works.

Chapter 11 presents the major steps or phases in the AL process and provides best practices based on the authors' experiences as well as the research literature. A number of real-world case studies from around the world and representing a variety of applications illustrate how each of the steps was planned and executed.

In chapter 12, readers are invited to look into the future through the perspectives of various stakeholders. In what we might call "social science fiction," readers will hear the predictions of a panel of consumers of AL representing manufacturing and technology global corporations; governmental, nongovernmental, and nonprofit agencies; the United Nations; human resources consulting firms; and universities. We hope that this fictitious account will inspire the reader to dream of what can happen and what he or she can become through the rigorous application of AL practices and principles.

At the end of each chapter (under the heading "Reflection Questions"), instead of providing a synopsis of the key points that readers should remember, we provide a few questions to encourage readers to reflect on what they have just read so that they can capture the learnings that are important and relevant for them (not the authors). This is in keeping with our general philosophy about how people learn best. We provide the programmed learning, but deeper, more profound, and more personalized learning comes through the process of questioning and reflection. We hope that the questions at the end of each chapter facilitate the reflective process.

A Truly Powerful Tool for Developing Leaders and Organizations

AL has quickly become a popular and powerful process for developing great leaders and great organizations in an increasingly complex world. We hope that the theories, principles, and practices presented in this book will enable the reader to realize the magic and wonder of this amazing method.

FOUNDATIONS OF ACTION LEARNING

Leadership and Organizational Change in the 21st Century

1

O rganizational and business leaders today fail at an alarming rate. Recent studies have indicated that 40% of new leaders fail within the first 18 months of promotion or appointment (Ciampa, 2005; Sessa & Taylor, 2000). Furthermore, the rate of failure seems to be increasing. Challenger, Gray & Christmas, an international outplacement firm, has reported that the turnover rate for chief executive officers (CEOs) in its database nearly doubled from 1999 to 2004. This alarming trend was confirmed when the firm reported that CEO turnover doubled again in 2005. Looking at another measure of the difficulties leaders face, Booz Allen Hamilton, a large management consulting firm, reported that the average tenure of CEOs decreased from 9.5 to 7.6 years between 1995 and 2005. What accounts for this discouraging rate of leadership failure? Primary among the various explanations for the difficulties leaders face is the reality that organizations throughout the world are encountering change at a staggering pace and on an unprecedented scale. Borrowing from the imagery of dangerous, rapids-filled rivers, Vaill (1996) referred to today's organizational environment as *permanent white water*. In order to survive leaders must navigate systems in which the organizational landscape is ever changing, in which events are often unpredictable and chaotic behavior becomes the norm (Stacey, 1992), in which authority is no longer heeded (Cohen

& Bradford, 2005; Helsing, Geraghty, & Napolitano, 2003), and in which the number of key stakeholders and key metrics for success (Kaplan & Norton, 1996) keeps expanding. As a result of these developments in organizational life, contemporary leaders must place as high a priority on learning as on results. The theories about and research on leadership from the mid-20th century onward have increasingly focused on the ability of leaders to learn not only new technical skills and industry-specific knowledge but also relationship skills as well as the expectations and needs of a very diverse group of stakeholders—customers, clients, constituents, employees, followers, markets (e.g., labor, financial, supplier), and even competitors.

Manchester, a firm specializing in leadership development and outplacement, reported survey results that indicated the following reasons for CEO failure:

-   failure to establish a cultural fit (75%),
-   failure to build teamwork with staff and peers (52%),
-   lack of clarity about what their bosses expected (33%), and
-   lack of political savvy regarding internal matters (25%).

These data give further evidence of the steep learning curve that contemporary leaders face as they learn their jobs at the next level of leadership.

The Importance of Learning for Leaders and Organizations

Paralleling the rate of change in the second half of the 20th century and the first years of the 21st, the importance of learning, both individual and organizational, has grown slowly but exponentially over the same time period. Until the mid-20th century, most authorities on leadership assumed that leaders were born, not made. These leaders had specific physical/personality traits and talents that destined them to become great (Carlyle, 1841/2003). Prior to 1950, the following traits and abilities were identified as characteristic of those chosen for leadership roles (Bass, 1990):

-   capacity—intelligence, alertness, verbal facility, originality, and judgment;
-   achievement—scholarship, knowledge, and athletic accomplishment;
-   responsibility—dependability, initiative, persistence, aggressiveness, self-confidence, and the desire to excel;
-   participation—activity, sociability, cooperation, adaptability, and humor; and
-   status—socioeconomic position and popularity.

Note that although many of these traits and abilities are the product of learning, none identify the ability to learn or to promote learning among followers. If people were not born as leaders, they learned most of the important leadership skills by the time they finished their formal education. The Duke of Wellington was said to have exclaimed that "the battle of Waterloo was won on the playing fields of Eton."[1]

An awareness of the importance of the ability to learn as a core leadership competency developed slowly as the world emerged from the postindustrial era (Leonard, 2003). During the 1950s and 1960s, management science emphasized the importance of setting clear goals and direction (Drucker, 1954/2006; Odiorne, 1965) as well as the ability to successfully manage the negotiation of financial and social rewards to maintain employee motivation and engagement (Adams, 1963; Homans, 1961; House, 1971). Herzberg (1968/2003) added an important dimension to the transactional process by demonstrating that some job factors (achievement, recognition, work itself, responsibility, advancement) were more effective as "motivators" than were other factors (company policy and administration, supervision, relationship with supervisor, work conditions, salary) that were often associated with job dissatisfaction but had limited ability to engage employees' intrinsic or personal motivation. The ability to motivate employees required managers and supervisors to spend time with them to learn what was important to them.

It also became apparent during this time period that the traditional directive, "command and control" leadership style had significant limitations in many situations. A number of thought leaders introduced situation leadership models that recommended applying different leadership behaviors or styles depending on the situation. In some situations, the traditional directive and task-focused style worked best, whereas in other situations a more relationship-focused and participative style was more effective. These observations introduced the notion of best "fit" between a leader's behavior and the leadership requirements that he or she faced (Chemers, 1997; Fiedler, 1964; Hersey & Blanchard, 1977). In a situational leadership model, managers and supervisors could no longer use one leadership style in every situation. Leaders needed to take the time to learn by listening,

---

[1]There is some debate over whether Wellington ever said these words exactly. The quote was published by Montalembert's *De l'Avenir Politique de l'Angleterre*, in 1855, a number of years after the battle of Waterloo. According to Count Montalembert, the Duke of Wellington, returning to Eton in his old age, exclaimed: "It is here that the battle of Waterloo was won." As often happens, the "playing fields" part of the quotation was added later for emphasis. Whatever Wellington's actual words, this quote emphasizes the importance of earlier school learning in the development of leadership skills.

questioning, dialoguing, and debating in the process of analyzing situational requirements.

Influenced by James McGregor Burns's seminal book on leadership, *Leadership* (1978), the next generation of thought leaders touted the ability to convey an inspirational and challenging vision and mission (Bennis, 2000; Bennis & Nanus, 1985; Kouzes & Posner, 1995) as the way to leverage the intrinsic motivators described by Herzberg (1968/2003) and referred to by McGregor (1960) in his Theory Y model for leadership and management. When leaders provided vision, passion, and caring for the development of employees, they were able to "supercharge" performance by evoking personal commitment and dedication in addition to the motivation provided by traditional extrinsic incentives, such as pay, promotion, status, and benefits (Bass & Avolio, 1990). Lowe, Kroeck, and Sivasubraniam (1996) persuasively demonstrated that leaders with vision who understood how to link employee goals for personal growth, achievement, and altruism with the organizational mission were much more successful in driving "transformational" change than were leaders who primarily relied on a "transactional" approach. To inspire individuals and teams to reach peak performance, managers needed to pay as much attention to learning what was important to organizational members—their values, interests, passions—as to learning what was important to customers and competitors.

Adding to the complexity and confusion about what makes for good leadership, the 1990s ushered in a new class of leadership behaviors and a new leadership buzzword, *empowerment*. New communication and data management technology typified by the Internet, networked computers (e.g., corporate Intranets, Enterprise Resource Plannings, Customer Relationship Managements), e-mail, project management software and groupware tools, relational databases, and telephonic and video conferences allowed companies to significantly "flatten" their organizational structure, outsource work to sites across the globe, and create lean global work teams that functioned 24/7. Close supervision became a thing of the past as the span of management control and distance between managers and employees increased dramatically. In these organizational environments, leaders needed to learn how to be more empowering, leading by example and providing the resources that would enable employees to be self-managing, self-leading, and collaborative (Bandura, 1986; Greenleaf, Vaill, & Spears, 1998; Manz & Sims, 2001).

The diffusion of responsibility for leadership necessary in contemporary, technology-rich organizations has shifted the focus from traditional, hierarchical leader–follower models to more lateral, collaborative, and shared approaches to leadership (Pearce & Conger, 2003). Pearce et al. (2003), using a factor analytic design, persuasively demonstrated that the four distinct leadership approaches described earlier (directive, transactional, transformational, and empowering) are indeed used by CEOs in contemporary organizations. Pearce and Sims (2002) also demonstrated that high-performing teams display more lateral, collaborative, and power-sharing leadership behaviors among team members than do lower performing teams.

These comparatively recent studies have provided empirical recognition for a trend that most organizational members, both employees and supervisors, have been experiencing for a number of years. The traditional hierarchical, top-down, and directive approaches to leadership are being supplanted by more lateral, collaborative, shared, and team-based approaches. Although this trend is especially apparent in the world of information work, it is also popular in manufacturing, in which self-directed work teams are used (Fisher, 1999).

The Case for Action Learning

It should be clear from the previous discussion that in contemporary organizations, all employees, not just managers, need to learn effective leadership skills. This is especially true if the organization uses teams to solve difficult and complex problems. We propose that Action Learning (AL) is ideally suited not only to solve problems but also to develop the kind of leadership skills that are needed in contemporary organizations.

In AL, a diverse team uses a problem-solving methodology that emphasizes asking questions to create a solution for a real problem that is both urgent and important, with an agreement from senior leaders in the organization that the solutions would be implemented if good and feasible. AL has two goals: (a) to provide a creative, innovative, and effective solution to the problem; and (b) to promote individual, team, and organizational learning. The learning that results from the AL process is optimized when the team is provided a well-trained AL team coach whose primary role is to promote learning by asking questions that ensure that the team will take the time to consider and reflect on what it is doing: What is the impact of the team's actions? What is working/effective? What can be improved? What will the team do differently in the future?

Through the AL process, participants learn the following kinds of leadership skills that lead to timely and creative solutions:

- when to lead and when to follow,
- when to be directive and when to encourage collaboration and consensus,

- how to use intrinsic as well as extrinsic motivators to keep people engaged,
- how to engage people's idealism and desire for personal development and growth to develop inspiring visions and passion,
- how to empower subordinates to use and develop their ability to self-manage and self-lead, and
- how to develop a mind-set for continuous learning throughout the organization.

AL recognizes that leadership skills must be flexibly applied to situations and must be practiced by everyone in the organization. Rather than promoting a specific leadership model for people to follow, AL encourages organizational members to develop a leadership style that is customized to the situation through a process of asking questions, reflection, decision making, and action.

Developing Leaders and Solving Problems With Action Learning at Microsoft
Authored by Shannon Banks, worldwide leadership development consultant, Microsoft, and manager of the Tier 1 ExPo program

Founded in 1975 and headquartered in Redmond, Washington, Microsoft Corporation has nearly 90,000 employees worldwide. To accelerate the development of high-potential employees within the Sales, Marketing & Services Group, Microsoft developed the ExPo program, which is designed around key drivers that provide significant impact—namely, building an expanded, diverse organizational network; providing visibility to current leaders and engagement with immediate management; creating a thoughtful and rich development plan; and enriching the on-the-job experience of managers.

ExPo is offered to employees in the top 4% of the Sales, Marketing & Services Group worldwide. These employees are identified by their executives through a rigorous, high-potential identification process as having the aspiration, commitment, and ability to be business leaders at Microsoft. ExPo's objective is to accelerate these members' development by providing additional experiences that create greater readiness for leadership. Although ExPo includes early-career individual contributors through experienced employees in functional leadership roles, the development they undergo is differentiated by career stage.

One of the core components of ExPo is Leadership in Action. The Leadership in Action experience uses the drivers of accelerated development and the AL approach to advance leaders' skills and capabilities while, at the same time, making a direct business impact. In preparation for Leadership in Action, ExPo members in senior leadership roles (Tier 1) attend a global launch event that explores the value of differentiation. At this event, these members consider how they can differentiate themselves as leaders by focusing on and delivering what matters most. The session helps these members to identify the "breakthrough problem or opportunity" within their role in which they can create the visibility and momentum needed to propel their careers forward. Members use a Member/Manager Contracting process and reflection following the launch to get their manager's support for their breakthrough problems.

Following this launch event, ExPo members can further their breakthrough problems while helping to develop other high-potential managers (Tier 2s) at Leadership in Action practicums. At these events, members are trained in and use several experiential learning techniques, including peer-coaching Learning Circles, innovation techniques, and single-problem AL. AL teams are comprised of one senior Tier 1 high-potential leader who joins a Tier 2 Learning Circle for an immersive AL and creative innovation session. Over the course of 3 days, these high-potential leaders work together on the Tier 1 breakthrough problem in an immersive session of AL, followed by innovation training. The Tier 1 problem presenters take away actions and inputs from the event and use them to significantly move their problems forward. At the end of the year, Tier 1 members reflect on their ExPo experience and return to their management teams, Learning Circles, and AL teams to present both actions taken on their problems and learnings.

Microsoft has seen great value from AL because it allows members to practice and develop leadership competencies, work together as high-potential teams, and learn to ask great questions as leaders, all while working on real, urgent business problems.

LEADERSHIP SKILLS FOR THE 21ST CENTURY

Most organizations have identified leadership competencies that they believe to be critical for the success of their enterprise. Although these leadership competency models vary from organization to organization, they generally have four large competency clusters.

- *Cognitive skills.* Skills and competencies in this cluster include seasoned analytical skills, strategic thinking, creativity, and global perspective.
- *Execution skills.* Skills and competencies in this cluster include customer focus, planning, program management, and focus on results.
- *Relationship skills.* Skills and competencies in this cluster include influencing, engaging and inspiring, managing talent, creating open communication, collaborating, and building relationships.
- *Self-management skills.* Skills and competencies in this cluster include the ability to establish trust, adaptability, impulse control, and curiosity and love of learning.

The actual behaviors that are appropriate for each of these basic skills vary considerably depending on the scope and level of responsibility of the position. For instance, in relation to the strategic thinking competency, first-line supervisors need to understand strategy, middle managers must act strategically, executives who lead business units need to think strategically, and the most senior executives in the organization are responsible for shaping strategy.

Solving complex organizational problems requires the use of all of these competencies at one time or another in the problem-solving process. Not everyone, of course, needs to be skilled or expert in all of these skills. One great strength of AL is that the process teaches participants the value and benefit of diversity and shared leadership. The more effective the team is in leveraging all of the skills and knowledge among its membership, the better the product of its collective efforts. This fact demonstrates the reality of the popular Japanese proverb, "none of us is as smart as *all* of us." As the AL team becomes deeply involved in a complex problem, it invariably recognizes the need for most, if not all, of the leadership competencies noted above. Questions from the team coach and other team members help to identify who has the necessary skills and knowledge and to facilitate the integration of effort necessary for peak team performance.

LEADERSHIP DEVELOPMENT

Most organizations of any size have a formalized process for developing the leadership talent that will be necessary in the coming years. This process can be as simple as having each manager identify possible successors and give them developmental assignments, and as complex as sophisticated leadership development programs for cohorts of high-potential managers running over a period of 12 to 18 months. These programs seek to develop the leadership skills identified in the organization's leadership competency models.

Hicks and Peterson (1999) provided a model for the necessary and sufficient conditions for learning. These authors identified a "development pipeline" composed of insight, motivation, skill development, real-world practice, and accountability. Each element in the pipeline represents a key "active ingredient" that determines the amount of development that actually results from any particular training or development program. In addition to being a critical success factor for learning, each element also represents a potential "pinch point" for development. In other words, a leadership development program with superb classroom training content and materials delivered by highly skilled and qualified faculty and trainers will have limited effectiveness without opportunities for real-world application and practice or organization practices and policies that provide consequences, both good and bad, for demonstrating the new skills on the job. A more in-depth discussion of the elements of the Hicks and Peterson model as it pertains to demonstrating the advantages of AL as a general developmental strategy is provided in chapter 3.

COMPARISON OF LEADERSHIP DEVELOPMENT APPROACHES

Popular leadership development approaches can be analyzed and evaluated using the Pipeline for Leadership (Hicks & Peterson, 1999) model.

Test-Based Developmental Assessments With Individual Development Plan

This approach provides results from skills and personality assessment instruments that are used to develop an Individual Development Plan (IDP). These programs provide excellent insight on the basis of results from paper-and-pencil tests of mental abilities, personality, interest inventories, and so forth. However, the feedback provides inconsistent motivation because some managers doubt the validity of the assessment tools. In addition, when involuntarily involved in such programs, participants generally resist and resent the process. The IDP provides goals, but there is no specific process for developing these skills, there is little opportunity to practice new skills, and there are no consequences, either positive or negative, identified for demonstrating new skills.

Mentoring

This approach consists of formal or informal pairing of managers with mentors who are outside of the manager's reporting chain. Mentors give useful insight regarding organizational culture and politics but generally don't have comprehensive information about the manager's skills and abilities. Depending on the stature of the mentor, the manager may be highly motivated to use the mentoring relationship. However, mentors have limited opportunity to develop new skills, and the relationship offers few opportunities for real-world practice of skills. Because the mentoring relationship exists outside of the reporting chain, accountability in mentoring relationships is weak. Further, because they hear about the challenging issues primarily from the mentees, mentors are unlikely to be working from a comprehensive understanding of the context, the full complexity of the issues, the interests and behaviors of other involved parties, or a comprehensive understanding of the direct and indirect consequences of the mentees' actions.

360-Degree Feedback With IDP

This approach provides information from survey feedback from bosses, subordinates, and peers that is used to develop an IDP. These programs are strong in providing insight regarding current skills and are generally motivating because the feedback comes from bosses, subordinates, and peers. There may be a limited executive coaching component that is designed to help participants make sense out of and apply the results of the 360-degree feedback. However, there is no focused or systematic skill development component other than reference to reading materials or external training programs (cf. *The Successful Manager's Handbook* [Nelson-Neuhaus et al., 2004]), there is no opportunity to practice skills and receive feedback, and there is limited formal accountability for improving specific skills.

Traditional Leadership Programs

These programs typically provide formal classroom instruction in two areas: (a) the organization's structure, mission, strategy, practices, products, and so forth; and (b) the leadership skills that are understood to be critical and necessary in the organization and at a new level of responsibility. This is a universal prescriptive approach. Motivation is inconsistent; some participants are highly engaged and excited with the new challenges, whereas others see the processes as largely irrelevant and part of a "ticket-punching" process or feel that they have been "sent to be fixed." In these programs, participants are largely passive, receiving fact-based or abstract conceptual and theoretical information from the faculty. There is little opportunity for real-world practice and limited accountability for actually demonstrating the skills on the job.

Semitraditional Leadership Development Programs, Including IDP

These programs are similar to the traditional classroom programs except that they include more experiential components so that the participants are more actively engaged. Typically, participants complete an IDP primarily on the basis of a 360-degree feedback survey. Because participants are more actively involved, they are typically more engaged in the learning, but a number of participants still see these programs as ticket-punching exercises because of the lack of direct accountability for applying the learning on the job. Although these programs usually include individual and group exercises as well as short simulations, there is limited opportunity for real-world practice.

Simulation-Based Developmental Assessments With Feedback, Including IDP

These assessments provide realistic simulation of new or projected jobs and responsibilities along with performance feedback. Participants generally complete an IDP following this experience and get feedback from other participants in the simulation(s). The immediate feedback and realistic quality of the simulations provide valuable insight and are generally quite engaging. Feedback from faculty and other participants also provides a moderate degree of skill development. The high fidelity quality of the

simulations provides a realistic job tryout, allowing participants the opportunity to practice new skills in a realistic setting. Strong accountability, however, is difficult to achieve.

Development Assignments

These assignments allow participants to learn new skills in an extended job tryout. Because these jobs are seen as the next step in eventual promotion, participants are quite motivated and feel accountable for their performance. Although participants get general insight about their performance, they typically do not receive the kind of comprehensive and detailed feedback possible with 360-degree feedback and test-based assessment. As a result many managers are not in the position long enough to be reliably assessed by 360-degree feedback, and receiving test-based feedback requires special test interpretation skills that are not typically available for informal developmental assignments.

Coaching

Coaching is an intensive, one-on-one, developmental experience that is focused on a small number of goals for personal growth and development (usually two or three) over a period of 6 to 12 months. Coaching provides focused and real-time insight regarding participant behavior and provides highly targeted instruction and skill development. Skilled coaches are able to build strong personal rapport with participants, which results in a high degree of motivation and engagement. Because of the high investment by the organization and participant in personal coaching, there is a moderately high degree of accountability. Coaching programs, however, cannot be viewed as comprehensive leadership programs because they focus on only a subset of necessary leadership skills. Also, most coaching goals are focused more on development needs[2] than on examining how to build on current skill strengths (Buckingham & Clifton, 2001). Further, the data with which the coach works comes primarily from the person being coached. As such, the self-reported information may be biased, self-serving, distorted, or incomplete.

Action Learning

AL provides an opportunity for participants to analyze and provide solutions for important complex organizational issues with an agreement from the organization that the solutions be implemented if good and feasible. Skilled AL team coaches ask questions that encourage reflection,

---

[2]Although many coaches encourage participants to select skills that are strengths that can be further leveraged, the majority of participants focus only on the skill areas where they are weakest.

insight, and skill development. In addition to building the broad leadership skills identified earlier in this chapter, AL develops the collaborative and shared leadership skills that are necessary for high-performing teams and organizations. The importance and criticality of the issue ensures motivated and engaged participants. By the very nature of the process, AL provides all participants with the opportunity to practice new skills in a real-world environment. A particular strength of AL is the ability to generate accountability. Nothing galvanizes participants more than the reality that the team will get significant "face time" with the CEO and a panel of other senior executives to present their solution to significant and complex organizational issues.

Table 1.1 presents a summary of estimates of the degree to which popular leadership development approaches satisfy the requirements of each element of the pipeline for development.

ACTION LEARNING AND CAREER CHALLENGES

Another strength of AL is that a consistent developmental strategy can be used to teach appropriate leadership skills at any point in a manager's career (Freedman, 1998; Mahler & Wrightnour, 1973). Charan, Drotter,

TABLE 1.1

Estimate of Effectiveness of Typical Leadership Development Methods With Respect to Hicks and Peterson (1999) Leadership Development Model

Type of program	Insight	Motivation	Skill development	Real-world practice	Accountability
Test-based developmental assessments with IDP	S	M	W	W	W
Mentoring	M	S	W	W	W
360-degree feedback with IDP	S	S	W	W	W
Traditional leadership development programs	S	M	M	W	W
Semitraditional leadership development programs including IDP	S	M	S	M	W
Simulation-based developmental assessments with feedback including IDP	S	S	M	M	W
Developmental assignments	M	S	M	S	S
Individual coaching with trained coach	S	S	S	S	M
Action Learning	S	S	S	S	S

Note. W = weak; M = moderate; S = strong; IDP = individual development plan.

and Noel (2001) identified six levels or "passages" in a manager's development as the *Leadership Pipeline*. It is common for participants in leadership development programs to be based on the same leadership competencies regardless of level in the managerial hierarchy. As noted earlier, however, the challenges faced and skills required vary greatly when employees move from frontline supervisor, through middle management, to executive level positions (Kaiser & Craig, 2007). With a "one approach fits all" approach to leadership competencies, entry-level supervisors, for instance, may receive training in leadership competencies and skills that are inappropriate or even dysfunctional for challenges they face at that level (Leonard, 2005).

Because AL coaches do not teach any particular leadership model or stress specific leadership skills, participants learn the skills and develop theories that are local or "indigenous" (Day, 2005) to their particular organization and at the level at which they are working or will be working. Well-crafted questions asked by AL coaches focus on what actions are working well in addition to what actions would improve the team's problem-solving process given the team, the team's goals and the participants' level of responsibility in the organization of responsibility. As a result, when they participate primarily as team members, employees quickly learn useful shared leadership skills that are appropriate to their level in the organization. Executives, on the other hand, learn how to be both collaborative colleagues as well as forceful leaders, a difficult balance for leaders at that level. As managers rise in the organization, questions and the reflective process will spotlight new skills that must be mastered, current behaviors and skills that are still valued and need to be retained, as well as current behaviors that need to be reduced, de-emphasized, or eliminated because they have become liabilities or even dysfunctional at a new level of responsibility (Freedman, 2005).

Action Learning and Organizational Change

As noted earlier, the external environments within which organizations of all types must operate have become unstable and can be expected to continue to change—constantly. This conundrum extends through all sectors: public, private, nongovernmental, and nonprofit. Changes in any organization's environmental landscape come in a bewildering variety of permutations and combinations. Environmental changes include technology, local and global economics, financial, politics, legislation, ecology, labor and customer demographics (and their preferences), competition, global terrorism, and pandemics, among others. Each change presents both threats to and opportunities for any given organization.

To survive and thrive, organizations must recognize and adapt to their unique environments' particular demand characteristics. Invariably and inevitably, organizations must continuously reinvent themselves; that is, they must learn what to change and how to change. The demand for change is not optional; it is essential for the organization's survival. Most of these requisite changes have no historical precedents; that is, the changes are discontinuous with the organization's past experiences and established adaptive mechanisms and problem-solving processes. Thus, organizations must invent solutions to cope with ambiguous circumstances in which both the adaptive goals and the pathways to those goals are uncertain.

However, leaders may not have anticipated or may be ill-equipped to cope with the particular configuration of environmental changes challenging their organizations. Understandably, leaders seek external resources that appear to correspond to the nature of the environmental change that seems to be most urgent and significant.

Thus, leaders typically seek outside assistance in the form of management consulting firms that can deploy technical experts or "techsperts" (Freedman & Zackrison, 2001) whose credentials and experiences seem to be most relevant. Thus, if confronted by a financial crisis, financial techsperts are recruited. If the crisis is caused by the perceived need to design and install a contemporary enterprise resource planning software platform system, a team of IT techsperts are brought in. If inefficiencies and counterproductive redundancies in some of an organization's business processes are detected or suspected, techsperts specializing in business process reengineering are sought.

In their search for expert guidance and advice, depending on the prevailing issues, leaders may choose techsperts specializing in such areas as strategic planning, downsizing, restructuring, mergers and acquisitions, global management, cross-cultural communications, executive succession, performance management systems, labor relations, diversity management, and stress management. In general, these techsperts are specialists in technical or structural (or techno-structural) change. On the surface, this strategy of seeking external, specialized expertise seems logical, reasonable, and efficient.

There is, however, a significant problem. Most techno-structural interventions that are designed and implemented by external techsperts frequently fail to achieve their intended results, or they greatly exceed their budgets, or they take far more time than originally scheduled, or they provoke complex and vexing side effects, or they expose and exacerbate previously ignored benign systemic problems (Freedman, 1997). Estimates vary, but the range of failures and shortfalls seems to be between

40% and 70% for techno-structurally driven organizational change initiatives with one or more of these difficulties (Schaffer & Thompson, 1992; Spector & Beers, 1994).

This is not to say that specialized techspert consultants are incompetent or not necessary. Far from it. Rather, such techspert consultants may be essential but, by themselves, not sufficient for enabling organizations to deal effectively with unprecedented and discontinuous environmental changes. Techsperts, however, often act as if they are the primary agents in creating and driving solutions for change.

Revans (1980) noted not only that technical expertise was not sufficient for producing good solutions but also that too much focused and narrow expertise can produce inferior and even disastrous problem solving. As a child, Revans heard his father, a member of the commission investigating the Titanic disaster, relate how the need to gain and retain approval from other engineers stifled dissent and prevented available knowledge about the vulnerabilities of the "unsinkable" ship from surfacing during the design of the liner. Later, Revans observed similar face-saving/preserving behavior that prevented normally creative individuals from taking risks or confronting authority in problem-solving activities. From these insights, Revans proposed that optimal problem-solving requires a diversity of skills and levels of expertise when dealing with complex problems.

Solving Problems and Building Teams With Action Learning at Morgans Hotel Group

The Morgans Hotel Group (MHG) is a hospitality company that operates, owns, acquires, and redevelops boutique hotels in the United States and Europe. In 2007, senior leadership at MHG identified several key issues that would require the talents and ideas of managers from throughout the organizations to resolve issues such as the role of the concierge, leadership development, the human performance matrix, employee recognition, and the award system for frequent guests. AL was determined to be the most effective way not only to solve these problems but also to build a stronger and more cohesive culture among the employees of the hotels.

Eight managers were selected to be trained as AL coaches to work with the MHG project teams. The AL teams worked for 2 days to develop strategies that were then presented to the project sponsors and key MHG leaders. The results were amazing and the teams worked fantastically, according to Kathy Chalmers, executive vice president for human resources, who said, "Action learning has truly been an extremely valuable tool in examining and resolving important challenges at Morgans Hotel Group." The organization estimated that millions of dollars were saved in hotel renovations as a result of AL.

ACTION LEARNING AS AN ORGANIZATIONAL DEVELOPMENT AND CHANGE PROCESS

AL is frequently used to bring about complex organizational change and, therefore, can be viewed within the context of organizational development and change (OD&C). OD&C consultants understand that attention to the impact of technology and other structural changes on the human or social system within an organization is necessary for any organization change intervention to be successful (Davenport, 1995).

According to Cummings and Worley (2005), OD&C is "a systemwide application and transfer of behavioral science knowledge to the planned development, improvement, and reinforcement of the strategies, structures, and processes that lead to organizational effectiveness" (p. 1).

The central principle of OD&C practice is that the more all involved parties actively participate in all phases of the organizational change process, the more likely they are to experience an emotional investment in the change and to feel a strong commitment to support the execution of the implementation plans. They are less likely, therefore, to resist the change initiative. Further, OD&C theory informs the use of methodologies that enhance the capacity of all involved parties to learn from their individual and collective experiences with the change process.

ACTION LEARNING AND OD&C AS COMPLEMENTARY AND SYNERGISTIC PROCESSES

There is a very strong relationship between the practice of AL and of OD&C. These are complementary, potentially synergistic practices, not redundant disciplines. Practitioners trained in AL and the principles of OD&C understand that people who will be affected by change must be included in developing change solutions. In both disciplines, practitioners understand that they are the catalysts rather than the drivers for change. Practitioners in both disciplines strive to enable stakeholders to create or design their own change strategies rather than provide them with a sophisticated and expert plan to follow. Both disciplines have explicit strategies for encouraging deeper reflection on the problem(s) that organizational stakeholders are grappling with. OD&C practitioners conduct action research to provide the relevant data that organizational stakeholders need to make well-informed decisions, whereas AL practitioners ask questions to encourage AL team members to gather and reflect on data that are relevant to the problem(s) they are addressing.

In addition, both disciplines are invested in and promote learning at all levels in the organization (i.e., individual, interpersonal, team, interteam, organizational). Learning is a primary objective of AL, and OD&C professionals understand that learning must take place for organizational change efforts to succeed. Both AL and OD&C practitioners work at three levels of potential organizational learning. At the first level, they help individuals in the organization learn how to achieve the desired or intended results of the change effort in the most efficient manner. Argyris, Putnam, and Smith (1985) and Argyris (1999) called this *single-loop learning.*

Second, both disciplines help individuals in the organization learn how the manner in which they diagnose, plan, implement, monitor the implementation, and identify and deal with "predictable surprises" (e.g., side effects and the emergence of nascent issues) that inevitably occur can either enhance or inhibit the effectiveness of the change effort. Argyris and his associates referred to this as *double-loop learning.*

At the third level, OD&C and AL practitioners assist all involved parties (including the techspert consultants) in learning about themselves from their experiences with the change effort. That is, they learn how their beliefs, assumptions, attitudes, and preferences are often related to their professional work experiences, roles, and status. This influences how they perceive what they believe is (and what they believe is not) pertinent for the change effort and, subsequently, what they think, how they feel, and what they do on the change effort. This can be referred to as *triple-loop learning* (Freedman, 2006). Techsperts typically focus on single-loop learning. AL and OD&C practitioners focus on all three levels of learning.

By viewing the problem and related issues through the lens of OD&C, AL team coaches can ask questions that encourage the team to discover, develop, and apply its collective wisdom and potential to deal effectively in determining how to best achieve the team's technical objectives while simultaneously considering the impact on specific end-users as well as on the global social and organizational system. The questions asked by the AL team coach facilitate reflection and dialogue not only about the capabilities of technological and structural changes but also about the impact of and required changes in the social and human systems of the organization. In this way, the changes proposed by the AL team are more likely to be accepted rather than resisted because the people who are affected by the changes have active involvement in the way technology is implemented.

Reflection Questions

1. What differences do you see between what is required to be an effective leader 10 years ago and what is required by today's organizations?
2. Given this direction, what leadership skills will become more important in the next decade?

3. How effective is your organization's leadership development process in preparing leaders for the next leadership level? Where are the gaps in their preparation? What questions would you ask senior leadership to help them reflect on the consequences of not addressing these leadership development needs?

4. Why is AL so effective in developing the leadership skills that will be important for leadership in the organizations of today and tomorrow?

5. How much is your organization relying on outside experts and techsperts to provide solutions for your organization's most urgent problems? What have been the consequences, both positive and negative, of this reliance on outside expertise? How can an AL coach challenge teams regarding the overreliance on outside experts and techsperts?

6. What are the common barriers to learning in your organization? How does AL remove these barriers?

Fundamentals of Action Learning and How It Works | 2

As we noted in chapter 1, Action Learning (AL) is a problem-solving tool that simultaneously builds leaders, teams, and organizations. Since Reg Revans first introduced AL in the coal mines of Wales and England in the 1940s, multiple variations of the concept have emerged, but all forms of AL share the elements of real people resolving and taking action on real problems in real time and learning while doing so. To optimize the full power of AL, we propose that the following six components are necessary:

1. important and urgent task, problem, or project;
2. diverse group of four to eight members;
3. questioning and reflective communications process;
4. development and implementation of action strategies;
5. commitment to learning; and
6. AL team coach.

Not all AL programs conducted worldwide, however, incorporate all six of these components. Most AL programs assign important problems and expect the team to produce a useful solution. Most use diverse groups with from four to eight members, have goals that include personal learning, and encourage the use of questions and reflection. The other components are applied less universally. Many programs do not include true AL team coaches. Often teams are provided with task facilitators or coaches who have a personal interest in the problem (many would be considered expert sponsors). In a few cases, a trained AL team coach is not provided at all because of the assumption that this role would emerge naturally if necessary. In some programs, the importance of generating a good result greatly outweighs the importance of creating an outstanding learning experience. The apparent assumption is that good performance automatically translates into good learning. Finally, whereas many programs note the importance of asking questions, they don't have a ground rule that requires coaches and participants to lead with questions rather than with statements.

We hope that the following sections provide the reader with compelling arguments for adhering to each of the six components previously summarized. These sections provide a fuller description of and rationale for including each component into the AL design.

The Project, Problem, or Task

AL centers on a problem, project, challenge, issue, or task, the resolution of which is of high importance to an individual, team, and/or organization. The problem should be significant, be urgent, have no easily identifiable solution, and be the team's responsibility to solve. It should also provide an opportunity for the group to generate learning opportunities; to build knowledge; and to develop individual, team, and organizational skills.

For AL, problems are seen not only as a challenge but also as an opportunity for learning and for developing individual, team, and organizational capabilities. Problems are not just burdens but also occasions to sharpen the wit as well as the skills of the problem solvers. A fundamental premise of AL is that individuals learn best when undertaking some action, which they then reflect on and learn from. The main reason for having a problem or project is that it gives the group something to focus on that is real and important, and that is also relevant to them. It creates a challenge on which to test stored-up knowledge. Solving the problem should make a significant difference to the individual or the organization. The more urgent and important the problem, the greater will be the group's energy, excitement, and commitment to solving it. If the problem is unimportant or too simple (or perceived as either), the group will not put as much effort and energy into solving it, and the group's capacity to be an effective problem-solving team will not be tested. In addition, the group may feel that the organization or individual does not have a great deal of confidence or trust in them. As a result, the group's time and resources will not be well used, nor will the group's potential be fully tapped.

PUZZLE VERSUS PROBLEM

The issue that is addressed by AL should be a problem, not a puzzle. Puzzles generally have one acceptable solution. The task of the problem solver, in this instance, is to come up with the correct solution. This is generally the case in schools and classrooms. Teachers provide homework that includes problems for which there is one right answer and an infinite number of incorrect ones. In real life, however, there are rarely situations for which there is one and only one correct solution. Solutions to most real-life problems are a good deal messier than the simplified problems typically provided in classes and courses. Managers, in particular, face conflicting and cross-cutting priorities that make perfect problem solving nearly impossible. Every solution has strengths and liabilities depending on which priority is being considered.

WHEN TO USE AND NOT USE ACTION LEARNING

By definition, the most important and critical problems in organizations have no known solution. If a simple solution to the problem existed, the organization would quickly solve it. In addition, the true source of the problem is initially unclear. Experienced problem solvers understand that the presenting problem is rarely the root or source problem. When the root of the problem is unclear, the goals for the problem-solving process are also unclear or ambiguous. As a consequence, defining the problem is far more difficult than is usually the case with a puzzle or typical classroom exercise.

Figure 2.1 presents a classification of problems based on whether a pathway to a solution is known and whether the goals for the problem are clear.

AL is an ideal problem-solving process when there is no known solution, or when the solution is uncertain but the problem goals are clear and specific (Quadrant B). The presenting problems frequently identified by senior leadership, however, are often vague and general. A problem that falls into Quadrant D (no known solution and ambiguous and unclear problem goals) will need to be refined by either senior leadership or, more commonly, the AL team (thereby moving the problem into Quadrant B) before it is a feasible problem for the team to tackle.

The solutions already exist for problems in Quadrant A. For instance, common negotiation problems can be approached more efficiently and practically using well-known negotiation strategies. AL would be inefficient and inappropriate in this situation. In these cases, why reinvent the wheel?

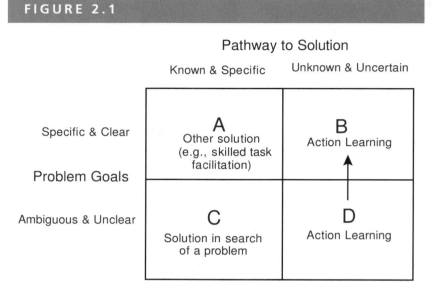

FIGURE 2.1

Classification of problems based on whether pathway
to a solution is known and project goals are clear.

Quadrant C is a curious but important situation. In this case, in which there is a known solution but the goals are ambiguous and unclear, we find a solution in search of a problem to solve. One of the authors became aware of a consulting firm that was offering a free organizational assessment that included recommendations for solving the problems identified in the assessment. Somewhat later it was discovered that the same recommendations were offered regardless of the identified problem. And, as you can guess, that solution happened to be the main service that this firm offered. In other words, when all you have is a hammer, every problem looks like a nail!

The tendency to use old tools to solve new problems is a related problem. Team members enter AL programs with a set of problem-solving tools and habits that have worked for them over the years. In many cases, team members have built their reputations and careers on being experts in using these tools. Without an AL team coach to challenge "the way we have always worked," team members are likely to slip into old and familiar problem-solving habits without duly considering whether a new or different approach might work better.

Finally, the problem should be one for which the group has been given the authority and power to solve and to implement action. If the group is not able to take the action, it will not know whether its ideas, strategies, and learnings really work. And if the group has been notified that it is merely making recommendations that may or may not ever be implemented, its members may have lower energy levels, be less creative, experience frustration and/or apathy more easily, and skip meetings or not undertake tasks they agreed to do.

An Action Learning Group or Team

The core entity in AL is the AL group, team, or set[1] that ideally has four to eight members. The group should have a diversity of backgrounds and experiences so its members are able to acquire various perspectives and encourage fresh viewpoints. Depending on the AL problem, groups may volunteer or be appointed, may be from various functions or departments, may include individuals from other organizations or professions, and may involve suppliers as well as customers.

Diversity of group membership is extremely valuable and contributes immensely to the power and success of AL, especially when the group is dealing with complex, adaptive problems. The diverse group has a greater ability to solve complex problems as well as to pose a wider array of strategies. Weick (1995) noted that teams and organizations need requisite variety if they are going to be able to adequately understand and successfully adapt to the complex environment around them. Thus, the more complex the problem, the more important and necessary are diversity and diverse thinking. Various perspectives provide the opportunity to generate many, rather than just one or two, possible solutions. As individuals, we are all subject to mind-sets and assumptions that limit the scope of the ideas we are able to generate. People with different perspectives will challenge our mind-sets and basic assumptions. Therefore, whenever possible, levels of experience, business unit location, gender, age, and ethnicity should be balanced to add diversity and richness to AL groups.

Tim Brown (2007), CEO and founder of IDEO, a well-known design firm, has also identified the importance of diversity in creative problem solving.

> The more you encourage serendipity—say, by bringing together different people—the more you'll get rich answers. The more you put a group together that sees the world the same way, the

---

[1] The terms *group, team,* and *set* are used interchangeably in this book. In the United Kingdom, following Revan's terminology, AL groups are often termed sets. In the United States, given the long-standing interest in teams and team process, AL groups are more frequently termed teams. In some instances, a set refers to one session or meeting of a group or team. Because there is some confusion about the definition of a set, we will usually refer to AL groups or teams rather than sets.

more conventional the outcome. We try to put teams together that have varied backgrounds—not just disciplines, but life experiences. (p. 32)

AL groups, because of the intensity and strong cohesiveness generated by the six components and two ground rules (to be discussed shortly), are unlike any other type of problem-solving group. Intensive learnings, deep sharing of personal perspectives, critical responsibility, and direct accountability create great growth for the group. The high level of teamwork and team-thinking that is created via the reflective inquiry process and the interventions of the AL team coach make group solidarity very important. Once its membership has been established, the group should stay intact as is throughout its existence. Putnam (2000) noted that the most complex problems can only be solved by a group that has developed a strong social bonding. Therefore, it is preferable that the group meet fewer times when everyone is present than more often when any of the members are absent.

There may be occasions when outsiders join the group for part of a particular session or sessions. They should be invited when the group determines that they can help by providing information or support relative to the resolution of the problem. Usually, AL teams will need to interact with outside people between AL sessions as they seek information, identify resources, and pilot-test action strategies.

A Process That Emphasizes Insightful Questioning and Reflective Listening

AL emphasizes questions and reflection over statements and opinions. By focusing on the right questions rather than the right answers, AL focuses on what one does not know as well as on what one does know. AL tackles problems through a process of asking questions first to clarify the exact nature of the problem, reflecting and identifying possible solutions, and only then taking action. The focus is on questions because great solutions are contained within the seeds of great questions. Questions foster group dialogue, build cohesiveness, generate innovative and systems thinking, and enhance learning results.

The quiet time between questions and responses provides opportunities for group members to examine assumptions and to find common perspectives. For reflective inquiry to occur, there must be space for people to stand back, reflect, and unfreeze their presuppositions and basic assumptions. Reflection usually does not come easily or naturally. In most group settings, attempts to create reflection fail. However, in AL, reflection is continuous and natural. AL deliberately carves out the time and creates the conditions for reflecting and listening. When group members are expected to ask questions and carefully listen to the responses, they develop the habit of reflective inquiry for use in the group and also in their day-to-day lives.

Reflection and the Learning Process

Revans (1982a) posited that Learning (L) is a function of Programmed knowledge (P; i.e., the accumulated and shared knowledge and experience of each team member and of the organization) + Questioning (Q; critical analysis applied in a social setting). To this familiar L = P + Q formula, others (Marquardt, 1999; Pedlar, 1996; Yorks, O'Neil, & Marsick, 1999) have added the process of critical reflection (R; i.e., L = P + Q + R). Although the act of asking questions naturally encourages reflection, these authors believe that it is the role of the AL team coach to extend and increase the depth of questioning to encourage the discussion of norms, values, beliefs, and especially assumptions. Reflection at this level fosters double- and triple-loop learning (Argyris, Putnam, & Smith, 1985).

Kolb's (1984) well-known learning cycle also highlights the importance of reflection in the learning process (see Figure 2.2).

FIGURE 2.2

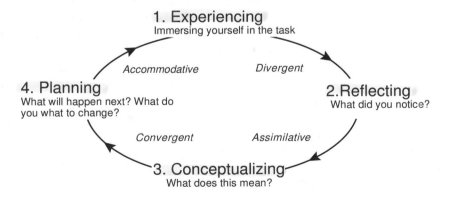

The Kolb learning cycle. From *Experiential Learning: Experience as a Source of Learning and Development* (p. 42, Figure 3.1), by D. Kolb, 1984, Upper Saddle, NJ: Pearson Education. Copyright 1984 by Pearson Education. Reprinted with permission.

The priority given to insightful questioning and reflective listening ensures that individuals and the team do not jump from experiencing to acting without first reflecting on their experience—what is working/effective, what the group can improve, and what changes the group wants to make. The core questioning/reflection process tempers the bias toward action that is so common in the early stages of problem solving in teams.

Reflection and dialogue combine to foster an individual's or a team's ability to generate the deeper changes associated with learning. There are three different levels of reflection, each successively more challenging and sometimes more powerful. The three levels are reflection, critical reflection, and metacognition.

REFLECTION

Reflection is an exercise in individual exploration of the meaning of experience, thoughts, feelings, and actions. Kolb (1984) noted that reflection is the process through which individuals make sense of their experiences, which yields a basis for future action and initiates new or adapted ideas in the process. Boud, Keough, and Walker (1985) defined reflection as a "generic term for those intellectual and effective activities in which individuals engage to explore their experiences in order to lead to a new understanding and appreciation" (p. 19).

Raelin (1997) stated that reflection takes time, involves thought, and can turn inward and focus on self. This focusing on oneself can be an uncomfortable experience for some individuals. Various reasons for this discomfort have been given; lack of familiarity and practice or trust level with fellow team members are two that are often cited (Dilworth & Willis, 2003).

Mutual trust is a necessary condition for reflection to take place within a group. An ideal environment for reflection learning is open and supportive. Bandura (1977) noted that environments that promote interpersonal interaction facilitate reflection. Social interaction may enhance motivation and prolong engagement with the task. Social interaction would almost certainly bring forth more information and ideas that could be shared and perhaps result in deeper thinking about the subject. This interaction might take place during the learning activity or occur later in formal or informal group discussions.

CRITICAL REFLECTION

Whereas simple reflection may or may not be purposeful, *critical reflection* is used with a goal in mind. Critical reflection in the context of learning is the purposeful reinterpretation, analysis, and evaluation of any given experience leading to a change in the learner. Reflective learning involves assessment or reassessment of assumptions. Reflective learning becomes transformative whenever assumptions or premises are found to be "distorting, inauthentic, or otherwise invalid" (Mezeirow, 1991, p. 7). John Dewey defined critical reflection as an "active, persistent and careful consideration of any belief or supposed form of knowledge in the light of the grounds that support it, and the further conclusion towards which it trends" (1933/1997, p. 4). In a general sense, critical reflection is simply thinking about and challenging what we know and how we know it (Usher & Edwards, 1994).

Brookfield (1987) suggested that four activities are central to critical thinking: (a) identifying and challenging assumptions, (b) contextual awareness, (c) imaging and exploring alternatives, and (d) reflective skepticism. The ability to critically reflect on one's experience, to integrate knowledge gained from experience and knowledge possessed, and to take action on insights is considered by some to be the distinguishing feature of the adult learner (Brookfield, 1987; Ecclestone, 1996; Mezirow, 1991; Stein, 2000). Table 2.1 presents Brookfield's four activities central to critical reflection along with useful questions that AL team coaches can ask to facilitate critical reflection.

TABLE 2.1

Critical Reflection Process (Brookfield, 1987)

Activity	Description
Analysis of assumptions	This is the first step in the critical reflection process. It involves thinking in such a manner that it challenges our beliefs, values, cultural practices, and social structures in order to assess their impact on our daily proceedings. Assumptions are our way of seeing reality. Questions such as, ▪ What do you know or believe about this issue, the company, each other? ▪ What did you not know before? ▪ What are you still curious about?
Surface context bias	Realizing that our assumptions are socially and personally created in a specific historical and cultural context. ▪ Does everyone agree? ▪ How do you see it? ▪ How did we come to that conclusion?
Imaginative speculation	Imagining alternative ways of thinking about an issue in order to provide an opportunity to challenge our prevailing ways of knowing and acting. ▪ What if . . . . this were changed? ▪ What if . . . . we tried something different? ▪ What if . . . . . . we did nothing?
Reflective skepticism	Questioning universal truth claims or unexamined patterns of interaction. It is the ability to think about a subject so that the available evidence from that subject's field is suspended or temporarily rejected in order to establish the truth or viability of a proposition or action. ▪ What is really important—now? ▪ What is not being said? ▪ What is not obvious about the data? What data are missing? Untrue?

METACOGNITION

Metacognition is the act of thinking deeply about one's assumptions in the context of one's choices or alternatives. It is generally identified as higher order thinking involving active control over the cognitive processes engaged in learning (Flavell, 1987). Metacognition theory focuses on (a) the role of awareness and executive management of one's thinking, (b) individual differences in self-appraisal and management of cognitive development and learning, (c) knowledge and executive abilities that develop through experience, and (d) constructive and strategic thinking (Paris & Winograd, 1990).

Whereas reflection and critical reflection might lead to change that impacts the problem at hand, metacognition (literally, thinking about your thinking) leads to a change in the learners themselves. Metacognition, by definition, involves double- and triple-loop learning (Argyris, 1993; Freedman, 2006). During AL debriefing sessions, metacognitive questions encourage learners to examine their beliefs, assumptions, and mental models. This examination makes these normally implicit thoughts explicit and therefore subject to change. Metacognition refers to higher order thinking that involves active control over the thinking processes engaged in learning.

USING REFLECTION TO IMPROVE DIALOGUE

A number of authors have made a distinction between debate and dialogue (cf. Bohm, 1996; Isaacs, 1999). Debate is typically used to understand the components of a problem, to identify distinctions between these components, and to justify and defend assumptions and positions. Debating generally involves persuading, selling, and telling. The ultimate aim of debate is to achieve agreement on one meaning and solution (Elinor & Gerard, 1998). Most of us are skilled in debate because this is the primary form of discourse and discussion used and encouraged in school or problem-solving activities.

People tend to be much less skilled and practiced in the process of dialogue. Through dialogue, we are able to see the whole among the parts as well as the connections between parts. Rather than defending assumptions, dialogue encourages us to inquire into or even challenge assumptions. Learning and inquiry are encouraged in dialogue rather than persuading, selling, and telling. Dialogue is a powerful tool for creating shared meaning among the many possible meanings (Elinor & Gerard, 1998).

Effective dialogue requires the suspension of opinions and criticism and promotes a creative exploration of issues and problems. Dialogue promotes collective thinking, a positive "team think" process. The group now has the potential to cocreate meaning as a common understanding is developed among its members. Dialogue brings people to a new way of perceiving an issue that may be of concern to all. That new understanding might include an identification of which actions or decisions should be taken individually and collectively (Dixon, 1996). Dialogue also involves a relationship. Central to the concept of dialogue is the idea that, through the interaction, people acknowledge the wholeness, not just the utility, of others (Dixon, 1996). The focus is on acquiring greater understanding and attaining shared meaning. Dialogue is based on the principle that the human mind is capable of using logic and reason to understand the world, rather than having to rely on the interpretation of someone who claims authority through force, tradition, superior intellect, or divine rights.

Dialogue is an affirmation of the intellectual capability of not only the individual but also the collective. It acknowledges that everyone is blind to his or her own tacit assumptions and needs the help of others to see them. It acknowledges that each person, no matter how smart or capable, sees the world from a given perspective and that there are other legitimate perspectives that could inform that view.

Isaacs (1999) noted that dialogue is more than a set of techniques for improving organizations, enhancing communications, building consensus, or solving problems. It is based on the principle that conception and implementation are intimately linked, with a core of common meaning. According to Isaacs, during the dialogue process "people learn to think together—not just in the sense of analyzing a shared problem or creating new pieces of shared knowledge, but in the sense of occupying a collective sensibility, in which the thoughts, emotions and resulting actions belong not to one individual, but to all of them together" (p. 358). Through dialogue, people can begin to move into coordinated patterns of action and start to act in an aligned way. They can begin to see how to fit parts into a larger whole.

ACTION LEARNING, CRITICAL REFLECTION, AND DIALOGUE

It should be clear from this discussion that the active questioning, probing, and inquiring process that is inherent in AL naturally promotes critical reflection and dialogue. Particularly in the early phases of problem solving, the use of open-ended questions creates divergent conversations that expand what is being communicated by uncovering many different perspectives. AL promotes the sense-making conversations to which Weick (1995) referred.

This is not to say that debate has no place in AL. At the back end of the problem-solving process, debate plays a key role in bringing issues to closure, in critiquing options, in creating implementation plans, and in assigning accountability. In this phase of problem solving, the appropriate use of debate and closed questions (i.e., questions with limited options, such as *yes* or *no*) is necessary to deliver an actionable solution. The appropriate use of questions to encourage dialogue as well as debate is covered in greater detail in chapter 5.

Reflective dialogue uses all three levels of reflection to generate learning in a social context. Individual reflection and metacognition are examples of dialogue with oneself. A central assumption of Revans' AL formula (1982a) is the presence of a true dialogue—dialogue that is powerful enough to put into words a team member's knowledge (P) as well as his or her thoughts, feelings, intentions, and assumptions. In the experiential sense, learning occurs when a concrete experience (e.g., a surprising problem, a new opportunity, an especially challenging conversation with a colleague) occurs, and this experience causes us to stop and reflect to think about the problem, our actions, and the challenges we expect. This moment of reflection is a dialogue either within ourselves or with our group and is an essential first step in the learning process because it generates the awareness of what we do not know, of a lack in our mental models or schema. This outcome requires a robust and honest dialogue, and that type of dialogue requires intention, practice, and courage.

REFLECTION AND THE PROCESS
OF DRAWING INFERENCES

Argyris and Schön (1978) noted that people often make inferences about what they experience (i.e., Why is this happening? What is their motivation? What will happen if I take a certain action?) without being aware of, much less critiquing, their inferring process. Argyris and Schön developed the *ladder of inference* to graphically capture the process of making inferences and drawing conclusions (see Figure 2.3).

Questions help members of the AL team stop and reflect on the various components of the inferencing process that they use to draw conclusions and make decisions. Properly framed questions encourage members of the team to identify what data they are drawing from, the assumptions they are making in attaching meaning to the data selected, what logic is applied to ascribe causation and draw conclusions, and what beliefs or generalizations are developed as a result of these conclusions. Focusing on the various components of the inferencing process also serves to dampen the enthusiasm and drive to draw rapid conclusions to support the often premature push for solutions and action.

FIGURE 2.3

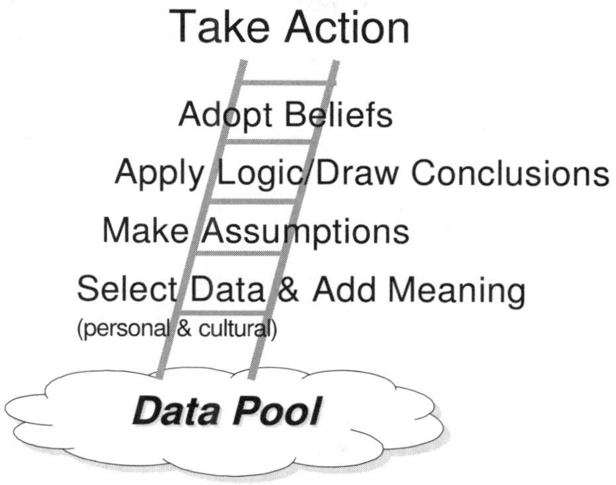

Take Action

Adopt Beliefs

Apply Logic/Draw Conclusions

Make Assumptions

Select Data & Add Meaning
(personal & cultural)

Data Pool

The ladder of inference. From *Overcoming Organizational Defenses: Facilitating Organizational Learning* (p. 88, Figure 5.1), by C. Argyris, 1990, Upper Saddle, NJ: Pearson Education. Copyright 1990 by Pearson Education. Reprinted with permission.

USING REFLECTION TO IDENTIFY DISCREPANCIES BETWEEN "ESPOUSED THEORIES" AND "THEORIES IN USE"

Reflection involves recalling, thinking about, pulling apart, making sense of, and trying to understand. Reflective inquiry challenges one's programmed knowledge. Typically, programmed knowledge corresponds to what Argyris and Schön (1978) referred to as *espoused theories*. Espoused theories generally correspond to theories and methods that people think they should be using. People usually think that their actual behavior approximates the behavior advocated or promoted by programmed knowledge. Argyris and Schön noted, however, that the actual behavior of people, or their *theories in use*, do not correspond, in many cases, to the espoused theories that people claim guide their behavior. This inconsistency does not decrease the importance of programmed knowledge; rather, espoused theories represent aspirational or abstract theories that become modified in actual practice by contextual and practical considerations or factors beyond one's conscious awareness or consideration. Mezirow (1991) pointed out that reflection involves bringing one's assumptions, premises, criteria, and schemata into consciousness so that they can be vigorously critiqued.

Reflective inquiry generates mutual support within the team as group members listen intently to one another. It is the key to transformative learning (Mezirow, 1991). Schön (1987) described how reflection involves several elements: (a) diagnosis (ability to frame or make sense of a problem), (b) testing (engaging in experimentation and reflection to test alternative solutions), and (c) the courage to act and take responsibility for one's actions.

THE ROLE OF THE ACTION LEARNING TEAM COACH IN FOSTERING CRITICAL REFLECTION

Lewin (1946) emphasized in action research that knowledge should be gathered and produced in the service of action. AL is an action research approach to everyday life. It is a philosophy of continuous learning. The ongoing and conscious transformation of experience to learning is a large part of the whole point of AL. It follows, then, that questioning and reflection are essential elements of AL. Without it, an AL assignment is essentially a task force. Yet we have noted that for various reasons (e.g., time constraints, conflict avoidance, lack of skills), reflection may not occur in the work setting. In order to overcome barriers to reflection the AL teach coach will intervene to ensure the quantity, timing, and quality of reflection.

Quantity of Reflection

The AL team coach plays an important catalyst role in generating opportunities for reflection. The coach's interventions encourage the team to take the time reflect. In playing this catalyst role, the team coach is aware that he or she can only affect the conditions for learning, not the learning itself. "Only learners themselves can learn, and only they can reflect on their own experiences . . . the learner is in total control" (Boud et al., 1985, p. 19).

Timing of Reflection

According to Schön (1987), there are two types of reflection: reflection-in-action and reflection-on-action. Reflection-in-action helps us as we complete a task; reflection improves our ability to share data, innovate, assess options, and observe results. As such, reflection is used throughout the AL experience. Reflection-in-action is generated spontaneously when a surprise or a problem occurs. Reflection-on-action takes place in the quiet spaces between action and, at the end of a project, involves the team thinking back on what it has done in order to discover how its actions impacted the results.

Quality of Reflection

The AL team coach takes care that reflection should consider both feelings and thought. As noted by Kofman and Senge (1995), "Action is critical, but the action we need can spring only from a reflective territory that includes not only cognition but body, emotions, and spirit as well" (p. 17). Boud et al. (1985) stated that any reflection that does not address either cognition or feelings is incomplete. Dilworth and Willis (2003) noted that reflection is a dialogue with one's self. Reflection can lead to a self-catharsis where one truly listens to his or her innermost self.

GEMS: AN ACTION LEARNING REFLECTION MODEL

The pace of life in an organization works against the routine practice of reflection. This lack of practice can lead to a lack of skill. It has been said that reflection is a simple and understandable process that most of us do not do, or do not do very well or with any frequency (Duley, 1981; Gustafson & Bennett, 1999). This lack of skill to engage in reflection is an important challenge for AL team coaches. Most teams need assistance to use the reflective skills needed to transform experience into knowledge and learning. The following framework is designed to provide practical guidelines for encouraging reflection in AL groups. There are two factors to consider in this framework: the expertise of the learner(s) and their resulting level of autonomy related to learning.

Expertise of the Learner(s)

The expertise of the learner(s) factor describes the AL participant's depth of knowledge, competence, and confidence relative to the task at hand. For example, when a particular problem or issue is first raised, many participants are low in all three areas. Later, participants gain more knowledge, competence, and confidence through asking questions, reflecting, and engaging in dialogue. It is expected that an AL team will consist of people who have varying degrees of knowledge of the subject matter at hand when they begin to address a problem or issue.

Level of Learning Autonomy

The level of expertise relative to the learning situation affects the capacity and capability of the learner to independently direct his or her own learning through reflection. Grow (1996) suggested that the capacity to engage in self-directed learning is situational and that it is the AL team coach's job to match methods to the student's needs.

Following Grow (1996), there are four stages of learner autonomy with respect to AL:

- Dependent learners are novices with respect to a topic or problem area and, therefore, may lack confidence and are temporarily dependent on the knowledge, skills, and experience of others.
- Somewhat self-directed learners are more confident in their ability to learn but are still not familiar with the topic or problem area.
- Intermediate self-directed learners have attained some skill and knowledge with the topic or problem and are willing to explore it. These learners are willing and able to engage in critical-thinking strategies.
- Highly self-directed learners are self-confident about their knowledge, skills, and understanding of the topic and problem, and they take responsibility for their own learning and thrive in an atmosphere of autonomy.

The expertise of the learners and their learning autonomy work together to provide a framework or hierarchy of reflection questions. Each level of reflection builds on the responses to the level below and ensures that the reflection is rooted in experience and culminates in learning.

- *Gather data*: Begin with questions related to the concrete experience. What did participants do, observe, read, and hear? Who was involved? What was said? What happened as a result of their work?
- *Evaluate*: In the evaluation level, the coach asks questions that encourage team members to explore their cognitive and affective experience. What did the experience make them think? How did it change their thinking about . . .? What did they learn? What worked? How did the experience feel? What did it remind them of? How did their apprehension change or their confidence grow? Did they feel successful, effective, and knowledgeable?
- *Meaning*: Critical reflection generates new data and, during the meaning phase, the team integrates that new data so that it changes knowledge, awareness, or understanding, which affects how members see things and, ultimately, how they will act.
- *Speculate*: Finally, the participants can engage in imaginative speculation, a type of rehearsal for future behaviors. Questions here might include: What will you do differently next time?

Definitions and examples of the GEMS framework are provided in Figure 2.4.

Guided critical reflection uses reflection and critical reflection to enhance the potential for deeper, transformative learning. As the coach uses the process, participants gain knowledge from experience. They also

FIGURE 2.4

State of the Learner(s)	Autonomy	GEMS Coaching Framework
Expert High knowledge High practice High competence High confidence	**Autonomous**	**Speculate:** Use dialogue to encourage Imaginative speculation, identify alternate applications. • Future focused, what might happen when? • What would you predict/infer from...? • What ideas can you add to...? • How would you create/design a new...? • What might happen if you combined...? • What solutions would you suggest for...? • What is the most important...?
Experienced High knowledge High practice Some competence Some confidence	**Intermediate Self-Direction**	**Meaning:** Use metacognition to accommodate and assimilate experience into knowledge. • How can you leverage what you know? • How is...an example of...? • How is...related to...? • Why is...significant? • What is surprising about your results?
Conceptually Aware Some knowledge Some practice Low competence Low confidence	**Some Self-Directed**	**Evaluate:** Critically reflect to evaluate and analyze the experience. • What worked and what didn't and why? • What were your assumptions around what would work? • How does...compare/contrast with...? • What evidence can you list for...?
New area of learning Low knowledge Low competence Low practice Low confidence	**Dependent**	**Gather:** Coach encourages team to reflect remembering and describing data. • What happened first (sequential)? • Who said what? • Where did it happen? • When did it happen? • How did we accomplish this task?

GEMS Coaching Framework.

increase their personal learning autonomy. There are certainly other factors that affect the capacity for learners to learn from reflection in the context of AL. These other factors may include individual learning styles, team member roles, power, previous learning experiences, overwhelming demands, or the accountability for practicing what has been learned. The GEMS framework takes these factors into account. It has been explicitly designed to assist the AL process to foster affective reflection on action. It is built on an understanding of adult learning and the personal practice of a number of AL facilitators.

Taking Action on the Problem

AL requires that the group be able to take action on the problem it is working on. Members of the AL group must have the power to take action themselves or be assured that their recommendations will be implemented (barring any significant change in the environment or the group's obvious lack of essential information). If the group can only make recommendations, it may lose its energy, creativity, and commitment. There is no real meaningful or practical learning until action is taken and reflected on; one is never sure an idea or plan will be effective until it has been implemented. Action enhances learning because it provides a basis and anchor for the critical dimension of reflection. The action of AL begins with taking steps to reframe the problem, then determining the goal, and only then formulating strategies and taking action.

Groups and individuals may choose between two sharply contrasting approaches to problem solving: (a) analytic/rational or (b) integrative. Proponents of the analytic/rational form of problem solving believe that there is one right solution to a problem. The group should develop a strategy on the basis of a careful analysis of the situation and then determine in a logical fashion the causes of the problem and the solutions to it.

Advocates of the integrative approach believe that there may be multiple right answers. Learning while taking the action, and acting out the thinking and learning, are equally important. Solving the problem is only part of the goal; learning from the opportunity is another part. The group attempts to collect a variety of insights in a holistic manner and to integrate these various possibilities. Intuition, open questions, and free associations are all tools of the integrative process of problem solving. Finding interrelationships between problems and solutions becomes valuable for the current problem as well as future problems (Hodgkinson & Clarke, 2007).

A Commitment to Learning

Solving an organizational problem provides immediate, short-term benefits to the company. In the long term, these immediate benefits are leveraged and multiplied as the individual and team learnings are applied more extensively throughout the organization. Thus, the learning that occurs in AL has greater value strategically for the organization than the immediate tactical advantage of early problem correction. Accordingly, AL places equal emphasis on the learning and development of individuals and the team as it does on the solving of problems; the smarter the group becomes, the quicker and better will be the quality of its decision making and action taking.

A number of conditions and circumstances created within the AL process generate high levels of learning and knowledge creation. Of greatest impact is the carefully planned, created, and sustained environment for learning generated by each of the six elements of AL, most especially by the actions of the AL team coach. The AL team coach is granted the authority and power to intervene whenever he or she senses there is an opportunity for the group to learn. Through a series of reflective questions, the coach guides the group in its learning. The coach acts as a facilitator, helping group members become more competent by (a) gaining new knowledge and information; (b) reasoning differently; (c) behaving more effectively in groups; (d) gaining greater understanding of their motives; (e) altering beliefs, values, and basic assumptions; and (f) acknowledging feelings and their impact.

The actions of the AL team coach help to provide a safe environment or "practice field" for reflection and learning to occur. Within the team, it is safe to be vulnerable, to learn, and to take risks. Failure in solving the problem or within the group is seen as an opportunity to learn rather than as an event that must be hidden or ignored.

Members are encouraged to recognize the potential in all situations to provide learning opportunities. Individuals are provided the time to reflect on their effectiveness and helpfulness to the group. Problems and crises are seen as valuable occasions for learning and development instead of as situations to be avoided (McGill & Beatty, 1995).

Because everyone in the AL group knows that he or she is there to learn as well as to solve the problem, there is a disposition within the group to learn. Learning is highly prized, and group and individual efforts are rewarded through improved performance. Team members are expected to contribute to each other's learning. The urgent and important problem serves as an energizing impetus to build their learning capabilities.

The questioning process within AL leverages learning opportunities and creates the physiological and psychological conditions for maximizing learning. In addition, the requirement for the group to take action forces the members to transfer ideas and theories into action. Because everyone is expected, strongly encouraged, and assisted to learn, the group environment is highly conducive to change and learning. As Sandelands (1998) observed, having a group of colleagues who bear a collective responsibility (i.e., comrades in adversity) creates synergies that amplify learning and performance.

AL encourages self-critical reflection as well as frank and honest feedback from fellow team members (Zuber-Skerritt, 1995). Further group learning is promoted as members discuss, share, and pool their ambitions and experiences, creating an environment that promotes group synergy.

An Action Learning Team Coach

Coaching is necessary for the group to focus on the important (i.e., the learnings) as well as the urgent (i.e., resolving the problem). The AL team coach helps the team members reflect on what they are learning as well as how they are solving the problem. Through a series of questions, the coach enables group members to reflect on how they listen, how they may have reframed the problem, how they give each other feedback, how they are planning and working, and what assumptions may be shaping their beliefs and actions. The coach also helps the team focus on what they are achieving, what they are finding difficult, what processes they are using, and the implications of these processes. The coaching role may be rotated among members of the group, or it may be assigned to one person throughout the duration of the group's existence.

Although it certainly would be possible for any group member to focus on the learning and to ask the questions assigned to the AL team coach, the reality is that these tasks are rarely, if ever, performed unless someone is designated to concentrate on them. In the absence of a designated coach, the reflective learning questions are simply not asked, and if they are, their quality and timing are poor.

To maximize individual and group learning, a person must be designated to focus exclusively on that task. Problem solvers (i.e., the group members) are focused, as they should be, on the urgent problem. The urgency of the problem always overwhelms the importance of learning (Covey, 1989). Thus, a person who has power must be assigned this important role or else it gets lost because of time and the pressures (and tyranny) of the urgent.

AL is dependent on a few simple rules and processes. The AL team coach ensures that these norms and learnings and processes are followed. The central role of the coach is to ensure that the group takes time to learn. The coach must take on this primary role because it is unlikely that the team by itself would take the necessary time to reflect and capture learnings. Without an AL team coach, the team would likely slip into the familiar pattern of activities that characterize task forces. In this environment, team members can easily go on "autopilot," mindlessly displaying habitual behavior that has been well-rehearsed and reinforced over years of organizational life. The coach creates and sustains the atmosphere of learning and reflective inquiry. It is simply too much to expect anyone to manage the learning as well as the problem.

If no one is assigned the role of AL team coach, and hence everyone becomes responsible for it, the learning questions will either get asked too often in too many ways or not asked at all. And the questions will probably be asked for purposes other than to help the group learn. In addition, it is important to note that group members may resent or be uncomfortable with anyone in the group arbitrarily assuming the role and functions of the AL team coach. They would likely challenge someone taking over this responsibility in a spontaneous way.

Two Ground Rules That Empower Action Learning

The need to balance chaos and order explains why AL, with its flexibility and search for innovation, requires clarity and stability. Because the power of AL is based on two key behaviors—reflective inquiry and continuous learning—establishing the following two ground rules to help ensure that the following fundamental tenets of AL are practiced is critical for success.

STATEMENTS SHOULD BE MADE ONLY IN RESPONSE TO QUESTIONS

Because questions provide so many benefits (as is illustrated in more detail in chap. 5), this AL ground rule assists all the group members in making the important transition from advocacy to inquiry. This ground rule does not prohibit the use of statements; as a matter of fact, there may still be more statements than questions during AL meetings because every question asked may generate one or more responses from each of the other members of the group, or from 5 to 10 statements per question. In addition, the percentage of statements versus questions often rises over the course of an AL process as the team moves from definition, analysis, and idea generation to critique, solution development, and implementation.

In the latter stages of problem solving, the percentage of statements and assertions that debate solution ideas increases, and the use of closed questions that bring discussion to closure so that decisions can be made becomes more important and frequent.

However, requiring people to think "questions first" transforms the overall dynamics of the group. The natural impulse to make statements and judgments changes to the impulse to listen and reflect. Once the problem or task has been introduced to the group, the members must first ask questions to clarify the problem before jumping into statements to solve the problem. AL recognizes the near direct correlation between the number and quality of questions and the final quality of the actions and learnings. Balancing the number of questions and the number of statements leads to dialogue, which is a proper balance between advocating and inquiring.

THE ACTION LEARNING TEAM COACH HAS THE POWER TO INTERVENE

The AL team coach focuses all of his or her energy and attention on helping the group learn but is not involved in working on the problem. The coach looks for opportunities to enhance the learning of the group so that its ability to solve the problem and develop innovative action strategies is increased. As noted earlier, too frequently the urgent drowns out the important, underscoring the necessity of ensuring that the important will not be forgotten or neglected. If the AL team coach is not empowered, the urgency of the problem will always win out over the importance of the learning. To maximize group learning, the coach must have the power to intervene whenever there is an opportunity for the group to learn, to improve on what is not going well, and to encourage the group to continue behaviors that are conducive to solving the problem.

In following this ground rule, when the AL team coach decides to intervene, the group should temporarily stop working on the problem, listen to the questions of the AL team coach (who only asks questions), and respond to those questions. Only when the coach indicates to the group that the questions are finished should the group resume problem solving. It is vital that the AL team coach be careful and economical in the timing of the intervention as well as in the amount of time used. The coach should be cognizant that the group members will subconsciously continue to work on the problem during and following the intervention. As a result, when returning to the problem, the group will appear rejuvenated and the team's performance will be noticeably more effective and creative.

The AL team coach also controls the conclusion of a session, letting the group know in advance when the problem solving will end at that session. He or she then uses the last 10 minutes to capture the learnings of that session and urges the team to consider how these learnings might be applied as individuals, as a team, and to the organization.

Australian Government Department Embraces the Power of Questions in Action Learning

"I can't stand it any longer! I have to make a statement!"

Sometimes during the first AL session, at least one participant blurts out this reaction. But as the staff of the Australian Federal Government Department of the Environment, Water, Heritage and the Arts works through the sessions, participants quickly begin to see the strengths and benefits of AL—and realize the power of asking questions.

The Department's Leadership Development Program uses AL as a key enabler for skills building and encouraging progress on the real-life problems that the staff manages on a day-to-day basis. At each Leadership workshop, staff self-select into groups of seven people and each group is supported by one of the Department's Senior Executives, who acts as the AL coach. At first, people struggle with the two ground rules of AL and with controlling their urges to give solutions. Initially, questions may be closed-ended or statements dressed up as questions. With each AL session, the quality of questions improves. The group moves faster to the real problem, and individuals focus more successfully on practicing their designated leadership skill.

Following the Leadership Development Program, the groups continue to meet in AL sessions on a monthly basis, still with the Senior Executive in the AL coach role. Progress reports are heard from the problem's presenters. The Australian Federal Government Department of the Environment, Water, Heritage and the Arts has found AL to be very useful, powerful, and effective.

Multiple-Problem and Single-Problem Action Learning Groups

AL groups may be formed for the purpose of handling either a single problem or several problems. Members of single-problem groups focus their energy on solving that problem. In this type of AL, both the membership and the problem are determined by the organization. The primary purpose of the group is to solve the problem assigned to them by the organization. The group may disband after handling just one problem or may continue for an indefinite period and work on a series of challenges. Membership in the AL groups is determined by the organization on the basis of the type of problem and the aims of the programs. For example, if the organization is seeking to create networks across certain business units, members from those units will be appointed to the team. If the development of high potential leaders is the goal, then these future leaders will be placed in these AL programs. If the issue is more focused, then participants may be selected according to their interests, experience, and/or knowledge. In some in-company AL programs, individuals may be allowed to volunteer, but the organization reserves the right to confirm or not confirm the final composition of an AL group.

In multiple-problem teams (also referred to as open-group or classic AL), each individual member brings his or her problem/task/project to the group for fellow members to help solve. The members self-select to join the group and support and assist each other on the problems that they bring. During each AL session, time is allocated for the group to work on each member's problem. Thus, a six-member group that meets for 3 hours would devote approximately 30 minutes to each person's problem. In open-group AL, the members may meet on a monthly basis for a few months or a few years. Open-group AL is usually voluntary and has more limited funding. Thus, the groups often meet on their own time and rotate the coaching role among the members. Over time, new members may join as older members withdraw. The members are usually from a variety of organizations and may include independent consultants and people who are no longer in the workplace.

Duration of Action Learning Programs

The duration of AL programs varies. Some teams are able to address the problem in a single meeting of several hours. In some cases, one meeting is all the time that is available for developing a solution.

In most situations, however, the team will meet multiple times over the space of a week or a number of months. In a massed program, an AL team may meet intensively (full time) over a period of a week. The Work-out process developed at GE (Davids, Aspler, & McIvor, 2002) is a good example of a massed program. In these programs, team members meet intensively over the course of a week to develop a solution that will be presented to a senior management team (usually including the CEO) at the end of the week. A typical AL process that is included in a longer leadership development program for high potential leaders can be described as a spaced program because the team meets intermittently on a weekly, biweekly, or monthly basis over 3 to 4 months (cf. Leonard & Goff, 2003).

The advantage of a massed program is that scheduling is simplified and members have less difficulty juggling their AL and regular job responsibilities. It is understood that, during the limited period that the team meets, all other responsibilities are suspended. The downside to a massed program is that there is often insufficient time to do both the research and development work necessary to develop an optimal solution. Frequently, shortcuts and compromises are necessary to meet the tight timelines. Spaced solutions, on the other hand, provide sufficient time to complete adequate research and to design high-quality, creative solutions. However, getting everybody together for each meeting can be a real challenge when managers are already struggling to meet the expectations of their regular job. In addition, bosses and managers often pressure their team members to treat the AL program as an outside activity (i.e., to participate as long as it does not interfere with their regular job). This expectation places the AL team members in a difficult double bind in which they are required to make choices between their job and their learning. These organizational issues are discussed more fully in chapter 7.

Formation of the Group or Team

The group may consist of volunteers or appointees and may be working on a single organizational problem or each other's individual problems. As discussed in the previous section, the group will have a predetermined amount of time and number of sessions, or its members may make decisions regarding these choices at the first meeting.

Exhibit 2.1 lists questions that should be considered in selecting members for AL teams.

Selection and Presentation of a Problem or Task to the Group

Problems (in single-problem designs) are typically selected by the organization and then assigned to the teams. Typically, senior management will identify a different problem for each AL team formed. Less frequently, the organization will form a team of high-potentials managers and authorize them to conduct research to identify an important and critical problem facing the organization. The issue of problem selection is covered in more detail in chapter 7. Exhibit 2.2 provides a list of the questions that should be considered in selecting a problem or project for AL teams to address.

EXHIBIT 2.1

Checklist for Selection of Members for Action Learning Teams

- Will membership be by choice or appointment?
- What will be the size of the Action Learning team?
- Will members from outside the organization be included?
- Will the groups operate on a full-time or part-time basis?
- How often will the groups meet?
- Are the most appropriate people in the group?
- Are the members clearly oriented to the principles of Action Learning?
- Are the members aware of how Action Learning is different from task forces and other problem-solving groups?
- Is the role of the Action Learning team coach clear and accepted?
- Are there any specific organizational or individual learning goals?
- Will single or multiple problem groups be used?
- Have team members agreed to processes and norms relative to air time, asking questions, and reflection?
- Is there agreement on ground rules relative to confidentiality, starting and stopping time, being supportive, and taking action between meetings? Have the members agreed on future dates for team meetings and committed to attending them regularly?
- Is there access to the necessary outside resources and knowledge?
- Is there a sense of ownership and responsibility for the problem? Have members identified a place convenient for participants?
- Does the team have a sponsor and are members clear about that person's role?

EXHIBIT 2.2

Checklist for Selection of Problem/Project for Action Learning Teams

- Who will choose the problem/projects—the organization or the individual managers or the group members?
- Who will be presenting the problem?
- Do the problems meet criteria for Action Learning problems?
- Are the problems feasible in terms of scope and scale?
- Are the problems urgent and important?
- Do they provide opportunities for learning and development?
- Is there a time frame for completing the projects?
- Do the problems or program need to be discussed with top leadership?
- Do managers and participants understand the time involved in working on these problems?
- Is this an exercise or a true problem (i.e., does management already have a suitable solution)?
- Does the organization have restrictions on possible strategies?
- Will teams work on single or multiple problems?

Capturing Learnings

Throughout and at any point during the session, the AL team coach may intervene to ask the group members questions that will enable them to reflect on their performance and to find ways to improve their performance as a group. Exhibit 2.3 provides a list of the questions that should be considered when helping a team capture the learnings that result from its experiences in AL.

How to Use Action Learning— A Real Case

A large energy company needed to develop a new work schedule that ensured the facilities would be covered 24 hours a day. The present system was one that sapped the earnings, energy, and morale of the workers and often left the company unable to meet the demands of customers. Management's imposition of a 6-day-per-week schedule was a burden to the workers and their families, especially because many of the workers needed to drive more than 2 hours per day to the remote mines. Frustrations and anger abounded on all sides, and everyone saw the problem in a different way. The situation demanded action.

EXHIBIT 2.3

Checklist for Ensuring Learning in the Action Learning Process

- Have the learnings been applied to situations in the workplace? broadly across the organization?
- What is the quality of individual development and learning? of team development and learning?
- Are the greater, long-term benefits and leveraging of learning valued?
- Has there been a review of the learning?
- Has there been a systematic analysis of how the learning has been applied to other parts of the organization?
- What were the major benefits to the members of the Action Learning program?
- Have verbal or written reports been prepared for clients, managers, and other interested parties?
- How can future Action Learning programs in the company be improved?
- What follow-up actions or activities have been planned?

Management brought together a diverse group of eight people to find a new solution to this problem over a 2-day period. After the group received a brief introduction to the six components of AL, the group began diagnosing the problem and soon saw it as a stimulus/opportunity not only to design and take effective action but also to learn how to work better as a team and become more competent leaders. The AL group consisted of a wide variety of individuals—technicians from different work sites of the company, a senior administrator, and a manager from another industry. The eight members included new employees as well as older, experienced workers. Some were actually experiencing the problem, whereas others needed to understand why it was a problem. There was pressure to solve this problem and high hopes placed on performance improvement. Management indicated that the group could indeed come up with the solutions and that everyone's ideas were needed; if group members could ask good questions and learn from each other, the problem could be solved.

Initially, members asked questions hesitantly and reluctantly. Many wanted to use statements and push for their solutions. Occasionally, the AL team coach asked them to turn their statements into questions and to listen and reflect before answering. Everyone became involved; often the younger, inexperienced members had better questions, became more confident, and received more support. Gradually, the group came to realize that the issue was as much a feeling that employees had no say in the changes as it was the difficulty of finding a solution that met the needs of workers, customers, and management. The members quickly moved from focusing on individual solutions to seeking what would be best for the organization.

Following a systematic examination of numerous issues, potential impacts of actions, and likelihood of success, the group developed three possible solutions that were submitted to employees at the affected sites as well as to top management. The alternatives were tested as well as refined. Four weeks later, the plants shifted to new schedules that resulted in improved morale among workers, higher satisfaction for customers, and better earnings stability—a measurable performance benefit for management.

The members of the group were advised that this activity was both a problem-solving as well as a learning program. If they could learn and share together, they would reach a truly innovative solution. Also, they were expected to learn about themselves as leaders and professionals and to identify learnings that could be applied to their particular work sites and to the organization as a whole. The climate and expectations were established to increase learning and performance; group members were to learn from each other and to be aware of the presuppositions and filters that hindered or helped their learning. Consequently, everyone could and did become concerned with helping each other learn and with developing themselves.

Throughout the sessions, the AL team coach focused on helping the group reflect on learning. The coach's presence alerted everyone that time and effort would be spent on learning and that they would be assisted as they applied "breakthrough" thinking to create new strategies. The coach served as a model by asking only positive, supportive questions to help members understand and improve the work of the group and apply their learnings throughout the organization.

Reflection Questions

1. Why are all six components of AL needed to optimize the power and speed of AL?
2. AL problems should be urgent. What happens to the learning, the group, and the results when the problem is not urgent?
3. How and why can the AL coach enable a group to simultaneously work on both action and learning?
4. How is the AL coach similar to and different from a task facilitator? What would be some difficulties you would face in moving from a facilitator role to a coaching role?
5. Would you consider introducing both single project and multiple project AL programs into your organization? What would be the impact and benefits?
6. Does your organization encourage a questioning culture? How could such a culture build better teams and greater leaders?

The Interdisciplinary Foundations for Action Learning | 3

R eg Revans, the creator of Action Learning (AL), was an empiricist. He did not build his theory and methods from studying adult learning, participative problem solving and decision making, executive development, or the effect of asking questions on the quality of team results. He learned primarily from his own evolving experience and practice. From these, Revans developed an effective, pragmatic approach to dealing with critical organizational issues while concurrently educating and training participants in his strategies and tactics.

Nevertheless, the core processes that we have identified for the AL process are supported by the research and theory developed in a broad spectrum of disciplines ranging from the behavioral and organizational sciences to related disciplines such as adult education and business. Although in-depth knowledge of these theories is not necessary for effective practice as an AL team coach, an awareness of the research and theory that supports the practice of AL will bolster the confidence of AL team coaches and help them resist the ever-present pressure to deviate from the principles that will rapidly produce high-performing teams and creative and innovative solutions.

Kurt Lewin pointed out that there is nothing quite as practical as a good theory (Marrow, 1969). This chapter provides some additional ideas and "mental models" (Argyris, 1993;

Johnson-Laird, 1994) that the AL team coach can apply when crafting questions that foster reflection on an issue or dynamic that the team is grappling with. O'Neil (1999, discussed in more detail in chap. 10) described some of the mental models that AL team coaches draw on in their work. It is our position that being familiar with and able to access useful mental models in real time is an extremely valuable AL team coaching skill.

As O'Neil (1999) pointed out, experienced AL team coaches have a set of mental models that they rely on in trying to make sense of what is going on. Coaches typically rely on the mental models they learned in their academic and professional training. This is true whether the coach's background is in psychology, organization development, education, counseling or psychotherapy, business, medicine, engineering, or the physical sciences. It is only natural that people draw on the models that they have learned and applied to problems and that fit how they see and relate to the world.

The aim of this chapter, then, is to broaden AL team coaches' repertoire of mental models so that they can be more flexible in the way they view the process before them. By extension, being able to see the problem from different angles or frames helps AL team coaches to ask better questions that encourage and foster more innovative and creative solutions. Good questions illuminate the learning opportunity for team members, stimulate them to reflect on their unfolding experiences, and enable them to improve their individual and team efforts to achieve their goals while also acquiring and practicing their leadership competencies (Marquardt, 2005). The questions that we offer following each theory or conceptual model are not definitive. Rather, we present the kinds of questions that can illuminate the theories for AL team members. AL team coaches should strive to learn how to craft their own good questions. These questions may be generated in the moment or after reflecting (and perhaps after reading this chapter) between sessions.

How People Learn: Foundational Theories of Learning

The process of learning has been studied intensively for more than a century. Learning was one of the first processes explored by the science of psychology that emerged from the academic discipline of philosophy in the latter half of the 19th century. Many of the early theories have become so embedded in contemporary practice that people may hardly pay any attention to them. We provide a brief review of these theories, highlighting the elements that have particular relevance to AL.

CLASSICAL OR PAVLOVIAN CONDITIONING

Many people are familiar with the famous experiment by Pavlov (1927) in which he paired a neutral stimulus (e.g., the sound of a bell) with a stimulus that provided a predictable behavior (e.g., the sight and smell of meat, which stimulates an autonomic response of salivation in a dog). After pairing the bell with the meat for a number of repetitions, the sound of the bell alone produced salivation in the dog. The natural response of salivating at the sight and smell of food had become conditioned to or associated with the sound of the bell.

This principle of associating one stimulus with another so that a previously neutral behavior (i.e., one that had little meaning) attains specific meaning and a predictable response can be observed in the way the team responds to the AL team coach. Because AL team coaches are given the special power to intervene whenever they perceive a learning opportunity, their words take on special meaning. When the coach pulls a chair forward in order to say something, individuals in the team become conditioned to stop talking and listen intently.

Although this sort of conditioning has a positive effect in amplifying the impact of the AL team coach, it can have a less desirable effect with other issues related to status. For example, when the contributions of some members are overvalued or devalued because of their role or status in the organization, the AL team coach may choose to intervene to ask questions that challenge the linkage between formal roles and status and the value of their contributions.

OPERANT CONDITIONING

Operant conditioning, also known as respondent or Skinnerian conditioning (after the famous experimental psychologist B. F. Skinner), is often associated with rats pressing levers to receive food pellets. The key principle in operant conditioning is that behavior that is rewarded (by something desired by the subject) becomes reinforced, such that, the behavior is more likely to occur in the future (Skinner & Ferster, 1957). Behaviors that are not reinforced by receiving a reward disappear or become extinguished over time. The scheduling of reinforcement is also important. For instance, a behavior does not have to be rewarded every time to maintain the link between the behavior and the reward. If the goal is to eliminate an undesirable behavior, such as leading with statements rather than with questions, then the violation of the basic ground rule that statements always follow questions must be noted each time it occurs. Otherwise, people's reactions to the statement will reinforce the statement-leading behavior, and the pattern of leading with statements will be retained as an informal norm.

Because of their special role and power, AL team coaches need to be very aware of which behaviors they reinforce and reward by a comment and, perhaps more significantly, which behaviors they let occur without a comment. If dysfunctional behaviors such as domination of conversation by a few, favoritism due to status or power, or scapegoating of unpopular views are allowed to occur without continuous intervention by the AL team coach, these behaviors will be sustained. The coach needs to note dysfunctional behaviors immediately after they occur. Addressing this issue later will only make it more difficult for the team to deal with the problem.

EXPERIENTIAL LEARNING

The self is not something ready-made, but something in continuous formation through choice of action.

John Dewey (1916, p. 408)

We could have begun this section with an historical review of experiential learning by discussing Socrates and his method of asking leading questions (which, for the most part, he already had the answers for). However, we chose to begin with John Dewey. He articulated the theory that—perhaps because of the human capacity for creating symbols (i.e., language) that represent things, people, activities, events, and situations—people learn when they conceive of some plan of action to achieve some desired end result and then put that plan into action (Dykhuizen, 1973). Dewey pointed out that such learning takes place only as people interact with their social and physical environments. They learn action sequences that result in the achievement of their desired consequences or end results. Argyris (1993) identified these learned sequences as mental models and theories of action (i.e., to achieve result A, in situation B, take action C). Without external validation and corroboration, people may create idiosyncratic theories of action composed of the accidental juxtaposition of several events that may correlate with one another. Although people may assume that one event causes the other(s), there may not be any fundamental causal relationship. AL team coaches must be alert when AL team members apply or construct their implicit mental models.

AL team coaches should enable individual team members to surface and make their implicit mental models explicit, thereby making them accessible to critical assessment and possibly to modification. For example, a team member might suggest an action that is based on her mental model. The AL team coach might ask, "What is your theory?" or "What do you think would happen as a result of taking that action?"

Theoretically, mental models that inform planning and action and that frequently enable people to achieve their intended goals are retained, stored in memory, and applied to other situations that are perceived to be similar. Action plans that consistently fail to achieve desired results are usually discarded (extinguished) fairly quickly. As noted earlier, actions that occasionally achieve a person's desired results—even though they mostly fail to do so (intermittent reinforcement)—are the most difficult to extinguish. These flawed, implicit mental models are used persistently, usually inappropriately and ineffectively, but with considerable intensity. Over time, people develop a repertoire of both effective and ineffective mental models that inform their perceptions, thinking, feeling, and actions. Generally, people do not reflect upon or distinguish between those mental models that are effective and those that are not. Instead, they habitually (if not compulsively) apply their unexamined, flawed mental models that inform their efforts to achieve their intended purposes in various situations. They often act as if they were addicted to their nonconscious mental models.

AL team coaches can create learning opportunities when team members' actions clearly do not produce the desired consequences. A question might be, "What did you expect?" This could be followed up with "Why did you expect that?" or "What is the basis of that expectation?" Such questions must be asked sincerely and in the spirit of genuine inquiry and curiosity, not sarcastically.

As Argyris (1993) stated, "Learning occurs whenever errors are detected and corrected. An error is any mismatch between intentions and actual consequences" (p. 49). People who have addicted themselves to ineffective, flawed mental models seem to have considerable difficulty in recognizing their own errors that result in a mismatch between their intentions and the actual consequences. They are most likely to attribute such mismatches to bad luck or the lack of cooperation or skill of other persons. Thus, they make it difficult for themselves to learn from their own experiences. Argyris (1993) also pointed out that

> theories of action are governed by a set of values that provide the framework for the action strategies chosen. Thus, human beings are designing beings. They create, store, and retrieve designs [mental models] that advise them how to act if they are to achieve their intentions and act consistently with their governing values. (p. 50)

Established patterns of perceiving, thinking, feeling, and acting reveal themselves at work (with colleagues, peers, superiors, and subordinates as well as with customers and suppliers), at home (with spouses, parents, and children), with their extended families, in informal social situations, at political events, at religious gatherings, and in their communities. Under relatively predictable circumstances, people are rarely curious about how their behavior is perceived by and affects other people. They take it for granted that their actions achieve their desired results—without adverse consequences or side effects. They see no pressing reason for reflection and introspection. The question then is, What does it take for such people to recognize that some of their habitual mental models are suboptimal and do not serve their purposes? Phrased differently, How can we encourage people to examine and reflect upon the ladder of inference described by Argyris and Schön (1978) and discussed in chapter 2 (see Figure 2.3)?

ANDROGOGICAL LEARNING— MALCOLM KNOWLES

Perhaps the best-known advocate for andragogical or adult learning is Malcolm Knowles (1978, 1984a, 1984b). His classic differentiation between pedagogy and andragogy illustrated the distinctions between some forms of traditional training and development and the AL approach that we recommend for leadership development and organizational change (see Table 3.1).

AL team coaches must enable team members to adjust to an andragogical orientation to learning as they work on their task. Many AL team members enter their first team meeting with an implicit expectation that the coach will function as a team leader. As such, they may be prepared to adopt a passive, dependent role that is subservient to the coach. The AL team coach may make one or two declarative statements about her role at the beginning of the first session. Basically, these are restatements of the two basic rules of AL: (a) no statements without a question and (b) the team must agree to stop whatever they are doing when the AL team coach announces that he or she has a question. By leaning back and observing, the AL team coach indicates that the AL team members are to, once again, take responsibility for themselves. As they discover that they cannot rely on the AL team coach to lead them, they learn to rely on themselves and each other and to take responsibility for their work. This is an application of Knowles's first principle of andragogy.

As they work together (e.g., to clarify the issue they are confronting, set a goal, adopt a strategy to achieve this goal, develop an action plan), AL team members discover that they each bring useful information, perspectives, interests, and concerns. They typically discover that one of their process challenges is to identify and utilize the team's human resources. This discovery process is accelerated when the AL team coach and, gradually, the team members ask open-ended questions of one another and then listen respectfully to the responses. This is an application of Knowles's second principle of andragogy.

To apply Knowles's third principle, AL coaches must wait until the AL team members become aware that they have exhausted the knowledge

TABLE 3.1

The Contrast Between Pedagogical and Andragogical Learning

Pedagogy	Andragogy
1. Students are dependent, submissive, and follow directions. Teachers make all decisions—what is to be learned as well as how, when, and where. Teachers also determine whether students learn the subject matter.	1. Adult learners are self-directed, responsible for their own lives. They need to be perceived and treated by others as capable of taking responsibility for themselves. They resent and resist others imposing their will when they have not had a chance to participate in decisions that affect them.
2. Students have little real-world experience that is relevant to what is taught; they have little of value to offer as learning resources.	2. Adult learners enter educational activities with a great amount and variety of pertinent experience. They are rich learning resources for one another. Their life experiences are a major source of their sense of identity; if these experiences are ignored, not valued, or not used, the person feels rejected.
3. Students are ready to learn when told what they have to learn to achieve some extrinsic result (e.g., good grades, promotion).	3. Adults are ready to learn when they feel a need to know or to do something that helps them perform more effectively in some area of their lives.
4. Students see learning as the acquisition of prescribed subject matter (content).	4. Adult learners enter educational activities with life-centered, task-centered, or problem-centered orientations. They learn to perform a task, solve a problem, or live a better quality of life.
5. Students are motivated by external pressure (e.g., from parents, bosses, teachers, competition with peers, fear of failure).	5. Adult learners are motivated internally (e.g., by the desire for and awareness that they are learning to enhance their self-esteem, social recognition, quality of life, self-confidence, self-realization, or competence).

and skills they brought with them into the team and feel stuck. To get unstuck and to progress from this point, they become aware that they need to proactively seek new knowledge or skills. They may or may not have a clear idea of how to locate and acquire the necessary knowledge and skills. The AL team coach may then ask, "What specific knowledge (or skill) do you think the team needs?" and "Where might the team locate this needed knowledge (or skill)?" The AL team coach may then ask, "OK, who has the next question?" These kinds of questions fulfill Knowles's third principle of andragogy.

The focus of the AL team coach's attention is on helping team members to achieve their goals, reflect on their collective experiences, learn how to work more effectively, learn about themselves, and develop and practice new skills. Thus, the essence of Knowles's fourth andragogical principle is satisfied.

As AL team members learn and develop proficiency in the application of new, relevant knowledge and skills, they feel increasingly confident (in themselves), competent, and comfortable—aspects of what Bandura (1997) referred to as *self-efficacy*. They are mastering the process of learning how to learn, and this makes them feel powerful—as individuals and as a team. As a result, they increasingly seek new challenges, take considered risks, explore, discover, reflect, and learn. This becomes a self-reinforcing, positive cycle of growth and development that expands and enhances the basis of the AL team members' self-esteem and self-worth. This process fulfills Knowles's fifth principle of andragogical learning.

Pedagogy is clearly, but not exclusively, appropriate in enabling children to learn. There are times when pedagogy is also relevant and useful for adults. Knowles (1984b) pointed out that pedagogy is appropriate when adult learners enter "a totally strange territory of content . . . they may be truly dependent on didactic instruction before they can take much initiative in their own learning" (p. 13). This corresponds to Revans's insistence that learning is a function of programmed knowledge, experience, and questions. This also corresponds to the evident need to provide inexperienced members of AL teams with information, theory, and skill development opportunities that are relevant to their tasks—before and during the AL process.

HABITS OF LEARNING

AL coaches should understand the various habits of adult learners. First, they need to understand the learning experience over a lifetime. Children learn rapidly (compared with adults) and in predictable stages (cf. Piaget, 2000). In the first few years, kinesthetic experience of the world presents infants with endless opportunities to learn through their five senses or through sensorimotor learning. With the acquisition of language, children enter a new phase focusing on auditory stimuli. In this preoperational phase, the child perceives, uses, and creates symbols to represent thoughts and tangible reality. As children enter formal educational systems, the concrete operational phase begins. Reading is emphasized, and information is accessed via the visual arena. Learning is characterized by reasoning and memorization.

Starting at about age 11, abstract thinking, imagination, and critical reasoning are increasingly important factors (Piaget, 1966/2000). Abstract conceptual thinking represents an important shift in the learner; it makes the capacity to think about one's own thinking possible. It gives the learner control over what is learned. This is one of the pivotal shifts marking the difference between adult learning and child learning. What follows is a lifetime of potential learning. Retaining the capacity to learn in the face of adult challenges and responsibilities, however, requires conscious practice and safeguarding against loss of the habits that promote learning. These habits include personal adaptability, an abiding sense of wonder, reflective practices, critical thinking skills, and metacognitive exploration.

Various authors have described these habits, linking them in important ways to learning in adulthood. These are some of the essential habits of learning that form the core skills of adult learning agility. Brief definitions for each of these habits are presented in Table 3.2. The processes of

TABLE 3.2

Habits of Learning

Habit	Description
Adaptability	■ Adaptive learning is demonstrated when individuals acquire knowledge, solve problems, or learn to act in a situation in which tasks, goals, and other conditions are given (Ellström, 2002).
A sense of wonder	■ Wonder is experienced when one is overcome by awe or perplexity, such as when something one assumes is familiar becomes profoundly unfamiliar or when something occurs that is totally unexpected (Van Manen, 2002).
Reflection	■ Reflection is "active, persistent and careful consideration of any belief or supposed form of knowledge in the light of the grounds that support it and the further conclusion to which it leads." (Dewey, 1933/1997, p. 9) ■ Reflection is the process through which individuals make sense of their experiences and that yields a basis for future action and initiates new or adapted ideas in the process (Kolb, 1984). ■ "Reflection is a generic term for those intellectual and effective activities in which individuals engage to explore their experiences in order to lead to a new understanding and appreciation." (Boud et al., 1985, p. 19) ■ Schön (1987) identified two types of reflection: reflection-in-action (thinking on your feet) and reflection-on-action (retrospective thinking). Practitioners use reflection when they encounter situations that are unique and when individuals are not able to apply known theories or techniques previously learned through formal education.
Critical reflection	■ Critical reflection is a process "comprising praxis of action, reflection on action, further action, and reflection on the further action and so on in a continuous cyclical loop." (Brookfield, 1987, p. 93) ■ Critical reflection is "carried out individually or interactively with others in order to optimize individual or collective practices, or analyze and try to change organizational or individual values, mental models, beliefs or attitudes." (Van Woerkom, 2003, p. 186)
Metacognition	■ Metacognition refers to higher order thinking that involves active control over the thinking processes engaged in learning (Flavell, 1987). ■ Metacognitive theory focuses on (a) the role of awareness and management of one's thinking, (b) individual differences in self-appraisal and management of cognitive development and learning, (c) knowledge and abilities that develop through experience, and (d) constructive and strategic thinking (Paris & Winograd, 1990).

reflection, critical reflection, and metacognition were covered in more detail in chapter 2.

Learning is a direct result of learners' capacity to extract meaning from their interactions, reflective thoughts, acknowledged needs, even from their fears and hopes. People develop life-long habits of learning and, particularly in the unsettling wake of discontinuous experiences, test the utility of these habits. Agile adult learners develop and consistently use learning habits that transform their experiences into useful knowledge.

AL team coaches can help team members to learn from their individual and collective learning experiences by asking them to reflect on and record their experiences in a personal journal and then to examine those experiences by applying some of the questions they may have learned from the coach.

For example, early in a discussion, the AL team coach might promote the habit of adaptability by asking questions that help team members to see the problem differently. Using techniques suggested by Gordon (1961), the AL team coach can help team members see relationships between the problem and other knowledge and experiences by asking the following questions: How is this problem like other problems? (direct analogy); What associations do team members have to personal experiences? (personal analogy); What additional problems are embedded in the identified problem? (compressed conflict).

To promote a sense of wonder, the coach can ask team members: What is the most fascinating aspect of the problem? What baffles you most about this problem? Why has it been so hard to solve this problem?

To promote critical reflection, the AL team coach may ask questions suggested in Table 2.1: What do you know or believe about this issue? (analyzing assumptions); How do you see it? (surfacing bias); What if . . . were changed? (encouraging imaginative speculation); What is not obvious about the data? What data are missing? What's untrue? (encouraging reflective skepticism).

To encourage metacognition, the AL team coach might ask: How do you see the problem now? What has changed? (double-loop learning); What are the critical success factors/governing variables for reaching the team's goal? (double-loop learning); What have you learned about yourself in working on this problem? (triple-loop learning).

The AL coach might choose to ask the team as a whole only one or two (certainly not all) of these questions. In such instances, it would be useful and illuminating for team members to write down their responses in their journals and then read the responses aloud. Continuing this line of questioning, the coach can ask the team members to assess whether the responses are essentially the same or different. Without inviting or requesting any discussion, the AL coach could then ask, "OK, who has the next question?"

Barriers to Using the Habits of Learning

Many adults continuously experience or create barriers that discourage or prevent their own learning. Some of these barriers are described in Table 3.3.

AL team coaches need to recognize these barriers to adult learning if and when they emerge and interfere with their AL team's effectiveness. Some elaboration, as follows, may be useful.

Passivity and Dependence

Many highly talented and strategically critical people at all levels of all kinds of organizations have learned how not to learn. For example, when the AL team coach observes a team member actively engaged in

TABLE 3.3

Barriers to Adult Learning

Barrier	Description
Passivity and dependence	Most people learn how to be taught; they have not learned how to learn. The pedagogical model that is appropriate for concrete operational learning fosters dependence on an instructor and passivity in the learner (Knowles, 1984a).
Defense systems	Highly successful people get that way because they are seen as good at solving problems. Thus, they rarely fail and therefore have no mechanisms for learning from failure (failure is caused by others or circumstances; Crossan, 2003).
The "cost" of learning	The psychological cost of acknowledging the absence of competence in learning something new is a major barrier. People see such gaps as weaknesses (Atherton, 2005).
Overwhelming demands	Managers are often so overwhelmed and absorbed by day-to-day expectations and demands that they have difficulties reflecting on their goals, deciding what really matters, and making sure the right things happen. Time for reflection and therefore learning is scarce (Bruch & Ghoshal, 2004).
Unexplored choices	Focused on the demands and constraints of their jobs, most managers develop tunnel vision and concentrate on immediate needs and requirements. They do not perceive or exploit their freedom to make choices about what they could do and how they could do it. No experimentation, no learning (Bruch & Ghoshal, 2004).

pedagogically teaching something that he knows and presumes the others do not know, the learners become passive and dependent on the "teacher." Sometimes such pedagogy is appropriate and useful—for example, when one team member possesses useful information that others lack. However, in many instances pedagogy is tolerated as a tedious but accepted cultural norm and discussions sound like a series of monologues that do not add value to the team's deliberations. If the coach perceives the latter situation, he or she might ask the following:

- How can we determine if this is an effective way of exchanging information among team members?
- Write down in your journals what you think the speaker has been saying. Let's have each person read what they have written.
- To what extent do we have agreement about what was communicated?
- What can we learn from this?
- How might we determine if everyone needs this information?
- Who already possessed this information?
- What did you decide to do when you realized you already knew what was being explained? Why?
- Is there a more effective way to exchange information among team members?

This line of inquiry enables team members to reflect and consider if they have fallen into a pattern of docile dependency.

Defense Mechanisms

Consider the emergence of defense mechanisms that people use to avoid anxiety associated with a challenge to their sense of competence and self-esteem. The experience of being members of AL teams generally tests participants' implicit assumptions that their habitual behavior patterns are universally effective. If a participant spontaneously exhibits one of his habitual behavior patterns, others may perceive that behavior as inappropriate, counter-productive, ineffective, or unacceptable and react in a critical manner. They may offer the participant critical feedback about the impact of this behavior on them and on the team's performance. This is most likely to occur when, at the end of a session, the AL team coach asks the team, "What can we do better next time?"

Perhaps a team member responds by saying, "We can allow each other enough air time for each of us to contribute our ideas and opinions before we act as if a mutually acceptable decision has been made." Several other team members may express agreement with this. The AL team coach or another team member might then ask, "What is it about our performance today that led you to suggest this particular way of improving?" The response may be a discussion of how some members have suggested a particular course of action and immediately acted as if the entire team had agreed.

However, they may say nothing at the time. The person in question may or may not be pointed out. Nevertheless, the other AL team members will have disconfirmed the person's previously unchallenged assumption that her preferred behavior pattern was always effective and appropriate. In such ways, solicited or unsolicited feedback can stimulate questions about the effectiveness of any participant's habitual behavior patterns.

The means by which people defend themselves against the anxiety that is created when their nonconscious assumptions are challenged or disconfirmed are many and varied. AL team coaches have options: Address the defenses (obvious or subtle) explicitly and directly or leave them alone. If a team member's defenses interfere with his own learning, the option is clear. Our preference is to leave them alone. We are not in a contracted psychotherapy relationship; we are engaged in a practical learning experience. If the person's defenses intrude on and disrupt the learning, the AL team coach would be obliged to address the issue privately with the team member.

The "Cost" of Learning

All learning that goes beyond simple adaptation requires risk, even if it is the relatively low-risk act of admitting a lack of knowledge or expertise. Self-reflective awareness or insight prompts the admission to self and/or others of acknowledged "chinks in the armor" that creates the potential for learning. Without insight that something is not known, people just do not initiate learning. The dilemma is clear: To develop and learn, people must adopt a vulnerable position, ask for feedback, take a close look at their own performance, and experiment with their behavior (Van Woerkom, 2003).

A predictable situation ensues when people move back and forth between two quite dissimilar organizational contexts: routine activities and participation in an AL team. Usually, their routine work objectives are reasonably precise and measurable, their daily role responsibilities are well established and clear, they are reasonably competent in the use of their tools and work processes, and their relationships with colleagues are generally predictable. Their status is understood, accepted, and respected by others.

In contrast, AL team members are often recruited by senior managers who consider them to have executive potential. Participants often come from the ranks of middle management or are highly esteemed and specialized individual contributors. They are used to being influential leaders in their respective contexts. However, AL team members are asked to work collaboratively—as a team of equals—in coping with unfamiliar (unprecedented or discontinuous) issues, settings, people, and work methods as well as with unusual group structures.

Many AL team members know how to operate as leaders in their respective areas of responsibility but may have little recent experience in a team of equals. They may or may not be aware of their incompetence in participating as members of such a team. AL team members are often confused when they engage the unprecedented issues with ambiguous goals and uncertain strategies to achieve those goals. Team members are asked to collaborate with previously unknown participants in an unfamiliar context, the AL team, in which the other participants' areas of expertise, experience, roles, and status are different and often unfamiliar from their own.

Participants are often surprised to discover that their preferred habitual behavior patterns, which have been reasonably successful in their familiar organizational contexts, are often counterproductive in the AL team. So, when their implicit assumptions and expectations are disconfirmed, AL team members often consider the question, Shall I persist with or shall I change my behavior?

To change their habitual behavior patterns, people must acknowledge, to themselves and to others, what they consider a deficit, defect, or inadequacy. This may carry the risk of a loss in self-esteem and prestige. They may also anticipate that they would look foolish if they tried to change or that changing is too complex a problem. They may think changing behaviors would take too much time and force them to sacrifice their work. This may be seen as too great a cost for some people to pay. Alternatively, many AL team members feel relieved to disclose their problem; let go of their unproductive habitual behaviors; and experiment with acquiring new, more effective behaviors.

AL team coaches can help AL team members deal with this issue. Coaches may ask the following questions: What are the risks you would have to take if you chose to continue to behave as you usually do? What are the risks you would have to take if you decided to change and experiment with acquiring new behaviors? How can you determine whether these anticipated risks are realistic?

Overwhelming Demands

Very busy people need to make space in their work lives to fully participate in AL team experiences. This can be accomplished in several ways, each of which has its advantages and disadvantages. One way is to have the AL project manager, with the support of the project's sponsors and champions, negotiate with the AL participants' managers for reduced work expectations. (The individual AL team members may not have sufficient leverage to conduct these negotiations alone.) Furthermore, the performance management system must be modified so that participation in the AL project is a significant component of each AL partici-pant's performance goals. These modifications should be made for all participants, including team members, sponsors, and champions. This must be coordinated between the AL participants' managers and the organization's human resources department.

Managers frequently expect those participating in AL programs to also meet all of their regular work responsibilities. Thus, a workweek that is already 50 hours to 60 hours in length expands to include late evenings and weekends to stay apace of the demands from both sets of responsibility. (As one wag put it, "What else do they have to do between midnight and 6 a.m.?") This may be thought of as a test of the AL team members' loyalty, endurance, and dedication. However, in our experi-ence, this is thoughtlessness that actually punishes AL team members for good behavior. It is also generally accepted that working excessive hours (60 to 80 hours per week) is actually less productive than work-ing normal hours.

The AL coach may assist the AL team to explore whether this is a common issue. If many team members are affected, the coach may ask, What might you, as a team, do to surface and deal with this issue? Fur-thermore, the AL project manager might explore the conditions under which all AL team members agreed to participate in the project and, if appropriate, elevate the issue to the organization's executive manage-ment team.

We have heard about an interesting policy operative in Singapore. According to Judy Willis (personal communication), when a new respon-sibility is added to a person's job, two existing responsibilities are taken away to make room to learn to perform the new responsibility.

Unexplored Choices

Some people habitually have a very narrow task focus, sometimes called *tunnel vision*. They ignore both the broad systemic and the long-term strategic implications of their work. They keep their heads down and focus only on what is in front of them. This may be a consequence of temperament (Keirsey & Bates, 1984; Kroeger, 1992). It may also be a protective (defense) mechanism that keeps the person from experienc-ing the anxiety that would result from recognizing broad and deep chal-lenges with which he or she does not feel competent to cope. That is, it may be a form of denial.

AL team coaches might approach this issue by asking the following questions: How does this team's work affect other parts and levels of this organization? How does what is going on in other parts or levels of this organization affect the work of this AL team? In what ways does this AL team's work contribute to the realization of the larger organization's strategic objectives?

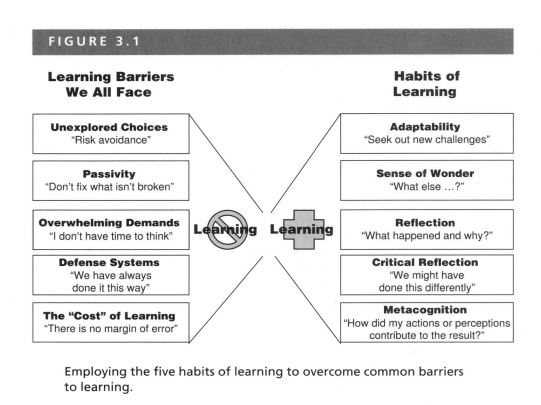

FIGURE 3.1

Employing the five habits of learning to overcome common barriers to learning.

Figure 3.1 is a graphic representation of how the five habits of learning provide an effective antidote to the common barriers to learning discussed previously.

How Action Learning Improves Learning Agility

The necessity of dealing with ambiguity and nonrepetitive tasks comes with the territory for most organizational leaders. The pace of change in a given industry's competitive environment demands resilience and learning agility at all levels. The ability to learn effectively is a greater predictor for leadership success than either intelligence or technical skills and a great competitive advantage for the firm. However, few leaders have the luxury of an extended learning curve for their personal leadership development. AL is a practical approach that puts learning how to learn and how to lead directly in the context in which leadership must be practiced. AL improves learning agility through the conscious mastery and application of the habits of learning (Marquardt, 2005; McNulty & Canty, 1995).

During the AL experience, team members have multiple opportunities to practice all of the transferable skills or habits associated with learning agility. The AL process requires an environment in which being a novice is encouraged and in which the risk-taking associated with learning and development is one of the measures of success. AL team members experience the luxury of an extended process of inquiry. This environment relieves them of the burden of feeling they have to play expert roles. It encourages them to spend more time than they ordinarily would to craft great questions and to generate the best possible responses before converging on an answer.

Action Learning at Regional Energy Services Corporation

For 160 years, a regional energy services corporation has been an energizing force throughout the southeastern United States—bringing power and fuel to homes and businesses, stimulating economic growth, spurring innovation, and enriching local communities. Faced with growth in customer demand, significant turnover from pending retirements, and rapid technology changes, the organization identified strong and well-aligned leadership as a significant driver of successes.

The Horizons leadership development system is an annual initiative designed to encourage collaborative leadership and to increase social networking, knowledge transfer, business acumen, and continuous development. Twenty-four high potential executives are invited to participate each year. The Horizons leadership development system is a 6-month, integrated process that includes AL, assessment, training, and opportunities for practice.

Prior to the first workshop, participants receive a package that includes selected articles, an executive summary of the upcoming workshop, and links to online assessment instruments. Participants are also encouraged to meet with their managers to review the learning objectives and identify a focus for their development. During the first 3 months, participants in the Leadership Horizons program operate as leadership teams of a simulated business. The challenges and opportunities they face in the simulation are drawn from real issues that may be encountered by leaders at any organization. The simulation, coupled with peer coaching, gives them real time feedback about how their leadership behavior affects their on-the-job performance. Trained AL team coaches debrief each simulation event to draw out the participants' own insights as they help each other learn. Brief tips and techniques sessions provide additional content models and tools to give the participants new ideas and skills to try out in the simulation. The overall simulation experience gives participants the opportunity to learn by doing, thus reinforcing success, and trying new behaviors and techniques within a safe but challenging environment.

During the final 3 months of the Leadership Program, AL is launched. Three AL teams of eight participants address important organizational issues. The organization's CEO is actively involved and supportive, identifying the issues, attending the launch, meeting with the teams, and providing resources where needed. Each team is assigned an AL team coach. Participants are asked to produce an initial problem statement as well as to develop a pilot test for potential solutions and a final set of recommendations. These recommendations are presented to an executive panel at the end of the AL cycle.

SOCIAL CONSTRUCTIONISM AND POSTMODERNISM

The notion of social constructionism developed in the disciplines of social psychology and sociology as a reaction to the philosophical belief that ideas and facts have universal meaning. The essential idea here is that reality is a social construct (Berger & Luckmann, 1966; Festinger, 1954) and is probably not the same from one group of people to another and is certainly not the same from one society or culture to another. According to social constructionism, reality is an invention or artifact of a particular culture or society. Reality, therefore, is whatever a collection of people agrees that it is.

Postmodernism also rejects the universality of truth, aesthetics, or cultural virtues. To simplify the postmodernist perspective, truth and virtue, as well as beauty, are in the eyes of the beholder (Lyotard, 1992). A related notion is that individuals, groups, organizations, societies, and cultures develop grand narratives that obscure the underlying complexity, contradictions, ambiguity, diversity, and interconnectedness of experience. Postmodern thought holds that the grand cultural narratives of previous eras (e.g., before 1950) have been "deconstructed" and replaced by mininarratives that are developed by much smaller social entities such as teams, organizations, and subcultures.

Weick (1979) implied social constructionism when he noted that "managers construct, rearrange, single out, and demolish many 'objective' features of their surroundings. When people act they unrandomize variables, insert vestiges of orderliness, and literally create their own constraints" (p. 243). In essence, not only are people's perception influenced by the social context but the way they organize their perceptions is also a social construct.

Without wading into the philosophical controversies connected with social constructionism and postmodernism, AL accepts the basic premise that development of individual, team, and organizational perceptions is a function of the social context and that the sensemaking process referred to by Weick (1995) involves the sharing and integrating of perceptions within the team and across the organization. The AL team coach helps the team understand the perspectives brought to the problem by asking questions that encourage dialogue rather than debate (cf. Bohm, 1996; Elinor & Girard, 1998). The coach also helps the team understand how it constructs reality by asking questions related to their inferencing process (e.g., the ladder of inference; Argyris & Schön, 1978; see Figure 2.3). The AL coach also assists the team in synthesizing a shared understanding of the problem by asking questions that focus on the process of achieving agreement about what problem the team is really working on.

NATIONAL ACADEMY OF SCIENCES REPORT ON OPTIMIZING LONG-TERM RETENTION AND TRANSFER OF KNOWLEDGE

In a report published by the National Academy of Sciences, Druckman and Bjork (1991)[1] provided a summary of the research related to how people learn and retain knowledge. The strategies provided in this report represent the best practices for curriculum designers to use in developing training programs. Six of the seven strategies are applied in the AL approach that we recommend. The seventh strategy, encouraging mental rehearsal, is frequently used by AL teams even if not directed to do so by the AL team coach.

Engage the learning in the process. This strategy is fundamental to AL. As noted by Revans, "there can be no action without learning, and no learning without action" (1998, p. 14). Because participants are constantly engaged in meaningful action, with inquiry and reflection, they cannot help but learn.

Integrate new knowledge with existing knowledge. This strategy is used specifically and strategically by the AL team coach. For instance, at the end of each session, the AL team coach asks questions that require team members to identify not only what they learned that can be applied to future meetings but also what they learned that can be applied in other parts of their lives such as in their regular jobs. In this way, new knowledge and innovation is integrated with current knowledge, understanding, and procedure.

Increase generalizability by practicing a variety of situations with increasing levels of complexity and difficulty. This strategy is used when the AL team coach asks how team members are going to apply what they have learned in their regular position or within the organization more generally. Early in the life of an AL program, team members grapple with some basic problems such as how to get organized, make decisions, and balance personal and team goals. These tasks and processes occur repeatedly throughout the life of the team and generally become more complex and complicated as the problem and goal are clarified and the solution begins to emerge. Thus, the team has many opportunities to practice and refine the necessary skills to achieve their team goals.

---

[1] Chapter 3 ("Optimizing Long-Term Retention and Transfer") of Druckman and Bjork (1991) contains a summary of the National Academy of Sciences report on the efficacy of training techniques.

Increase proficiency and mastery. Once the team knows the basics, they should continue to experience new challenges. Again, the team generally has numerous opportunities to practice the various team and problem-solving skills. Not only does the team find that the context becomes more complex and difficult toward the latter stages of the problem-solving process, but it also begins to recognize more nuances to the problem and team process. Having mastered the basic processes, team members have new opportunities to refine their behavior to reflect their increased sophistication.

Use spaced practice. The distinction between massed and spaced programs was discussed in chapter 2. One of the advantages of the spaced program is that it allows team members to integrate and practice new skills between sessions. Any artist or craftsperson knows that routinely practicing an art or craft several hours a day produces better results than practicing continuously for the same number of hours over a briefer period of time. It may seem more efficient to mass the practice, but the results are better if practices are shorter but more frequent with space between sessions. Also, by spacing opportunities for practice, team members can process their experience with the rest of the team, sharing their applied experience as well as receiving feedback and advice regarding problems they are encountering when enacting the skill.

Diminish external feedback. As team members learn and improve performance, AL team coaches should provide less feedback and teach them to provide their own monitoring and feedback. A primary goal of the AL coach is to encourage the team to manage its own learning. To paraphrase Saul Alinsky (1989), Chicago's populist guru of change management: Don't nobody do nothin' for nobody what they can do for themselves. This is a primary reason why AL team coaches only ask questions. As the team process unfolds, the questions and resulting reflections by the team become internalized by team members so that participants recognize learning opportunities and ask appropriate questions before the AL team coach feels that it is necessary or appropriate for her or him to intervene. As a result, the frequency of interventions by the AL team coach often declines as the team develops and learns to continually reflect upon and improve its performance.

Encourage mental rehearsal. Because AL team coaches only ask questions and do not give instructions, they cannot directly encourage team members to mentally prepare for and rehearse before important situations. However, coaches can indirectly encourage team members to rehearse by asking questions that evoke interest in reflecting on the best ways to prepare for important events and situations. This kind of question frequently prompts team members to consider what has worked for them in the past. These reflections will often surface ideas such as role-playing and mental rehearsal.

Why and How People Change

To learn means to change, either by adding new knowledge and skill to a person's repertoire or replacing anachronistic knowledge and skill with new, more pertinent information and more effective skills. Acquisition of new knowledge and skill is best accomplished in a safe, nurturing learning climate. For AL team coaches who intend to create a nurturing climate in which participants can learn and develop their capabilities, a first question to consider is: Why do people change? That is, what motivates a person to attempt to give up his habitual patterns of perceiving, thinking, feeling, and acting and strive to develop new, more effective behavior patterns?

Although no single answer is likely to be universal, some possible answers follow. First, people are likely to consider changing some of their habitual behavior patterns if and when they discover that these habit patterns fail to enable them to achieve their intended results. Second, people are likely to try to change their habit patterns when they discover that these patterns are detrimental to their relationships with others who are significant to them. Third, people may change if and when they discover and wish to emulate respected exemplars and, as a result, experiment and develop proficiency in using innovative, more effective behavior patterns. The AL team coach must consider and leverage these and other possible motives for individual and team change.

A second question naturally follows: How do people change? That is, how do motivated people actually modify their habitual patterns of perceiving, thinking, feeling, and acting?

If and when people decide to change, they soon discover that the process of enacting any alternative behaviors may be much more difficult than they imagined. The process is often awkward, frustrating, embarrassing, frightening, and threatening to one's self-esteem. In the face of such anxiety-provoking situations, people may give up their efforts to change, revert to familiar patterns, and try to endure the non-satisfying consequences.

We think of these habitual but counterproductive patterns of perceiving, thinking, feeling, and acting as "addictive." Thus, we extend the definition of *addictive behavior patterns* beyond the traditional applications of the term (e.g., alcohol abuse, overeating, smoking, drug abuse). We use the term *addictive* to encompass any behavior patterns that the individual uses (a) without making a conscious choice (i.e., applying them automatically or in a "knee-jerk" fashion), (b) persistently and frequently, (c) over an extended period of time, and (d) with little modification—regardless of the situations, conditions, or circumstances in which they are applied.

To gain insight into this process, we consider the work of psychologists James Prochaska, Carlo DiClemente, and John Norcross (1992), who have published some profoundly practical research results about self-initiated and professionally facilitated efforts to change the addictive behaviors of individuals. They identified a process that seems to be common to successfully modified addictive behavior patterns, regardless of the theoretical orientations or approaches used by the individuals or their professional facilitators. Thus, these results may be generalized to a variety of addictive patterns; hypothetically, their description of an effective process for withdrawal from addiction may be "trans-theoretical." This working hypothesis needs to be tested further.

FIVE STAGES OF INDIVIDUAL CHANGE

Prochaska et al. (1992) pointed out that successful modification, whether self-initiated or professionally facilitated, of habitual behavior patterns requires that the individual progress through five stages: precontemplation, contemplation, preparation, action, and maintenance. Further, they noted that individuals typically recycle through these stages several times before they learn to transcend their addictions.

Precontemplation

In this stage, people have no intention to change their behavior in the foreseeable future. These people are simply not aware that their addictive behavior patterns create problems in their relations with other AL team members; they are not aware of their addictiveness or its adverse consequences. Associates at work, family members, friends, or neighbors are often well aware that the precontemplators have problems, and that these problems impact both the precontemplator and their relationships with people with whom the precontemplator interacts. If these precontemplators seek assistance, they are likely to be accommodating to pressure from other persons, not from their own desire to change. For example, they may feel coerced by a manager who threatens to fire, demote, or not promote them if they do not get help. Precontemplators may change their behavior and maintain that change as long as the external pressure is on. Once the pressure is removed, they quickly revert to their old patterns.

Some precontemplators may wish to change, but this is quite different from intending to make or seriously considering a change within the next 6 months. The state of precontemplation is clearly characterized by their resistance to recognizing that they have a problem—that is, by denial. The individual, at this stage, is likely to say something like, "I may have my faults, but there is nothing that I really need to do about them."

Precontemplators may be considered *Unconscious Incompetents* or UIs (Howell & Fleishman, 1982). That is, they are not consciously aware of what they have not received disconfirming feedback and do not know because they do not have requisite knowledge and skills in some personal, interpersonal, team, or intergroup relationships. They are not as competent as they think they are or as they could be. They are not as competent as other, more competent people. Precontemplators may be blissfully ignorant. In his Johari Window, Luft (1961) said that this ignorance of incompetence of some habitual behavior is an element of their Blind Spot. Alternatively, precontemplators may be covering up their sense of incompetence. Luft said that what is covered up is an element of their area of hidden and avoided activities and that the cover-up itself is an element of a façade that precontemplators use to project an image of the person they want others to believe they are. Following are characteristics of UIs:

- The person is not aware of the existence or relevance of the skill area.
- The person is not aware that he or she has a particular deficiency in the area concerned.
- The person might deny the relevance or usefulness of the new skill.
- The person must become conscious of his or her incompetence before development of the new skill or learning can begin.

The aim of the learner and the AL team coach is to move the person into the Conscious Competence stage by demonstrating the skill or ability and the benefits that it will bring to the person's effectiveness.

Contemplation

At this stage, people are aware that they have problems with their habitual behavior patterns, and they are seriously thinking about overcoming or modifying them. However, they have not yet made a commitment to take action. Such people may keep themselves stuck in the contemplation stage for extended periods of time. The essence of the contemplation stage is that people know what they want to become but are not quite ready to begin a developmental process.

Contemplators weigh the pros and cons of living with or dealing with the problem as well as those of the available alternatives for solving the problem. They struggle with the tension between their perceptions of the advantages of maintaining the addictive behavior and the amount of energy, effort, and time they think it will cost them (i.e., the "loss") to overcome the problem behavior.

Such people are likely to say, "I do have a problem and I really think I should do something about it within the next 6 months."

Contemplators may be thought of as *Conscious Incompetents* or CIs (Howell & Fleishman, 1982) who consciously realize that they are not as competent as they thought they were—or as competent as they could be. Making the transition from UI to CI can be shocking and sudden. People can stay in this position for a long time. Luft (1961) might say that people are likely to keep their awareness of their incompetence as an element of their area of hidden and avoided activities. Following are characteristics of CIs:

- The person becomes aware of the existence and relevance of the skill.
- The person is aware of her deficiency in this area, ideally by attempting or trying to use the skill.
- The person realizes that by improving the skill or ability in this area, his effectiveness will improve.
- The person has a measure of the extent of her deficiency in the relevant skill and a measure of what level of skill is required for competence.

The person ideally makes a commitment to learn and practice the new skill, and to move to the Conscious Competence stage.

Preparation

Individuals at this stage have committed themselves to actually take some specific corrective action in the next 6 months. Such people have often unsuccessfully taken some sort of action at least once during the past 12 months. Some report small, often temporary improvements as a result of these efforts. However, they have not yet totally ceased or eliminated their problematic behavior patterns.

Such people might say, "I shall change my addictive behavior within the next 6 months."

This is the beginning of the process of becoming *Conscious Competents* or CCs (Howell & Fleishman, 1982). This process generally requires people to invest time and pay considerable conscious attention to learning about the particular area of behavior that they want to develop—through programmed or pedagogical learning and/or experience and reflection. Following are characteristics of CCs:

- The person achieves Conscious Competence in a skill when she can perform it reliably at will.
- The person needs to concentrate and think in order to perform the skill.
- The person can perform the skill without assistance.
- The person will not reliably perform the skill unless thinking about it; the skill is not yet second nature or automatic.
- The person can demonstrate the skill to another person but is unlikely to be able to teach it well.

Action

This is the stage at which people actually modify their behavior patterns, experiences, and/or environment. Action involves overt, intentional behavioral change. The person would be experimenting with new behaviors, either emulating some competent exemplar or creating new behavior patterns. Because they are visible to others as they enact new and unusual behaviors, such people are likely to receive considerable attention from others. To determine whether their experiments are effective, people who are acting in new ways must solicit or welcome feedback from others.

The corrective action that is taken in order to change may be confused with the actual results of the change effort. Considerable effort is necessary to maintain the changes achieved after the corrective action has been taken.

Successful alteration of an addictive behavior pattern means reaching some specific criterion—such as total abstinence from the counterproductive or dysfunctional behavior. Such people are likely to say, "I am working really hard to change my behavior."

This is the continuation of the process of becoming CCs (Howell & Fleishman, 1982). The process is likely to be uneven as people who are trying to become CCs learn, practice, get deflected, forget, regress, plateau, and repeat the process. Forgetting and regressing is particularly likely when people have been learning during a period of relative calm but are suddenly confronted by critical, urgent circumstances. Under such conditions, people are likely to relapse and regress to their "default setting" (i.e., their original habitual behavior patterns) primarily because these behavior patterns are familiar, comfortable, and can be applied quickly and automatically (without conscious, thoughtful attention).

The greater the complexity of the new behavior pattern that people are trying to master and gain proficiency in, the longer this process is likely to take. The person continues to practice the new skill, solicit feedback from other AL team members, and, if appropriate, commit to becoming Unconsciously Competent or UC with the new skill. Practice is the single most effective way to move from stage CC to UC.

Maintenance

This is the stage in which people work to prevent relapse and to consolidate the gains they have achieved during the action stage. Maintenance is a continuation of, not an end to, the change effort. The criterion is remaining free of the addictive behavior pattern and consistently engaging in new functional and socially approved behavior for more than 6 months. The new behavior would be incompatible with the old behavior patterns that the person is trying to extinguish. This stage extends to an indeterminable future period—it might last a lifetime.

Such people might say, "I'm trying to prevent myself from having a relapse. I may need a boost here and there to help me to maintain the changes I've already achieved."

Through repetitive practice with their new and more effective behavior patterns, CCs may eventually become *Unconscious Competents* or UCs (Howell & Fleishman, 1982). This is the point at which people no longer have to pay conscious attention to what they are doing or how they are doing it. Following are characteristics of UCs:

- The person becomes so practiced with the skill that it enters the person's unconscious and becomes second nature. Common examples are driving, sports activities, typing, manual dexterity tasks, listening, and communicating.
- The person can perform certain skills while doing something else, for example, knitting while reading a book (multitasking or parallel processing).
- The person might now be able to teach others in the skill concerned, although after some time of being Unconsciously Competent, the person might actually have difficulty in explaining exactly how he or she does it—the skill has become largely nonconscious.

This gives rise to the need for long-standing UCs to check their performance periodically against new standards (i.e., they must solicit and accept feedback on their performance).

There may be a fifth level of competence. Alan Chapman (n.d.) quotes David Baume who discussed *Reflective Competence*. He says,

> How on earth can I teach things I'm Unconsciously Competent at? I didn't want to regress to Conscious Competence. . . . So, *Reflective Competence*—a step beyond Unconscious Competence [suggests that I am] conscious of my Unconscious Competence . . . looking at my Unconscious Competence from the outside, digging to find and understand the theories and models and beliefs that clearly, based on looking at what I do, now inform what I do and how I do it. These won't be the exact same theories and models and beliefs that I learned consciously and then became unconscious of. They'll include new ones, the one's that comprise my particular expertise. And when I've surfaced them, I can talk about them and test them.

This notion of reflective competence is particularly relevant for training master AL team coaches, those qualified to train other AL coaches.

ACQUIRING NEW SKILLS

To make explicit our fundamental assumption, AL team coaches must retain in conscious awareness the reality that they are considering a person's set of behavioral skills and patterns. There is no single skill that enables people to become effective AL (or any other kind of) team leaders or members. Effective AL team members are those who have mastered a broad skill set that includes, for example, communicating, listening, participative team problem solving and decision making, managing and utilizing conflict, task leadership, emotional or maintenance leadership, identifying and utilizing team members' resources, recognizing and managing resistance, managing lateral interfaces between interdependent groups, and awareness of organizational political and power dynamics. AL team coaches must also be aware of the probability that different AL team members have achieved different levels of competence[2] with any particular skill going into their first AL team meeting.

In other words, some AL team members may be consciously or unconsciously competent in several but different relevant skills. However, it is extremely unlikely that any individual AL team member brings the same high level of conscious or unconscious competence or incompetence with every behavioral skill in a requisite skill set. Thus, a given AL team member may be a UI at the precontemplation stage with regard to skill A, a CI at the contemplation stage with regard to skills B and C, a CC at the preparation and action stages with regard to skills D, E, and F, and a UC at the maintenance stage with regard to skill G.

With effective coaching, every team member is capable of mastering and gaining proficiency in applying an entire set of specific behavioral skills in order to contribute to the realization of the purposes of the AL team.

OVERCOMING RESISTANCE TO CHANGE

The process of learning at all four levels does not go smoothly. Burley-Allen (1982) elaborated on the individual's internal experiences when integrating a new skill or behavior. *Internal experiences* include the following: (a) resistance—the natural tendency to stay with what is familiar; (b) uncertainty—feeling phony and tentative when starting to experiment with applying the new skills and behaviors; (c) assimilation—feeling less phony and more comfortable with the new skills and behaviors as people see themselves as becoming more proficient in their use; (d) generalization—beginning to apply what was learned in one setting or context to other, increasingly different situations; and (e) integration—reproducing the new skills and behaviors as called

---

[2]The reader may find the discussion of the GEMS model for promoting and facilitating reflection and critical thinking in chapter 2 (Figure 2.4) helpful in understand how to gear questions to the level of competence of the team or particular team members.

for in any situation or setting, automatically, and without conscious attention (i.e., like a UC).

In their understandable urgency to achieve tangible results quickly, AL team members may inadvertently be tempted to ignore or avoid the realities that people resist change and that resistance has a number of positive purposes. For example, where there is resistance, there may also be opportunities to surface significant obstacles and impediments to organizational change. These may not be anticipated or recognized by the planners and implementers of organizational change. Resistance must not be avoided, ignored (denied), or suppressed. AL team coaches must be prepared to help team members to respect, understand, and make productive use of resistance.

Furthermore, individuals—just like intact work units and larger organizational subsystems—will inevitably regress and recycle through previous developmental phases before they integrate and become fully proficient in the application of new skill sets. AL team coaches must be alert to the possibility that such apparently counterproductive phenomena will occur, and they must intervene accordingly.

Prochaska et al. (1992) pointed out that each of their five stages represents a different set of tasks that people need to move from one stage to the following one. Insufficient attention by the AL team coach can result in incomplete mastery of these behavioral skill sets. This exacerbates both resistance and regression.

AL team coaches must craft interventions that will not evoke unproductive resistance and the tendency to regress. They must enable AL team members to acquire and become proficient in the use of the skill sets they need to progress from one stage of competence to the next. By enabling team members to evolve through the first three stages, team members can apply their newly acquired skill sets and perform effectively. They are then likely to feel they have learned and been successful, and feel gratified with their efforts.

AL team coaches may find the classification of interventions in Table 3.4 useful in helping AL team members learn what they need to facilitate and enhance the change process.

It is also useful for AL team coaches to understand when and where, within each of Prochaska et al.'s (1992) stages, these intervention technologies should be applied. Table 3.5 describes the results of Prochaska et al.'s research findings.

To counteract the tendency of AL teams to act prematurely and to enhance the quality of their plans for their organization's transformation, we believe that it is often useful for AL team coaches to consider these research-based guidelines as they help their AL teams to progress from one of the first three of Prochaska et al.'s (1992) stages

TABLE 3.4

Classes of Interventions

Process	Definitions
Consciousness raising	Seeking and collecting information about self and problem: observations, confrontations, consultations by third parties, reading pertinent books and articles
Self-reevaluation	Assessing how one feels and thinks about oneself with respect to the focal problem: value clarification, self-assessment (and assessments of self by others), questionnaires, feedback, imagery, corrective emotional experiences
Self-liberation	Choosing and committing to act or to believe in one's ability to change: active involvement and participation in team-oriented problem-solving and decision-making processes, clarifying advantages and disadvantages of changing and not changing, commitment enhancing techniques
Counter-conditioning	Substituting alternatives for problem behaviors: relaxation, desensitization, assertiveness, courageous risk taking, positive self-statements, reframing assumptions and interpretations
Stimulus control	Avoiding or countering situational stimuli that elicit problem behaviors: restructuring one's environment (e.g., removing objects such as alcohol, food, ash trays that are associated with and trigger "automatic" or "knee-jerk" displays of problem behavior), avoiding high risk cues, "inoculation" against unavoidable cues
Reinforcement management	Rewarding oneself or being rewarded by significant others for making changes: contingency contracts, overt and indirect reinforcement, self-reward
Helping relationships	Discussing problems openly and honestly with a respected, objective, caring third party: alliances, social support networks, self-directed groups of colleagues who have similar concerns and problems
Dramatic relief	Experiencing and expressing feelings about one's problems and alternative solutions: role-playing, role reversals, rehearsals, theater games, and psychodrama
Environmental reevaluation	Assessing how one's problem behaviors and alternative possible changes (solutions) affect one's social environment: seeking feedback from work unit members, bosses, colleagues, associates, friends and family members, training in empathy, reviewing documentaries on the subject
Social liberation	Making more alternatives for liberating activities available in society: advocating for rights of the disadvantages and oppressed, empowering subordinates and associates at work, enacting modifications in organizational policies, rules and practices

Note. From "In Search of How People Change: Applications to Addictive Behaviors," by J. O. Prochaska, C. C. DiClemente, and J. C. Norcross, 1992, *The American Psychologist, 47,* p. 1108. Copyright 1992 by the American Psychological Association.

to the next, and beyond. The various classes of interventions can be used to aid in this stage-to-stage progression. Furthermore, we believe that it is in the AL team coaches' enlightened self-interest to understand, accept, respect, and use Prochaska, et al.'s concept of the spiral pattern of change.

TABLE 3.5

Classes of Interventions in Relation to Stages of Change

Stage of change	Classes of interventions
Precontemplation	Consciousness raising, dramatic relief, environmental reevaluation
Contemplation	Self-reevaluation
Preparation	Self-liberation
Action	Reinforcement management, helping relationships, counter-conditioning, stimulus control
Maintenance	Continuous application of all action classes of interventions, social liberation

Note. From "In Search of How People Change: Applications to Addictive Behaviors," by J. O. Prochaska, C. C. DiClemente, and J. C. Norcross, 1992, *The American Psychologist, 47,* p. 1103–1104. Copyright 1992 by the American Psychological Association.

THE SPIRAL PATTERN OF CHANGE

The vast majority of people taking action to modify their addictive behavior patterns do not maintain their gains on their first attempt. Relapse and recycling through the stages occur quite frequently. Linear progression is possible, but it is a relatively rare phenomenon; relapse is the rule rather than the exception.

During relapse, individuals regress back to a previous stage. They reestablish their familiar, addictive behavior patterns. They may feel relieved yet see themselves as failures and feel embarrassed, ashamed, and guilty. They are likely to become demoralized and resist thinking about changing their behavior.

Although they can regress all the way back to the precontemplation stage and remain there for various periods of time, they usually recycle back only one or two stages. Most try to learn from their recent efforts, and they begin to consider new plans for their next action attempt.

The amount of success achieved tends to be directly related to the stage that people were in before attempting self-initiated or professionally facilitated action (Prochaska et al., 1992). Scientific evidence is needed to test the validity of this assertion.

To treat all people who want to change their addictive behavior patterns as if they were the same would be naive. Each time relapsers recycle through the stages, their chances for achieving the maintenance stage are increased.

The primary implication of this probability to regress for AL team members and for AL team coaches is the need to pay simultaneous attention to the action steps that team members plan and execute to achieve their goals (Argyris's [1993] single-loop learning), the processes that AL team members use in planning and enacting their action plans (Argyris's [1993] double-loop learning), and what individual AL team members have learned about themselves through the AL experience (Freedman's [2006] triple-loop learning).

Reflection Questions

1. AL derives its power because it incorporates and applies well-tested theories. In addition to the learning theories described in this chapter, what psychological, economic, management, and sociological theories are incorporated in the AL process?
2. Unlike any other leadership development tool, AL is able to incorporate aspects of all five learning schools—behaviorist, cognitivist, humanist, social learning, and constructivist. What makes this possible?
3. How could you use AL to overcome your barriers to learning?
4. Flavell (1987) describes metacognition as higher order thinking that involves active control over the thinking processes engaged in learning. What are some ways in which AL encourages/enables metacognition?
5. How does AL enable individuals to quickly and effectively go through the five stages of personal change (i.e., precontemplation, contemplation, preparation, action, maintenance)?

The Power of Action Learning to Develop Leaders and Learning Organizations

4

A s noted in chapter 1, the challenges and demands that organizations face today require a broader range of leadership skills than were required in previous eras. In addition to the directive and transactional (motivating through the use of rewards) leadership skills so useful in the past, successful leaders in contemporary organizations display leadership styles that engage people's values, passion, and desire to achieve great things (i.e., transformational leadership) as well as empower people to take more responsibility for self-leadership in their decision making. Pearce et al. (2003) provided convincing evidence that CEOs demonstrate all of these leadership skills in their stewardship of contemporary organizations.

Leadership Development

Pearce and Conger (2003) noted that leadership in contemporary, technology-rich organizations has shifted from traditional hierarchical, top-down leadership to more lateral, collaborative, and shared leadership approaches. Chapter 10 provides consistent evidence that Action Learning (AL) develops not only the hierarchical, top-down leadership skills (i.e., the ability to direct, motivate, and inspire people, teams, and organizations to achieve significant goals; Acker-Hocevar, Pisapia, & Coukos-Semmel, 2002; T. B. Lee, 2005; Raudenbush, Marquardt, & Walls, 2003) but also the lateral influencing skills necessary to lead without authority or to empower team members and employees (S. H. Kim, 2003; T. B. Lee, 2005). This evidence supports our proposition that AL is uniquely suited for developing both the lateral, shared leadership skills that are so necessary in today's lean, technology-rich organizations as well as the hierarchical, top-down leadership skills that were effective in the more traditional, hierarchically structured organizations of previous eras.

In addition to these strengths as a leadership development strategy, AL has the unique and remarkable capability of developing all of the important individual leadership competencies typically identified in organizational or corporate leadership competency sets. As noted in chapter 1, today's leaders require skills in four cluster areas: (a) cognitive skills, (b) execution skills, (c) relationship skills, and (d) self-management skills. Let's examine how AL develops each cluster.

Cognitive skills. Competencies in this cluster include seasoned analytical skills, strategic thinking, creativity, and global perspective. They also include the ability to submit one's own ideas and views to the critical scrutiny of others and to be open to new perspectives and viewpoints. AL is built around problem solving and decision making. Group members are continuously analyzing and reframing a problem, establishing challenging goals, and searching for and identifying powerful strategies. Systems thinking and seeing issues from a variety of diverse perspectives are essential as the group searches for breakthrough ideas. Analytical, intuitive, and creative ways of thinking are needed and developed during the AL process.

Execution skills. Skills in this cluster include customer focus, planning, program management, and focus on results. Making decisions and taking action are parts of each and every AL session. Urgent problems that have deadlines and clear expectations are the anchor of any AL program. Strategies are examined from customer/client perspectives. The development and testing of plans and strategies are part of AL. At the beginning of each subsequent AL session, the group examines the impact of actions and lessons learned. Learnings and return on investment are critical. AL always pushes for results.

Relationship skills. Skills in this cluster include influencing, engaging and inspiring, managing talent, creating open communication, collaborating and building relationships, and nonjudgmental inquiry. In AL, every group member learns how to work in teams and receives regular feedback on how he or she is interacting with others and the impact of those interactions. Group members see how they are engaging and inspiring their teammates through their questions and their active listening. Members encourage one another to express their perspective. Searching and guiding the group toward consensus is the modus operandi of AL groups.

Self-management skills. Skills and competencies in this cluster include the ability to establish trust, adaptability, impulse control, curiosity, and love of learning. In AL, an obvious integral component is the recognition that everyone must continuously learn so that the group becomes smarter and better able to quickly and competently solve the problem and develop great strategies. Everyone is responsible not only for his or her own learning but also for the learning of other group members. Trust is built among members through the quality of questions they ask one another. Individuals develop patience and self-control as they are required to listen intently and build on the goals of the group rather than meeting their own individual needs. Group members learn the value of asking open-ended questions to foster and promote dialogue and creative thought, and they learn when to use closed questions to critique ideas, select the best ideas, and limit discussion so that action can be taken.

How and Why Action Learning Develops Leaders

AL differs from normal leadership training in that its primary objective is to ask appropriate questions under conditions of risk rather than to find answers that have already been precisely defined by others—and that do not allow for ambiguous responses because the examiners have all the approved answers (Revans, 1982a).

AL does not isolate any dimension from the context in which managers work; instead, it develops the whole leader for the whole organization. What leaders learn and how they learn cannot be dissociated from one another because how one learns influences what one learns (Dilworth, 1998). Thus, when a person is involved in decision making with a group of people over whom he or she has no hierarchical power on a problem for which there is no known answer (as occurs in AL), the person can develop every leadership competency. Dilworth (1998) noted that global leadership development, as practiced by most organizations, will

> produce individuals who are technologically literate and able to deal with intricate problem-solving models, but are essentially distanced from the human dimensions that must be taken into account. Leaders thus may become good at downsizing and corporate restructuring, but cannot deal with a demoralized workforce and the resulting longer-term challenges. (p. 49)

Typical leadership development programs provide few of the social and interpersonal aspects of an organization and tend to focus on tactical rather than strategic leadership (Lynam, 2000). Conner (2000), in her discussion of global leaders at Colgate Palmolive, as well as Neary & O'Grady (2000), in their case study of TRW, observed that developing global leadership skills requires combining U.S.-based classroom teaching with real-life learning experiences from often uncomfortable locations around the world.

Revans (1980) recognized that managers in classrooms were relatively passive and lacking in energy but came to life when they discussed their own "back home" problems with one another. Managers are people of action who learn from action. Fellow managers, in the right environment, are prepared to help one another and share their limitations. In AL, managers learn as they manage (Revans, 1980). Keys (1994) noted that AL represents a "new and revolutionary" type of executive development that has become the leadership choice of organizations who "seek to both teach and learn from their managers" (p. 50).

AL does not isolate any dimension form the context in which managers work; instead, it seeks to develop the whole leader for the whole organization. What leaders learn and how they learn cannot be dissociated from one another, for how one learns necessarily influences what one learns.

Dilworth (1998) noted how AL provides leadership skills that encourage fresh thinking and thus enables leaders to avoid responding to today's problems with yesterday's solutions while tomorrow's challenges engulf us. McGill and Beatty (1995) pointed out how AL provides managers the opportunity to take "appropriate levels of responsibility in discovering how to develop themselves" (p. 37). Fox (1998) described the powerful impact of training Motorola global managers using AL.

HOW SPECIFIC INDIVIDUAL LEADERSHIP SKILLS CAN BE DEVELOPED IN ACTION LEARNING

The development of individual leadership skills is a common though not universal goal for AL. In chapter 1, we presented the necessary and sufficient conditions for developing skills suggested by Hicks and Peterson (1999). They are as follows:

- Insight—Do people know which skills are important and which skills they need to develop?
- Motivation—Are people willing to invest the time and energy?
- Skill development—Do people have the opportunity to develop the skills and knowledge they need?

- Real-world practice—Do people have opportunities to apply their capabilities at work?
- Accountability—Are there consequences for people for displaying and using new skills on the job?

We also presented evidence for the relative advantages of AL when compared with other typical leadership development strategies. The potential for leadership development will not be converted to actual development of leadership skills unless the AL team coach carefully structures the team experience to focus not only on developing leadership skills but also on helping individuals and teams capture what they learned about leadership vis-à-vis their leadership skill gaps. In addition, the coach must get commitments from members to take action to demonstrate and practice these new skills outside of the AL team meetings.

HOW TO DEVELOP INDIVIDUAL LEADERSHIP SKILLS IN EVERY SESSION

Here is an illustration of how individual leadership skills can use the Hicks and Peterson (1999) model to customize the developmental experience for each team member during each session of an AL program in which the development of individual leadership skills is a specific goal and priority.

Insight. First, each member of the AL group identifies the specific leadership skill(s) that he or she wishes to develop/work on during the AL program (e.g., the choice or determination may occur in a number of ways: via 360 degree feedback, performance appraisal sessions, leadership instruments, self-reflection).

Motivation. Next, each member is asked to explain why each skill is important for his or her leadership agenda.

Skill development. The leadership skill(s) is then placed on a flipchart at the beginning of the AL session for everyone to see and to be cognizant of. Group members are advised that during and/or at the end of each session, they will be asked by the AL coach to provide feedback on how each person has practiced and implemented her identified leadership skill. The AL coach first asks the individual herself how she perceives she has performed her leadership skill and to identify examples and situations where she did or did not practice the skill. Then the other group members are asked to identify specific occasions when this individual demonstrated the leadership skill.

Real-world practice. At the end of each session, the AL team coach asks members to indicate what they will do differently vis-à-vis their leadership skills and to identify situations outside of the AL team in which the targeted leadership skill(s) is useful or important. Most important, the coach asks members to indicate specific actions they will take to demonstrate or practice that skill(s).

Accountability. The AL team coach also asks members to identify the impact that demonstrating that skill(s) will have on their careers as well as on the organization.

How Action Learning Builds the Learning Organization

Perhaps no tool is more effective in building a learning organization than AL. Lex Dilworth (1995) called AL "the DNA of a learning organization" (p. 243) because AL both enables and forces organizations to continuously learn on an organization-wide basis and thereby be better able to adapt to the continuously changing environment. Marquardt and Carter (1998) observed that "perhaps Action Learning's most useful role is in creating learning organizations" (p. 69). Revans (1982a) stated that "the most precious asset of any organization is the one most readily overlooked—its capacity to build on lived experience, to learn from challenges and to turn in a better performance by inviting all and sundry to work out for themselves what that performance might be" (p. 286). In short, an AL group is a perfect model for a learning organization.

Leveraging and linking learnings from within the AL group to the organization represents the greatest benefit of AL. At the organizational or institutional level of experience, action learnings are systemically and informally diffused across the organization. Solving a problem and achieving a great goal may be worth a million dollars to the organization, but if the Action Learning group can transfer a great strategy to other parts of the organization for continual application, if it can transfer knowledge and intelligence to other people who could benefit from it, if it can apply the leadership skills to the organization on a daily basis for the next 20 or more years, and if it can identify ways to change the culture and processes within an organization, that may be worth hundreds of millions of dollars to the organization.

Through interventions by the AL coach, the group is regularly asked to identify the learnings, skills, knowledge, and strategies. that can be applied to other parts of the organization. Thus, Senge (1990) noted that because a learning organization must be able to integrate work with learning and to continuously reflect on activities, the AL group is a perfect, miniature learning organization. Revans (1982b) correctly pointed out that AL creates constant learning opportunities for people and generates a powerful culture and morale for learning.

Action Learning and Leadership Projects at Heinz

Heinz, a $10 billion global company, sells 650 million bottles of its iconic ketchup every year. Founded in Sharpsburg, Pennsylvania, in 1869, Heinz employs approximately 32,500 people around the globe. The company has spent 10 years consolidating a market leading position for many of its products. In recent years, market share increases had leveled off and increasingly innovative competitors were entering the markets. A long established tradition of focusing on bottom-line cost cutting measures had maintained profit margins, but a decline was predicted unless a change in strategy was implemented. Leaders across the organization had to increase their focus on the top line. New growth and innovation was needed. One key to this new strategy was a change in top-line leader behavior.

To respond to these challenges, a leadership development system including assessment, development planning, and learning workshops together with AL was designed (see Figure 4.1). Business and function leaders individually participated in an assessment process and then met with Personnel Decisions International (PDI) coach to set development plans and goals. Three months later these individuals were invited to attend a learning workshop. The learning workshop concluded with a half-day kick-off session for AL. AL teams identified opportunities for innovation and shared problems. Each team met frequently for 3 months. At the end of 3 months, a reunion of AL teams was conducted during which recommendations of each team were presented and the business case was evaluated.

At the end of the process, most of the recommendations of the AL teams were implemented. Leaders had the opportunity to learn something about themselves and the members of their team. At the end of the program year, they put together a "reward and recognition kit" that included a guide to what resources were available, a history of the "spot reward" program (supervisors

FIGURE 4.1

Leadership Assessment Participation	Development Planning Meeting	Active Leader Program Participation	Action Learning Ongoing Development
Gain insight regarding strengths and development needs	Set development goals and plan	Build and leverage skills; Create a learning network	Solve top work team challenge; Be part of a continuous learning network

Leadership development system

handing cash to administrative employees for outstanding work), and copies of books and articles on reward and recognition. They described their experience to the rest of the management program and its executive sponsors as a cautionary tale about tailoring and timing rewards and recognition. They worked, they learned, they questioned, they experimented, they analyzed results, they shared useful learning with others to improve other leaders' effectiveness.

ACTION LEARNING HAS THE POWER TO BUILD ALL DIMENSIONS OF A LEARNING ORGANIZATION

Four major dimensions or subsystems are necessary for a learning organization: (a) learning dynamics, (b) organization renewal, (c) people empowerment, and (d) knowledge management. Because these dimensions and subsystems interface and support one another, they are all strengthened via AL (Marquardt, 2004). Let's explore how AL builds these four dimensions.

How Action Learning Builds the Learning Subsystem

AL programs encourage and enable significant levels of learning to occur at the team and individual levels during the AL sessions. Perhaps there is no greater demonstration of true team learning than what occurs during AL team meetings in which the entire group is developing common basic assumptions, a common understanding of the problem, and common growth in developing new knowledge. Usually, at the end of the AL meeting, the group seeks to identify ways in which its learning can be applied to the organization and thereby create organization-wide learning.

All types of learning are sought and developed in AL programs. In reflecting on past actions, the group attempts to adapt the new action to better respond to the environment. Anticipatory learning is acquired through the group's analysis of a variety of possible future scenarios or impacts of various actions. Almost continuously, AL groups are generating innovative, new creative knowledge. Finally, the time and space allotted for deep and frequent reflection during the AL sets provides the avenue for single-, double-, and triple-loop learning (Argyris, 1999; Argyris, Putnam, & Smith, 1985).

AL provides the opportunity for people in the organization to build these learning disciplines. In AL sets, people can reflect on their actions and the assumptions that underlie them. AL promotes "a depth and intensity of dialogue that is uncommon in the normal life experience" (Dilworth, 1998, p. 37).

Revans (1982a) noted that it is the "social dimension of AL that provides the challenge to misconceptions and ingrained mental schemata which predispose a person to overlook the ways in which he/she needs to change" (p. 33). In AL, people can explore real problems in a non-defensive way with supportive colleagues who feel free to criticize, question, and advise. Inherent in this approach is the ability to acknowledge that individuals frequently act in ways that may be incongruent with what they espouse (Argyris & Schön, 1978).

How Action Learning Builds the Organizational Culture and Structure for Continuous Learning

The culture created in AL programs is one in which learning is the most important and valuable objective. Throughout the AL process, emphasis is placed on how the group can continue to expand on and speed up its knowledge and learning capacities. Members are encouraged and expected to take risks and try new ways. They recognize that many of the greatest leaps in learning have come from learning from mistakes made.

Garratt (1997) remarked how AL is particularly valuable in helping organizations develop a vision and culture committed to continuous learning. Schein (1997), a pioneer in understanding organizational culture and organizational change, noted that "for change [learning] to occur, the organization must unlearn previous beliefs, be open to new inputs and relearn new assumptions and behaviors" (p. 39). AL is a powerful tool in helping to change these values and create these new visions.

Learning organizations have a bias for reflection-in-action. The capacity to quickly take action and to generate information is critical to organizations. Senge (1990) observed that "learning cannot exist apart from action. Action provides a basis for the critical dimension of reflection" (p. 39). It is the expressed strategy of an AL program to build in time, space, and opportunities for learning. And no strategy is more powerful for producing organization-wide learning than that of involving large numbers of employees in AL programs.

The structure of an AL set is fluid and flexible. Keeping the flow of questions and knowledge as clear and complete as possible is critical in processes such as reframing the problem, identifying possible actions, and providing frank feedback to one another. Needless protocol and bureaucracy and "administrivia" are discouraged. Leadership flows easily throughout the group.

How Action Learning Builds the People Subsystem

AL recognizes the importance of involving people at all points along the business cycle including supply chain, production, and marketing and sales in the problem-solving process. AL sets are most effective when customers, suppliers, and interested community members come together to ask fresh questions and share fresh perspectives.

Empowering people to take responsibility for themselves rather than waiting for outside expertise is a key value of AL. Limerick, Passfield, and Cunnington (1994) pointed out that there is within AL programs "the explicit recognition that management's role is to provide continuous opportunities for employees' self-development" (p. 36).

Pedler (1991) noted that in learning organizations, a primary task of managers is to facilitate the staff's learning from experience. Through the experience of AL, group members recognize the importance of making time for seeking feedback, for obtaining data from a variety of perspectives, and for encouraging new actions for old and new problems. They also perceive the value in questioning their own ideas, basic assumptions, attitudes, and actions.

Building learning alliances helps organizations to achieve continuous improvement and develop the capacity to cope with discontinuous change. Learning from "fresh faces" is as critical for success in AL as it is in organizations. New partners and perspectives can

- enlarge the range of the continuous environmental scanning ability of those in the alliance,
- bring a wide analytical range and a wider range of assumptions to the learning process so that discontinuities are more likely to be recognized,
- help members recognize and overcome defensive routines so that they can be more transcendent,
- take place at multiple levels within the alliance and improve the learning of all members, and
- open up the boundaries of the organization and make possible completely new organizational forms constantly open to importing chaos and evolving new forms of order (Limerick et al., 1994).

How Action Learning Builds the Knowledge Subsystem

A learning organization has the ability to acquire, create, store, transfer, apply, and validate knowledge.

Acquiring Knowledge

AL organizations are information rich. In AL, set members recognize not only the importance of acquiring information from external resources but also the value of tapping the tacit, internal wisdom, and experience of each other. The internal networks developed in AL sets heighten the awareness of organizational resources, facilitate exchanging and sharing of ideas, and generate knowledge.

Creating Knowledge

Participants in AL programs understand that they should seek new ways of solving old problems and that the old knowledge may no longer be sufficient. Thus, members are constantly creating new knowledge to encourage the team to be more innovative. Nonaka (1994) suggested that information creation is a fundamental requirement for the self-renewing (i.e., learning) organization. An autonomous self-organizing group begins to be realized when members are given the freedom to combine thought and action at their own discretion and are thereby able to guarantee the unity of knowledge and action. The actions of AL clarify and generate meanings.

Storing Knowledge

Knowing what knowledge to store and knowing why it is stored is based on the organization's ability to make sense of the data encompassing and surrounding it. The organization must then develop sense-making categories for coding and retaining value-added knowledge. Through their ongoing reflection on learning and the knowledge acquired, AL programs lend themselves well to the Kantian school of thinking that "positions sense-making above mere sensing" (Botham & Vick, 1998). By reflecting on action, the AL team develops the ability to "make meaning" of the data collected and stored.

Transferring and Testing Knowledge

During the reflection periods, self-learnings become more explicit and intentional. Team members capture and store for themselves the knowledge and wisdom that will help them become better in both their professional and personal lives. Finally, AL groups continuously seek ways in which they can transfer the learnings, wisdom, and experience gained in resolving the set's problem(s) to the organizations and communities in which they work.

Other Benefits of Action Learning—Team Building and Personal Development

It is AL's ability to harness the powers of each diverse discipline that enables it not only to develop leaders and transform organizations but also to build teams and develop personal and professional competence.

Thus, just as the AL coach regularly asks people how the learnings and experiences within the group can be applied to the organization, he or she also regularly asks team-related and individually focused questions aimed at building teams.

BUILDING TEAMS VIA ACTION LEARNING

Most teams never learn because they do no reflect on their experiences as a total entity. AL groups, however, quickly become high-performing teams. AL teams continuously improve because of the actions of the coach. A valuable "teamthink and teamlearn" mind-set steadily emerges.

The group shares clear responsibility and accountability on real problems, causing a need for deliberative team unity and success. Learning (whether at the individual or collective level) requires reflection, and reflection requires questions. Groupwide learning improves the behavior and quality of actions of the group. This group reflection and learning occurs as a result of some of the following types of questions from the AL coach:

- How are we working as a team?
- What are we doing best as a team?
- What team skills enabled us to creatively and rapidly solve this problem? Develop these strategies?
- How could we practice these team skills in other groups of which we are a part?
- What would make us a stronger team?

The process of ongoing questioning and shared learning develops a number of important team strengths, including strong caring and cohesion among the members, consensus around problems and goals, clarity of communications, collaboration, and dedicated commitment. Let's examine how AL builds each of these important characteristics.

Cohesiveness and Caring

Effective teams have an underlying sense of "tightness," of being bonded together to achieve a common purpose that is both highly important and immensely personal. *Cohesiveness* refers to the overall attraction of group members to each other and the way in which they "stick together" and desire to be in the group (Beal, Cohen, Burke, & McLendon, 2003; Cartwright, 1968). Members have a sense of belonging and are dedicated to the well-being of the group. Cohesiveness also refers to the morale, teamwork, and spirit of the group.

A strong union is built in AL programs as people focus on seeking to clarify the real problem and acquire a commitment to action. In addition, when a person shares feelings about self-awareness, significant learnings, and frank appraisals of self and others, he or she develops powerful linkages with other group members. AL has the powerful effect of increasing trust levels in groups (Marquardt & Carter, 1998). As a result of sharing problems, members share important aspects of their lives with others in the set. This sharing generates a common understanding of the others' situation and creates a bond among set members.

Cohesiveness is also built by the egalitarian nature of AL teams. Dilworth (1998) pointed out how AL teams operate "without a designated leader. Any mantle of authority is left at the door." This makes AL a "good fit with self-directed work teams which are rapidly become a feature in organizations worldwide" (p. 37).

Clarity of Objectives and Purpose

Many teams fail because there are no clear objectives or there is confusion about what the group is attempting to accomplish. In most groups, there is an assumption that everyone understands the problem and goal and that everyone has a similar understanding of the problem and goal. However, this is rarely the case. Most groups struggle to convince each other that their perspective or understanding is the correct one.

AL groups, however, do not accept these assumptions. Members ask each other what they believe the problem is or what they understand the goal to be. If the coach believes that the team is moving ahead without sufficient clarity regarding its objective or purpose, he or she asks questions that require team members to share perceptions to make sure that they are clear about and in agreement concerning the problem that they are working on. Thus, clarity of objectives and purpose is achieved before the multiple strategies that might resolve the problem and achieve the goal are confronted.

Communications and Dialogue

High-quality communications are critical for the successful functioning of high performance work teams. AL helps to develop an underused and extremely useful form of communication—dialogue. As noted in chapter 2, dialogue is a deep form of communication that requires the free and creative exploration of issues and problems, a sincere listening to one another, and the suspending of one's opinions and criticisms (Bohm, 1996; Ellinor & Gerard, 1998; Isaacs, 1999). The focus in AL is not to get a member's ideas accepted, but rather for the member to be sure that everyone else's ideas are heard. Dialogue can be extremely valuable to the team during certain stages of problem solving, such as when divergent thinking and sharing of viewpoints can help the team to understand its connections to the problem, to generate a common understanding of the nature and breadth of the problem, and to develop shared meaning when evaluating and analyzing data and information.

AL fosters dialogue by emphasizing listening, by asking questions rather than posing solutions, and by encouraging the development of shared meaning rather than the imposing of one person's meaning. As a result of dialogue, team members are more likely to propose win–win solutions rather than advocating or convincing others, which often results in win–lose situations.

It is similar to how Japanese people in a Japanese restaurant focus their attention on being sure that everyone else's glass is filled, as opposed to how people in the United States tend to focus on seeing that their own glass is filled. Thus, in the United States, each person fills his own glass; in Japan, a person would never need to fill his own glass as everyone else is watching to be sure that it remains full. A similar phenomenon occurs in AL groups; everyone is dedicated to hearing the opinions and perspectives of others, and thus everyone is focused on asking others for their perspectives. Our experience indicates that people tend to hear what they have asked for and be resistant to what they have not asked for.

Dialogue is important in AL and in building teams because it promotes powerful collective thinking and communications. Dialogue allows the group to better tap its collective wisdom and see the situation as a collective whole rather than in fragmented parts. It forces group members to focus on how and why internal perceptions are influencing the way they perceive the problem.

Commitment to Task and Ownership of Results

In AL, the strategies developed will be implemented by the team itself or by the organization in the name of the team. Thus, the group is highly accountable and responsible for its actions, which all members of the group will have to live with.[1] In the first AL teams developed by Reg Revans, the coal miners knew that their ideas would have to be effective and safe, as they would be the ones who would have to go into the coal mines the next day to implement those strategies. Members need to seek ways in which they can work together, particularly if they are accountable as a group for the action to be recommended and taken by the group.

Teams will neither optimize the processes under which they are working nor produce quality results unless participants take responsibility and ownership for their products. People are thus committed to helping one another and to a high level of effort. AL develops strong com-

---

[1]As noted in chapter 1, accountability is a necessary and sufficient condition for learning. This is true for teams as well as for individuals.

mitment as a result of the intense personal sharings as well as the impact of the selected actions on one or all group members. Cooperation and collaboration are critical for the development of great strategies.

Creativity

AL teams are always searching for breakthrough strategies, ideas that will lead to a quantum leap in solving the problem and achieving the goal. Asking curious questions from a variety of perspectives, and building on each other's questions, inevitably leads to creative, systems-based strategies and solutions. The reflective questioning and accountable actions inherent in AL groups generate great results. People who have been in AL teams enthusiastically report those occasions to be among the most creative and exciting ones of their lives, during which difficult, complex problems got solved in wonderfully creative ways. AL enables teams to access their collective wisdom and ignorance, to work together in meaningful and reflective ways, and to coordinate action.

Continuous Improvement in Team Competence and Performance

Research and experience have demonstrated that action taken on a problem changes both the problem and the people acting on it (Revans, 1980; Tyre & von Hippel, 1997). Participating in the AL process helps team members develop the following knowledge, skills and abilities:

- ability to focus on process and product issues interchangeably as necessary;
- self-understanding and self-awareness gained from the feedback of others in the groups;
- questioning and problem-solving skills;
- ability to be an effective member of a group, learning how to work with others and to be supportive as well as challenging;
- new knowledge about the organization—products, people, and processes;
- facilitation, advising, and leadership skills; and
- communications skills, including giving and receiving feedback.

ACTION LEARNING AND THE DEVELOPMENT OF PERSONAL COMPETENCE

Weinstein (1995) noted that participants in AL achieve learning at three different levels: (a) understanding something intellectually, (b) applying some newly acquired skill, and (c) experiencing and thereby undergoing an inner development that touches on beliefs and attitudes and that leads to personal development. AL is particularly effective at this third level because it provides the opportunity for internal dissonance, whereas the problem or action may provide the external trigger. In AL, people become more aware of their blind spots and weaknesses as well as their strengths; they receive the feedback and help that they have requested. As noted in chapter 1, learning at this level can be described as triple-loop learning (Freedman, 2006).

AL generates tremendous personal, intellectual, psychological, and social growth. Butterfield, Gold, and Willis (1998) noted how AL participants experience "breakthrough learning" when they became aware of the need to reach beyond their conscious beliefs and to challenge their assumptions about their present worldviews. This readiness to change and grow is a prerequisite for development. The specific knowledge, skills and abilities that are developed by participating in the AL process include

- critical reflection skills, which are key to transformative learning for the individual (Mezirow, 1991);
- inquiry and questioning abilities that allow individuals to do more than just advocate and push personal opinions;
- systems thinking so that individuals begin to see things in a less linear fashion (Gharajedaghi, 1999);
- ability to adapt and change;
- active listening skills and greater self-awareness;
- empathy—the capacity to connect with others that, according to McGill & Beatty (1995), is one of the most valuable relationship skills developed in AL;
- problem-solving and strategy-selection skills; and
- presentation and facilitation skills.

AL promotes individual transformation that relies on a relaxing of the person's need for control within social settings. By participating in a variety of interpersonal sequences, a person learns that a viewpoint is just that. It is no more than a hypothesis for action (Argyris & Schön, 1978). This posture, however, can place the group member in a vulnerable state because rather than defend a point of view, he or she assumes a reflective response. The reflective response can be characterized by a number of attributes that are in direct contrast to a control position.

- Instead of maintaining unrealistic standards, one sets realistic expectations.
- Instead of expressing trepidation, one displays tolerance.
- Instead of concentrating on self-expression, one engages in deep listening.
- Instead of being self-absorbed, one conveys humility.
- Instead of feeling out of depth, one feels open to learn.
- Instead of feeling out of context, one becomes open to experience.

Professional development, according to McGill & Beatty (1995), demands "a complex weave of reflective practice and opportunities for development of knowledge and skill" (p. 37). The reflection on practice that takes place in AL is the "oil in the wheel" that enables effective personal growth as well as reconstructive and additive learning.

AL teams progress through distinct phases that inherently accentuate self-awareness and personal development. First, individuals are placed in unfamiliar settings and/or given unfamiliar problems. In these new settings, fresh questions are automatically and naturally induced. Being out of one's comfort zone forces individuals to look at things through a different lens. Once fresh questions are introduced, group members begin to unfreeze and reshape their underlying assumptions, thereby transforming how they see and respond to the situation(s). As these assumptions get questioned, they may be confirmed, modified, or rejected.

Individuals are helped to develop in the ways described above with questions from the AL coach such as the following:

- What have you learned about yourself?
- What enabled you to develop your personal skills?
- What is the quality of your questions?
- What are your best team skills?
- How do you learn?

Creating Personal Openness and Willingness to Change

Persons who appreciate the value and importance of asking questions will be more open to changing their basic assumptions and previously offered solutions. They may be more willing to see that the old ways may no longer work in a new world of chaos, uncertainty, and challenges. Kanter (2006) and others have remarked that the willingness to embrace and manage change is one of the most important competencies of today's worker.

AL can be a freeing experience. Participants discover that questions that arise out of curiosity, ignorance, or lack of knowing help them break out of rigidly held mind-sets (Revans, 1982a).

Butterfield et al. (1998), in their research on the key benefits of AL, discovered that participants referred to "breakthrough learning" when they became aware of the need to "reach beyond one's conscious belief and to challenge one's assumptions about his or her present worldviews" (pp. 493–494). AL causes a new awareness relative to the impact of reactions and interactions.

AL teams depend on members supporting and being concerned about the well-being of others. Beaty, Bourner, and Frost (1993) stated that "in order to have the energy and capacity to help solve another's problem, you need to care for the other person." You need to care enough about the other people in the team to "want them to succeed with their project and to learn from so doing" (p. 355). In AL, people begin to gain a sense of what it feels like to be that person with the problem; they develop an attitude that is curious and thoughtful about the way the problem owner feels about the problem. They develop a willingness to share another person's feelings and thoughts.

Building Organizations, Teams, and Leaders Via Action Learning

The ability to (a) build great organizations, (b) create teams, and (c) develop leaders, while (d) solving complex problems is the magic of AL. AL has proven to be more effective in accomplishing all four of these objectives than any single tool that focuses on just one of them. As noted in chapter 1, AL develops leaders better than any of the current leadership development methodologies now available. Similarly, there is no better way to create a learning organization than through AL. Moreover, AL develops high-performance teams more rapidly than do any of the team-building strategies currently used by organizations. In fact, an action to solve an organizational problem cannot be successfully implemented until (a) the leader/individual implementing the change is himself changed, (b) the organization's culture and operations are changed, and (c) the organization and leader are able to work effectively in teams.

Reflection Questions

1. What are leadership skills that you would like to improve? How would working in an AL group enable you to develop these skills?
2. Leadership competency involves cognitive, execution, relationship, and self-management skills. How does an AL program develop competencies in these categories?
3. Developing leadership skills requires insight, motivation, practice, and feedback. What are some ways in which AL does this?
4. What would be the major challenges in transforming your company into a learning organization? How could AL assist you?

5. Knowledge management is often stymied by the lack of human commitment to store and transfer valued knowledge. How could Action Learning overcome these obstacles?
6. What enables AL to build teams that quickly achieve great results while maintaining positive human interactions?

Asking Questions to Promote Reflection and Learning Throughout the Action Learning Team's Life Cycle

5

A sking great questions that promote valuable reflection is an art. Whether the questions are great depends on the Action Learning (AL) team coach's ability to accurately assess the challenges facing the team in its efforts to solve the problem it has taken on. These challenges will generally fall into two categories: (a) task challenges related to the team's problem-solving process and (b) human relationship challenges related to the interpersonal or group dynamics of the team. It is no coincidence that the nature of the team's challenges falls so easily into the two dimensions of leadership that have been identified by most researchers and theorists (Blake & Mouton, 1964; Katz & Kahn, 1951; Likert, 1961; Shartle, 1950).

The focus of this chapter is on intrateam processes and activities (primarily questions asked by the AL team coach) that promote reflection and learning within the team. Therefore, this chapter focuses on the problem-solving and team development phases that teams typically go through in developing and implementing solutions. In contrast, chapter 6, "Developing and Changing Organizations Through Action Learning," focuses on the phases that organizations or systems go through in changing or renewing themselves. Because of the systems change focus of chapter 6, the discussion is organized around the phases of the consultation process, a model that has proven to be very useful in the practice of organization development and change (OD&C) consulting.

Although the phases of the problem-solving and consultation processes generally parallel each other, the implementation steps for each phase can be quite different. The catalyst for change at the team level is good coaching, which is primarily characterized by asking phase-relevant questions. The catalyst for organizational or systems change, in contrast, is good consultation, which is characterized by the appropriate application of Action Research at each phase in the consultation process. A comparison and contrast of AL and Action Research is provided in chapter 6.

Task Challenges

The sequence of task challenges that AL teams encounter is usually correlated with the typical phases in the problem-solving process. Although the process of problem solving and learning is rarely linear, according to Koberg and Bagnall (1974), problem-solving teams are generally engaged in and often struggling with the following challenges:

- recognizing the problem,
- defining the problem,
- analyzing the problem,
- generating solution ideas,
- critiquing ideas,
- selecting best ideas,
- implementing best ideas,
- evaluating results, and
- identifying new problems that need solving.

Teams recognize questions as being great when they encourage and focus reflection on the primary challenges facing the team at any particular moment, particularly when they encourage team members to invent better and often novel ways to solve those challenges. Questions are frequently recognized as great when they focus the AL team's attention and stimulate the team to deal with some significant issue or relationship that has been overlooked or ignored. Team members think the object of the question is obvious once it has been asked. Great questions are invitational rather than critical and are experienced by the AL team members as helpful and practical.

RECOGNIZING A PROBLEM

This phase is often confused with defining the problem. In many cases the recognition and definition phases flow together so smoothly that it is difficult to distinguish between them. In other cases, however, helping a team recognize a problem, apart from defining it, is critical. For instance, many teams wait until all team members arrive before starting meetings, even though it is typical for one or more members to be late, sometimes significantly so. Team members chat with each other in the meantime, but little task work gets done. Consequently, over time, team members arrive later and later, significantly compressing the amount of time available to get the work done. When the AL team coach recognizes that this is a problem the team could address, he can ask the team to reflect on how it is treating precious time by simply calling attention to this behavior: "I notice that we are waiting longer and longer for all of our members to arrive before we begin our work." He can then ask the team, "Is this the best use of the team's time?" Although teams are typically defensive of their current behavior, often citing courtesy as a reason for waiting, this simple and direct question forces team members to reflect on their behavior and ask themselves or each other, "Is our behavior effective?" and "How can we manage our time better?" This simple question uncovers a problem that was previously unrecognized or, at least, not discussed.

PROBLEM DEFINITION

It is almost axiomatic in AL that the initial presenting problem is seldom the real problem after further analysis by the team. It is also typical for teams to accept the initial presentation as the root problem and to waste a great deal of time going down unproductive pathways. Because proper problem definition is so important, the first question asked in the initial session is usually, "Do we have agreement on the problem that we have been tasked to work on?" After team members have shared their views of the problem, the answer to this question is usually "no." Asking questions early in the process that focus on problem definition encourages the team to consider whether there is enough agreement on the issue before establishing goals of the AL process and before moving on to the analysis and solution-development phases.

Team members also have a tendency to provide solution statements that are disguised as problem statements when the coach asks them to share their perception of what the problem is. For example, a team member may say, "The issue is that marketing is not checking with production to determine if they can build what marketing is selling." When this happens, the AL team coach can get the team back on track with the following instructions: "Listen to my question carefully. What is the problem that you think the team should be addressing?"

PROBLEM ANALYSIS

Challenges in this phase often involve the tendency of problem-solving teams to jump to solution-development activities before fully exploring the issues. In addition, if a clear problem statement is not identified early, problem analysis tends to be unfocused and unproductive. Issues involving social status and participation become apparent; ideas from team members with greater status or technical expert consultants (techsperts) frequently receive greater consideration. The ideas from quiet or introverted team members may not be heard as the team rushes to get into brainstorming to generate solutions. The team fails to identify and challenge important assumptions in its rush to the idea-generation phase. As a result, many of the steps in making accurate inferences are skipped (see discussion of the ladder of inference in chap. 2, this volume). In many instances, team members may be taking a sterile analytic approach to the problem without considering the values that are embedded in their analysis. Here are some typical questions that are often helpful during the problem analysis phase of the team's work:

- Has the team gotten sufficient input from all team members? from all relevant stakeholders?
- What is the impact of having some people actively involved in the discussion while others are silent?
- Does the team see the problem that it is working on as being the same as it seemed in previous work sessions?
- What assumptions are being made in this analysis? Have they been tested?
- What data are the team attending to or excluding in analyzing this situation?
- What values are being used to interpret this situation? What is the impact of these values on the meaning that is being developed by the team?

After the team has completed its analysis of the problem, it needs to finalize the goals for the AL project. The AL team needs to consider not only what is desired by the organization and the team (often an idealized outcome) but also what is possible and feasible given the team's resources, power, and time availability. The scope and scale of the project are generally refined and summarized in the AL project charter, which is developed by the team and approved by the organization.

GENERATING SOLUTION IDEAS

Team members are generally very anxious to get to this phase of the problem-solving process. They may be so anxious, in fact, that earlier interventions by the coach may be to focus on the consequences of jumping to problem solving before fully defining and analyzing the problem. Although the basic principles of effective idea generation and brainstorming are well-known (Delbecq, Van de Ven, & Gustafson, 1975; Osborn, 1979), teams often violate most of the following basic principles:

- Defer judgment and criticism of ideas.
- Give priority to quantity rather than quality of ideas.
- Encourage participation by all team members.
- Build on the ideas of others and ask questions of all members, not just of the problem presenter.
- Tolerate pauses and silences.

Most participants on organizationally sponsored AL teams are successful managers. They get results precisely because they have developed the ability to focus on immediate needs and requirements. This focus on getting results drives out the "habit" of creative thought so critical to brainstorming. As a result, the basic principles of brainstorming are often violated. When the coach notes that these principles are being violated, he or she can easily generate questions such as the following to get the team to reflect on the consequences of these violations and to generate useful idea-generation ground rules:

- What is the impact on creativity/participation when ideas are immediately critiqued?
- What can the team do to minimize premature judgment and criticism during this phase?
- What is the impact of less than full participation by team members in the idea-generation process?
- What changes in process can the team make to ensure more complete participation?
- How can the team build on the ideas of others?
- Why are we cutting off discussion after only a few moments of silence?
- What would happen if the team let the silence continue longer?

Coaches for teams and individuals who have had some training in creativity and brainstorming will find that these questions quickly trigger recognition of effective idea-generation methods and adjustment in the team's process. In these cases, the team will almost immediately switch to an interaction style that is much more successful in generating creative ideas.

CRITIQUING IDEAS

After generating many ideas, teams face the challenge of organizing the ideas and evaluating them. It is during this phase that the abilities of team members with strong critical thinking skills should be tapped to cluster and set the criteria for evaluation. This does not always happen, however, and frequently the most vocal people, who often have personal interests in certain outcomes, dominate the discussion. When the coach observes a less than optimal evaluation process occurring, he or she can raise the following questions:

- What process is the team using to evaluate these ideas? Are there ways to improve this process?
- What would be some effective methods for organizing these ideas?
- What skills would be useful at this point in the problem-solving process?
- Who in the group has the skills that the team needs right now?

SELECTING THE BEST IDEAS

The AL process provides tremendous opportunities for teams to learn effective team decision-making processes. Teams typically struggle with team decision making (Levi, 2007). The practices they have learned in other parts of their lives don't often work well in teams. Autocratic decisions or decisions pushed through by a dominant few often suffer from a lack of creativity and almost always fail to generate "buy-in" and commitment from the members who did not participate in making the decision (Castore & Murnighan, 1978). Democratic decisions made by voting to reflect the will of the majority generally result in mediocre decisions and leave a significant minority dissatisfied with and resistant to the decision. Consensus decisions, in contrast, are the most creative and achieve the most commitment but take a long time (Hare, 1980). Although a number of decision-making models have been offered (Maier, 1970; Vroom & Yetton, 1973), they are complex, using a number of criteria (e.g., quality, speed, and acceptance or support [Johnson & Johnson, 1997]) and therefore are difficult for teams to use. It is no wonder that teams struggle with effective team decision making.

The AL team coach can help the team make better choices about how it makes decisions by asking questions that encourage members to reflect on how their decision-making process affects important aspects of team performance.

- How does the team decide how to make decisions? (This question brings a largely undiscussed process to the team's awareness.)
- How would you describe the team's decision-making style?
- How effective is this style? What are the pros and cons?

- What is the impact of the way decisions are being made?
- What choices does the team have in making decisions?
- How can the team improve its decision-making process?

In most instances, these questions will foster an understanding of the way that the needs for quality, speed, acceptance, and support determine the most effective methods for making decisions. Because the team begins making decisions within the first minutes of starting to work on a problem, these questions may be offered in any of the phases of the team's problem-solving efforts. It is often a good strategy to ask the first question (How does the team decide to make decisions?) early in the team's life and to return to this issue periodically so that the team develops an appreciation of the need to have a flexible approach to decision making. By approaching this issue gradually and systematically, the coach can effectively leverage the team's increased sophistication in this skill during the problem-solving phase when this skill is most crucial and prominent.

IMPLEMENTING THE BEST IDEA

There is currently an increased appreciation of the importance of implementation skills and planning for organizational change and improvement (Bossidy & Charan, 2002). Coming up with a good idea is of little value if the team does not have an effective plan to implement it. AL provides an excellent opportunity to build the execution and change management skills that are so prized in contemporary organizations. The AL team coach can promote and foster skills in this area by asking questions such as the following:

- How does the team plan to turn these ideas into real change in the organization?
- What will be the critical success factors for implementation of the ideas?
- What will be the impact of these actions on the organization?
- What factors will keep this plan from being executed successfully? Which stakeholders might feel that their interests would be threatened by implementing the proposed organizational changes?
- What resources are required to execute this plan?
- Where are these resources located? Who has the authority to make these resources available?
- What plan does the team have for selling the plan within the organization?
- What plan does the team have for identifying and dealing with resistance to the proposed changes?

Implementation of even well-conceived plans has always been difficult in the complex environments in which contemporary organizations must operate. This difficulty has been responsible, in large measure, for the emergence of OD&C theory and practice. Experienced AL team coaches recognize that arriving at good ideas is frequently easier than successfully implementing them. Chapter 6 deals in greater detail with the issues, tactics, and strategies necessary for successful implementation of AL solutions.

EVALUATING RESULTS

The process of evaluating results is built into every step of the AL process. During meetings, the AL team coach may ask the team to evaluate how well the team is working; at the end of each meeting, the coach asks questions to summarize and integrate the learning that occurred during the meeting; at the end of the project, the AL team coach raises questions that encourage the team to evaluate and capture both double-loop learnings (questioning assumptions, values, and practices to create and innovate; Argyris and Schön, 1978) as well as triple-loop learnings (what participants have personally learned about themselves as leaders and organizational change agents; Freedman, 2006).

The process of evaluating results during and at the end of AL sessions is covered in chapter 2. Here are some questions that would be useful in getting both the team and the organization to reflect on what happened as a result of the larger AL process. These questions can be asked effectively in a joint meeting with team members and organizational representatives (e.g., senior leadership, Human Resources, Organizational Development specialists, end-users, and other significant stakeholders).

- How has the organization been changed as a result of the AL process?
- What changes would this group recommend for the way this organization (a) conducts business, (b) develops leadership, (c) and approaches organizational change?
- What changes in the way participants (a) approach learning, (b) exercise leadership, (c) and view their strengths and development needs have resulted from the AL process?
- What actions will you take to improve the way you approach learning in your work and personal life?

IDENTIFYING NEW PROBLEMS THAT NEED SOLVING

It is somewhat of a cliché to note that the solution to one problem inevitably uncovers new problems begging to be addressed. Inquiry into new problems that are uncovered in the AL process can also be addressed in a joint meeting with team members and organizational representatives convened at the end of an AL cycle. Questions that would encourage reflection about new problems include the following:

- What important problems for the organization emerged with the completion of this project?
- From your perspective, what important and critical problems are linked to the problem that this team worked on?
- What other parts and levels of the organization may be affected by the newly identified problems and in what ways?
- How can the organization leverage the work of this team to solve new and emerging problems of great importance to the organization?

Human Relationship Challenges

AL team coaches will frequently notice relationship problems that are either being avoided or handled in ways that interfere with effective problem solving. A major strength of AL is that these issues can be addressed quickly by an alert and skilled coach to minimize dysfunction while treating the situation as a learning opportunity. In fact, the speed with which dysfunctional group dynamics are addressed may make it appear that several of the stages in Tuckman and Jensen's (1977) well-known group development model (i.e., forming, storming, norming, performing, adjourning) are avoided. Specifically, it may often appear that the team moves directly from forming to performing. On closer examination, it becomes apparent that the time in the storming and norming stages was minimized but not eliminated.

Changing the focus from problem solving to group development stages introduces some other challenges that teams typically face during development. Exhibit 5.1 presents the typical activities/goals, associated team challenges, and useful questions to help the AL team reach maturity as a high-performance team.

DEALING WITH COVERT AND DYSFUNCTIONAL TEAM BEHAVIOR

Early in the study of group dynamics, it was noted that group member behaviors were often motivated by motives and needs that were not consistent or aligned with the stated purpose of the group or team. Group members may appear to operate to satisfy personal agendas, some of which are conscious but unstated publicly. In other situations, team

EXHIBIT 5.1

An Integrated Model of Team Development

Launching/Forming

Activities/Goals	Team challenges
▪ Given charter from team sponsor	▪ Building interest/recruiting members
▪ Establishing team membership criteria for membership	▪ Coordinating schedules and priorities
▪ Time boundaries and initial meeting times provided	▪ Generating enthusiasm for the problem
▪ Clarification of purpose	▪ Understanding charter
▪ Building commitment	**Questions**
	▪ How do team members feel about this problem? How can the level of commitment be raised?
	▪ How is the team managing the time? On what basis is it deciding how long the meetings should be?
	▪ How do team members feel about the problem?
	▪ What would make the problem more interesting/exciting/challenging/valuable to team members?
	▪ How will the team make sure that the charter is supported by the organization?
	▪ How satisfied is the team with the charter?

Storming

Activities/Goals	Team challenges
▪ Common goals are clarified, forging a team identity	▪ Managing conflict
▪ Team learns how to deal with negative feelings generated by competitive work style and personality differences	▪ Building consensus
	▪ Developing dialogue
▪ Team roles begin to emerge	▪ Valuing differences
	Questions
	▪ What is the team's approach to managing/resolving conflict?
	▪ How well is the team managing/resolving conflict right now?
	▪ What can the team do to improve its management/resolution of conflict?
	▪ How does the team reach agreement on what to do?
	▪ What is the quality of the discussion?
	▪ How can the team improve communication?
	▪ How does the team deal with differences in values and styles among team members?

Norming

Activities/Goals	Team challenges
▪ Agreement on procedures for identifying tasks and resources and assigning subtasks	▪ Avoiding role "lock" or stereotyping
	▪ Finding the right balance between structure/procedure and spontaneity/experimentation

EXHIBIT 5.1 *(Continued)*

An Integrated Model of Team Development

Norming

■ Experimentation with different ways of working together leading to role differentiation	Questions ■ What ground rules or norms does the team have for its work? ■ What ground rules or norms would be useful? ■ What roles are necessary for the team to work effectively? ■ What are the consequences of people getting "locked" into static roles? ■ How can the team encourage the flexible enactment of roles on the team?

Performing

Activities/Goals ■ More efforts to give positive feedback, support, humor, and spontaneity ■ Spontaneous innovation and creative thinking	Team challenges ■ Avoiding overconfidence—team feels superior and able to accomplish anything ■ Balancing creativity with practical limitations Questions ■ How innovative or creative are the team's ideas of solutions? ■ What is limiting the creativity of the team? ■ How can the creativity of the team be improved? ■ Is the balance between innovation and practicality appropriate? ■ What does the team need to do to improve the balance between innovation and practicality?

Reviewing/Renewing/Adjourning

Activities/Goals ■ Facing realistic limitations of time, resources, and talents of the team members ■ Facing up to renewing its mission/charter or ending its existence ■ Group decides for itself what it can tolerate and accomplish, regardless of outside expectations ■ Grieve and mourn the termination ("loss") of the Action Learning team.	Team challenges ■ Facing realities and candidly reviewing progress ■ Performing without clear structure, norms, or roles ■ Becoming "self-managing" ■ Keeping from getting discouraged Questions ■ How would the team characterize its progress against the team charter? ■ How is the morale on the team? ■ What are the sources of low morale? ■ How can morale be improved? ■ How can the team maintain morale over a long period of time? ■ How well is the team performing according to its own norms/standards/ground rules?

From *The California School of Organizational Studies Handbook of Organizational Psychology* (p. 38), edited by R. Lowman, 2002, Hoboken, NJ: Wiley. Copyright 2002 by John Wiley & Sons. Reprinted with permission.

members and the team as a whole may seem to be behaving without conscious awareness of their motives or the controlling needs (Marshak, 2006). In most cases, these unconsciously motivated actions interfere with the team's ability to mature and reach levels of high performance. Although the AL process does not eliminate these instances of dysfunctional and immature behavior, the early intervention by the AL team coach can quickly (a) bring the issue to the conscious awareness of team members, (b) encourage the team to reflect on the consequences and sources of the behavior, and (c) promote team problem solving to improve performance and modify or discontinue the dysfunctional behavior.

Hidden Agendas

Unless there is a strong bond among team members as well as clear agreement and commitment to the team's mission (conditions not generally true at the start of AL programs), team members' behavior typically displays tension between the desire to reach and satisfy individual goals and needs and the commitment to achieving team and organizational goals. This natural dissonance can be dealt with productively through honest dialogue or unproductively through pursuing personal hidden agendas while publicly espousing commitment to the team or to the organizational goals expressed in the team's project. Of course, this conflict is not usually black and white. Most team members genuinely want to support the team's mission as expressed in the team charter, but their perceptions and behavior are also influenced by personal needs and agendas. Figure 5.1 provides some of the typical hidden agendas present during an AL project.

The AL team coach can promote dialogue in surfacing and discussing the conflicts between personal and team/organizational goals when they become apparent by asking questions such as the following:

- How is the team dealing with possible conflicts between organizational, business unit, and personal goals as it develops solutions to the team's problem?
- What is the impact of discussing the organization's goals as expressed in the team's mission without openly discussing the impact of team member interests and needs?
- What are the areas of shared or common interest between organizational, business unit, and personal needs?

Although team members may still not be totally honest and open about their personal interests and needs, at least the issue will have been raised for discussion.

Another form of hidden agenda is the undiscussable issues that exist in any organization. Most team members are aware of these issues but are reluctant to bring them up because of politics, personal rivalries, and

FIGURE 5.1

Action Learning Team Members Haunt Themselves With Ghosts That They Create

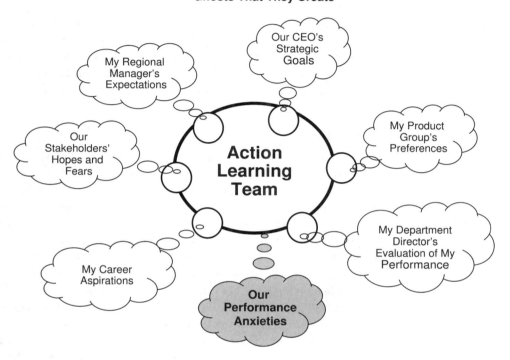

Example of hidden agendas for an AL team

a history of people getting "burned" in the past when bringing up these issues. These are the "third-rail" issues or the "elephant in the room" that everyone is aware of but no one will point out, much less discuss (Marshak, 2006).

Some of these issues will be obvious to the coach, whereas others may only reveal their presence by a conspicuous lack of discussion about a seemingly important issue or by the emergence of anxiety or tension any time a particular issue is broached (and usually dropped like a hot potato). Questions such as the following can be used to encourage discussion of undiscussable issues or topics:

- What are the sensitive issues in relation to this topic that are difficult for the team to discuss or consider?
- I notice that the topic of _____ seems to be avoided or discussion of the issue is dropped quickly. Are others noticing this? Why do you think this is happening?

- What are the consequences of proceeding with our work without fully considering these difficult-to-discuss issues?

Dysfunctional Team Behavior

Bion (1961) noted that teams spent much of their time operating "as if" the purpose of the team was other than that specified in its mission or charter. Bion referred to these behaviors as *basic assumptions* (the team is operating "as if" an unstated assumption were true). Bion noted the following dysfunctional, "as if" behaviors that are relevant to AL teams:

Dependency

The team is operating under this basic assumption when it behaves "as if" it needs a strong leader to take charge. When the team is in this operating mode, members act as if they do not understand the problem or how to develop solutions and look to the coach or other authority figures to provide guidance and leadership. Teams typically assume this basic assumption during the forming stage of team development. Teams operating under a dependency basic assumption can put a great deal of pressure, either directly or indirectly, on the coach to become more directive and provide task leadership. Coaches often feel internal pressure to intervene by providing task leadership because many are very good at task facilitation and feel confident that they know what needs to be done next in order for the team to move forward successfully. Sometimes a coach can be seduced by the team or the task to engage in subtle task facilitation by taking on the "scribing" role and keeping public notes on flip-charts.

In these situations, asking good questions such as the following will be the coach's salvation by keeping him or her from falling into the trap of becoming involved in facilitating tasks rather than fostering individual, team, and organizational learning:

- Why is the team looking to me (the coach) to provide guidance/leadership now? Is the team following the ground rule that the AL team coach is only responsible for the team's learning?
- What difficulty is the team having defining the problem and developing leadership within the team?
- How can the team do a better job defining the problem and generating leadership within the team?

Fight/flight

The team is operating under this basic assumption when it behaves "as if" it needs to fight or flee authority or attempts to direct the team. Because the coach does not take a directive role, the fight/flight behavior is not normally directed toward the coach. However, it is more common to see fight/flight behavior in the team whenever a team member takes the initiative and attempts to assume leadership. Fight/flight behavior is most frequently seen during the storming stages of team development (Tuckman & Jensen, 1977). The AL team coach can help the team deal more constructively with fight/flight behavior and learn how to accept and share leadership by asking questions such as the following:

- I am noticing that efforts to take leadership are often resisted by the team. Do others observe this? What is the impact of this behavior on team effectiveness? What can be done to reduce the resistance to leadership in the team?
- I am noticing a reluctance to take the initiative or express leadership in the team. Do others observe this? What is the impact of this behavior on team effectiveness? What can be done to encourage more leadership in the team?
- How do team members decide when to take leadership and when to accept the leadership efforts of others?

It is important to note that a number of these questions are prefaced by an observation. After making the observation, the coach asks a question to confirm the observation: "Do others observe behavior_____?"[1] If at least some members of the team confirm an observation, the coach can then ask additional questions to encourage the team to reflect on the consequences of these actions and to consider changes the team can make to eliminate the dysfunctional behavior. This sequence is often necessary because the behaviors may be covertly motivated and not consciously recognized by the team until the coach points them out. Even if the team denies that the coach's observation is accurate, the issue has been put on the table and the "elephant in the room" is no longer invisible. It is usually wise not to push the team to accept the observation as being accurate and valid. The team will often self-correct as a result. If not, other opportunities will emerge later to address the recurring behavioral issue.

The Search for a "Messiah"

Bion (1961) noticed that teams frequently looked for a subgroup (often a pair of individuals) that they hoped would rescue the team from its internal difficulties and incompetence and termed this a *pairing* basic

---

[1] The reader may recognize the technique of confirming an observation as similar to an intervention approach suggested by Schwarz (2002). Asking the team to confirm an observation not only gives permission to the team to disagree with the coach but also provides some useful assumption-testing for the coach to insure that his or her inferences are valid (Argyris & Schön, 1978).

assumption. Although this occurs occasionally in teams, it is more frequent for teams to look to experts outside the team to do the work that the team can do for itself and learn in the process. Team members are used to hiring outside experts in their regular job, and therefore it may seem normal and appropriate to do so in the AL team. In an extreme case, some team members will suggest subcontracting or farming out most aspects of the project. Because this proposal relieves the team from having to create solutions on its own (this reaction is a form of a dependency basic assumption), other team members are often quick to accept this recommendation. The coach can encourage the team to reflect on this behavior by asking questions such as the following:

- Why does the team believe that it does not have the ability to do this task itself?
- What are the pros and cons associated with outsourcing or hiring someone else to do this task?
- What factors are leading the team to believe that outside experts are needed?
- What experience do team member have with using outside experts?

Several other dysfunctional team behaviors are occasionally noted during extended AL projects.

Scapegoating

Teams often scapegoat members of the team or other parts of the organization when they have difficulty reaching consensus on important decisions or the direction to take or the merits of ideas or solutions. In these situations it is common for team members to idealize majority views and opinions and to discredit the merits of minority or unpopular views. Instead of evaluating the pros and cons of competing views objectively, the team splits the views into polarized "good" and "bad" viewpoints. When this happens, minority opinions do not get a fair hearing and individuals who hold these viewpoints are ignored, criticized, and encouraged (sometimes not so subtly) to keep quiet. Sometimes, if some AL team members are disappointed or angry that the AL team coach is not performing the task leadership functions that they expected but are reluctant to express this directly, they may direct their anger toward a vulnerable team member (often a lower status or less "popular" member) as a safe alternative target for their angry feelings. It is important that the AL team coach quickly intervene with good questions when he or she notices scapegoating because these primitive yet common team responses can be very destructive to team cohesiveness and effectiveness. For example, the coach might say the following:

- I am observing that the views of some team members seem to be consistently ignored or criticized. Do others observe this? What is the impact of this behavior on the team's effectiveness?
- I am hearing that the proposal supported by the majority has many advantages and few drawbacks. I am also hearing that the proposals forwarded by the minority have little or no merit. Am I hearing that correctly?
- If the team disagrees with this observation and offers more balanced assessments of the pros and cons of each side, the coach can follow up with questions that encourage the team to reflect on its splitting tendency: I am wondering if the team can come up with strategies for achieving more balanced assessment of the views of all group members.

If the team agrees with the observation but sees the polarized views as justified, the coach has several options: (a) stop pursuing the issue (the issue has been raised and the team cannot avoid considering it as a possible issue) or (b) if the coach is reasonably sure that scapegoating is going on because of the weight of the evidence or because it is a reccurring phenomenon, he or she can present the behavioral evidence and ask the team to make sense of it. This is a high-risk move and should be attempted only if the scapegoating is blatant, is denied by the team, is very disruptive to effective teamwork, and threatens the ultimate success of the team.

Violation of Norms for Effective Team Performance

From time to time, the coach will notice behavior that is not an example of typical dysfunctional team behavior, such as scapegoating or the basic assumption behavior noted by Bion (1961). Rather, the coach may note violation or, more often, a lack of appropriate norms for effective team performance. For example, let's say that Robert has just harshly criticized Laura by saying, "Laura, how can you be so stupid? That will never work." When such behavior occurs in a group, the members tend to become timid and fearful of also being attacked; they lose energy and look forward to the end of the meeting. No one knows how to handle Robert so nothing is said.

This situation, however, is a great learning opportunity for the AL coach to help the team reflect on the consequences of a particular type of behavior and to develop more effective norms to promote better team performance. The team coach might say, "I am observing that someone is attacking another member of the group. What is the impact on a group (quickly moving from the personal to the theoretical level) when one member attacks another?" The group will typically respond with comments that reflect a loss of energy, concern over another wasted meeting, fear, and a desire to "get out of here." The coach then asks, "How could a group handle such dysfunctional behavior?" Again, team members may respond with such statements as, "We all need to show respect for one another"; "We need to stay focused on working on the task"; "If someone behaves like this, we need to confront the person immediately." The coach then asks the group to return to the task by simply saying, "Who has the next question?"

Without recommending a ground rule or norm directly, the AL team coach has helped the team to recognize an informal norm (e.g., it's OK to be brutally candid and judgmental in critiquing an idea), to reflect on the impact of this sort of behavior, and thereby to encourage the team to develop explicit norms for behavior in this sort of situation. As a result of this coaching intervention, rarely, if ever, will this type of dysfunctional behavior occur again in that group because the group and the involved individuals have (a) become clearly aware of what has happened and the significant impact on the quality and speed of the group's work and (b) have explicitly established a norm that will minimize this kind of dysfunctional behavior in the future.

LEVERAGING DIVERSITY

Diversity in AL team membership is encouraged and usually intentionally planned. However, differences among team members along such dimensions as ethnic and cultural backgrounds, race, status, job responsibilities, technical education or training, gender, age, political views, values, work experiences, and even Myers–Briggs Type Indicator profiles can result in both challenges and learning opportunities.

Diversity in AL teams is critical in two distinct ways. First, it is critical in determining the composition of teams. Second, it is critical to manage diversity during the AL team's deliberations in order to leverage the benefits of diversity and limit the disadvantages created when diversity is mismanaged.

Team Composition

When teams deal with problems for which the goals are ambiguous and the solutions are initially uncertain, they must be as diverse as possible. Thus, in recruiting, selecting, and deploying team members, the problem champions, sponsors, and project managers must pay careful attention to the selection criteria that they use. For example, team members should be representative of the stakeholder groups that will be affected as a result of planning and implementing a specific organizational change. Team members should also be competent in applying knowledge and a broad range of cognitive skills that relate to the problem that the team is to address. Teams should be composed of a diagonal slice of the organization, including (as much as possible) all hierarchical levels and all functional, product, departmental, and regional subsystems. Team members should look and sound like customers and people employed in the organization's subsystems. Furthermore, teams should be reasonably large (i.e., five to eight persons), with members drawn from a reasonably large pool of potential team members. This increases the probability of creating AL teams with requisite cognitive and identity diversity.

However, if the problem has a specific goal with a well-known solution—or a clear pathway to find or create a solution—diversity among team members is not a critical factor. In fact, in such situations, AL would not be the most appropriate way to set goals and find or create solutions. Rather, such cases call for finding or recruiting the best individual performer.

Diversity in Action Learning Teams

AL teams must deal with issues that are illuminated by such surface-level diversity dimensions as race, age, and gender. Teams must also deal with less obvious diversity issues such as status, assertiveness, and pertinent knowledge. As Thomas (2008) pointed out, "In the midst of diversity, tension is inevitable" (p. 213). AL team coaches must recognize the sources of these tensions and enable team members to manage them effectively to learn how to leverage the beneficial values of diversity. There are at least two sources of diversity in teams: social identity and variety.

Diversity as Identity and Social Justice

Diversity is a frequent focus of attention because of increasingly widespread concerns for social justice in various societies in general and within organizations in particular. This is also a valid concern for AL teams. Among others, Bell and Berry (2007) pointed out that "women, minorities, and other non-dominant group members remain woefully underrepresented in key organizational positions, confined by glass ceilings and walls; held to higher performance standards; and sometimes subjected to virulent harassment, discrimination, and exclusion" (p. 21). AL teams may address this pervasive issue as a designated problem or deal with the consequences during their sessions and when developing their solutions to other designated problems that are influenced by their organization's existing diversity issues.

Diverse cognitive skills are distinct from such identity-based distinctions as race, gender, age, ethnicity, and so on. Page (2007) found that "cognitive and identity diversity often correlate empirically" because where and how people look for solutions "are the product of training, practice, and life experiences. How we see the world is informed and influenced by our values, our identities, and our cultures. . . . Diverse identities, therefore, often translate into diverse [cognitive skills]" (pp. 8–9).

Many advocates of an inclusive approach have promulgated a hopeful "value in diversity" argument to managing diversity. According to this argument,

> effective management of diversity could benefit organizations by reducing costs associated with low job satisfaction and high turnover; increasing organizations' ability to attract and retain employees; increasing organizations' ability to market to different types of consumers; and increasing creativity, problem-solving ability, and system flexibility in organizations. (Bell & Berry, 2007, p. 22)

However, tests of the validity of this argument seem to have yielded only mixed results.

Adding to the unique perspectives on diversity offered by Page (2007), Klein and Harrison (2007) offered the following suggestion:

> Groups rich in diversity of knowledge, heuristics, [interpretations,] and perspectives have more tools, more insights, and more estimates with which to tackle the problems assigned to them than do homogeneous groups . . . [which increases] the possibility that diverse individuals may combine their differing [cognitive skills] to create breakthrough solutions and innovations. (p. 27)

Diversity as Variety

Klein and Harrison (2007) combined Page's (2007) four dimensions of diversity into one category: diversity as variety. Page's dimensions are as follows:

- *Perspective.* Perspective refers to where a person looks to find new solutions to challenging, complex, or complicated organizational problems. Diverse perspectives are derived from team members' past experiences, for example, as members of their society's dominant or nondominant group; men or women; straight, gay, lesbian, or transgendered persons; older or younger persons; multiskilled, skilled, or unskilled workers; high-, middle-, or low-status persons; well- or less well-educated persons; long- or short-term organizational employees; persons with multicultural, foreign cultural, or strictly local backgrounds; persons experienced with several organizations or only one; and persons with single career or multiple career experiences. Page (2007) pointed out that, when searching for or creating solutions for problems, "someone from a different perspective will notice different *candidate* solutions" (p. 7).

■ *Heuristics*. Page (2007) defined heuristics as "methods or tools to find solutions . . . [that] vary in their sophistication from simple rules of thumb to complicated algorithms. . . . Diverse heuristics, like diverse perspectives, improve problem solving" (p. 8) and decision making that increase the probability of an innovative breakthrough. "Heuristics change how a person searched for solutions" (p. 8). For example, one person may experiment by taking the opposite of a more traditional approach to finding or creating a solution. One person may break a problem down into its component parts, whereas another person may reverse the sequence of tasks and activities involved in a business process. Some people prefer to map and analyze an existing set of interdependent activities (e.g., how a research institute hired senior scientists) and then identify flaws and inefficiencies (e.g., gaps and redundancies), whereas others prefer to start with a blank canvas and create an ideal process that is then compared with the existing process. Using different heuristics, people can "identify different candidate solutions, increasing the probability of a breakthrough." By "seeing problems differently (diverse perspectives) and by looking for solutions in different ways (different heuristics), teams, groups, and organizations can locate more potential innovations" (Page, 2007, p. 8).

■ *Predictive models*. AL team members should all be smart. That is, they should each be accomplished, accurate predictors. However, they should "differ in how they make predictions" (Page, 2007, p. 11).

■ *Interpretations*. "Predictive models rely on interpretations . . . the mappings we make from the real world into categories [that,] in turn, are conceptual boxes, or placeholders" (Page, 2007, p. 11).

> An interpretation categorizes part of the world. . . . A predictive model tells us what we think will happen. . . . Predictive models are thoughts. Heuristics are courses of action [that] tells us what to do. . . . A perspective . . . is a representation of the world. Each person possesses . . . perspectives, heuristics, interpretations, and predictive models. And each of us differs in the particular collection of these tools that we hold in our heads." (Page, 2007, p. 12)

CAVEATS IN CREATING DIVERSE ACTION LEARNING TEAMS

Klein and Harrison (2007) pointed out that "diversity is itself diverse" (p. 27). Cognitive heterogeneity (i.e., varying perspectives, heuristics, predictive models, and interpretations that are held by team members) represents only one form of diversity (i.e., variety). Variety is evident when every team member contributes some unique information to the team that is relevant to its task. However, teams are also diverse in terms of their members' values, assumptions, beliefs, interests, priorities, pre-occupations, and attitudes. It is quite possible, therefore, for one form of diversity (e.g., differences in values and beliefs) to nullify the benefits of other forms of diversity (e.g., variety of thought and perspectives). Consider the following situation:

> Valeen's team has been tasked with creating a new software application to be used by customer service reps and tech support consultants. He has created an AL team that has admirable diversity in terms of perspectives and thought—the team is composed of software engineers, customer service reps, tech-support consultants, and client end-users.
>
> During the second meeting, however, several members become silent and appear unwilling to participate for long periods of time. The AL coach notes the drop in performance but has no idea what is causing it. Midway through the meeting, the coach notes the behavior (the drop-off in participation by several members of the group) and asks the team what it makes of this pattern. Initially, all team members appear unwilling to discuss the "elephant in the room."
>
> Finally, one brave participant from the silent subgroup volunteers that she is offended by a comment made by another member and supported by others in the group. Through further discussion, it becomes clear that members of the silent group are members of a cultural minority. The comment that offended this cultural subgroup related to an issue of bitter contention between this cultural minority and the majority culture represented by the rest of the group. With the reason for the behavior uncovered, the coach asks about the impact on team performance of this issue and follows up by asking the team how it wants to handle this challenge. The team's performance improve immediately when the undiscussable issue is uncovered and the team is challenged to develop solutions for the problem.

This is a case in which diversity in several dimensions can, at least temporarily, create dysfunction in the team. The coach, applying the best practices discussed in this chapter, was able to get the team to identify a problem related to the team's diversity along a values dimension that allowed it to make adjustments in team and individual behavior so that the diversity along a second dimension—variety in skills and perspectives—could be leveraged.

Klein and Harrison (2007) termed this type of situation *diversity as separation*. This form of diversity is most evident when team members are bifurcated into two or more polar extremes. Separation results when subgroups are in conflict with one another, resulting in low group cohesion, coordination, and morale.

Klein and Harrison (2007) also identified another form of diversity (termed *diversity as disparity*) that can cross-cut and often nullify variety along diversity of other dimensions. Diversity of disparity occurs when one team member outranks the rest in status, prestige, power, technical knowledge, political connections, or aggressiveness or has control over other scarce resources. When there is great disparity along status dimensions, low-status team members' voices, participation, and sharing of information can be stifled because high-status persons override them—and low-status team members allow this to occur. In teams with a great deal of status disparity, self-interest dominates and political activity is triggered. Low-status team members either disengage and accept the influence and control of the more powerful or mobilize to overthrow those in power.

As in the previous example, the best practice in this situation is for the AL coach to (a) describe the observed behavior, asking whether the team members also are aware of the behavior, (b) demonstrate curiosity about the behavior—what might explain the behavior, (c) inquire about the impact of the behavior on the team's performance, and (d) ask the team how it wants to adjust its behavior to improve performance. Done properly, this complication caused by disparity in status can result in greatly improved performance and enhanced awareness of the presence and impact of diversity issues.

DEALING WITH DIFFICULT TEAM MEMBERS

By using the type of questions recommended earlier, the AL team coach can help the team quickly resolve most of the challenges that typically emerge in the various stages of the problem-solving process and team development. As noted earlier, a well-crafted question can make it seem as if the team has progressed directly from forming to performing (Tuckman & Jensen, 1977) without having to resolve the challenges presented in the storming and norming phases. Dysfunctional team behaviors (e.g., scapegoating, splitting, diversity issues) may require a more complex series of questions (because these issues are often driven by unconscious or denied processes), but a skillful coach is usually successful in helping the team move to a more effective and mature level of performance.

Occasionally, however, the AL coach will work with a team with a difficult team member who does not respond to the question and reflection method that is the heart of AL. There are two basic reasons for the imperviousness of the individual to good questions.

Misalignment Between Personal and Action Learning Goals

Some individuals enroll in AL for personal reasons that are at variance with the primary goal of AL, which is for individuals to learn how to be better problem solvers and leaders. The following case example illustrates this point.

Jamie seemed unwilling to following one of the basic ground rules—statements always follow questions. Jamie seemed intent on leading with recommendations for solving the problem despite the best efforts of the AL team coach. In a discussion during a break, the AL team coach learned that Jamie was on a job search and had joined the team to network with other team members. Jamie admitted that she was trying to impress the team with her expertise and problem-solving acumen. This behavior became increasingly self-destructive and counter-productive because the other team members felt increasingly frustrated with her and were less likely to see her as a good job prospect. The AL team coach took a directive coaching stance with Jamie, gently but firmly making it clear that her motivation for joining the team was inappropriate and that she needed to accept the goals and ground rules for the program if she wanted to remain on the team. Jamie decided to leave the team, much to the relief of its members.

Inappropriate Assignment

In other situations, the organization inappropriately enrolls people in AL programs. Some managers may believe that AL is a training course for people who have difficulty working in teams or being good team members. Examples of inappropriate remedial placement are painfully shy individuals who are terrified of speaking up or dominating and highly competitive people who have great difficulty working in teams in which they are not in charge. AL is not an appropriate method for "fixing" people. Inappropriate assignment of individuals to a team is best avoided by making sure that the organizational communications about whom to refer to AL programs are clear and explicit. Even with the best instructions for team assignment, however, an inappropriate assignment occasionally occurs. When it becomes clear that an individual is unable or unwilling to follow the primary ground rules or to participate in the discussions, the AL team coach needs to intervene with the organization and the individual to counsel the individual out of the program. Not to do so is unfair to both the individual and the other members of the team.

WHAT TO DO WHEN THE TEAM SEEMS STUCK

Coaches who are also strong task facilitators often feel frustrated when they observe teams that use dysfunctional processes and cannot seem to "invent" significantly better processes even when the coach asks all the right questions to encourage reflection. In these situations, coaches must balance the goal of helping the team develop creative solutions with their role in promoting learning. Sometimes the time and frustration necessary to let the team members discover best practices for themselves (i.e., to "reinvent the wheel") are not justifiable. After all, many of the effective practices and principles used in creative problem solving today took decades to develop through a laborious trial-and-error method. Is it reasonable to expect team members to discover these principles for themselves in the relatively short time they have to meet?

This is a ticklish issue. On the one hand, intervening to suggest a best practice prematurely robs the team of the opportunity to learn these principles for themselves. On the other hand, it is not desirable to jeopardize the project's success because the team gets stuck using a suboptimal process despite excellent questions by the coach. One solution that can be used sparingly while holding to the ground rules is to ask a question in the following form: Would it be useful to see a model that other teams have found helpful in this situation? In this case, the coach is not suggesting a solution to the problem at hand; rather, he or she is providing a framework for addressing the problem.

Fortunately, a skilled coach will need to use this questioning approach infrequently. In the vast majority of situations, teams are able to recognize and invent effective team problem-solving processes on their own. Asking the questions previously suggested often triggers participants' memories of previous trainings. In these cases, changes in the team's process can occur almost instantaneously. The skilled and experienced AL team coach will always be flexible enough to know when to offer a process model in the form of a question that will prevent a stalled team process from creating a poor solution and a negative personal experience.

Reflection Questions

1. In thinking about problem-solving teams you have worked with, how often did the team discuss the problem-solving process before beginning the work? What were the consequences? What kinds of questions could you, as a team coach, ask to get the team to reflect on the phases of problem solving and the implications for its work?

2. We have observed that quick intervention by the AL team coach when dysfunctional team behavior emerges greatly accelerates team development. What process makes this possible? Think of a recent team problem-solving meeting that got mired in conflict or counterproductive behavior. What questions could you have asked to move the process through storming and norming to performing?

3. It is common for teams to look to someone else to solve the problems the team is encountering. What assumptions are teams making when they farm out a problem to internal or external

techsperts? What questions could you ask as an AL team coach to challenge the team's decisions the next time you observe this behavior?

4. How can you improve the diversity of a project or AL team when the membership requirements (e.g., an engineering department) restrict diversity?

5. Think of a recent team meeting during which someone dominated the discussion and seemed oblivious to his or her impact on the process. What questions could you ask as an AL team coach to interrupt this process and improve team performance?

IMPLEMENTING ACTION LEARNING

Developing and Changing Organizations Through Action Learning $\Big|$ 6

n the previous chapter, we discussed how Action Learning (AL) team coaches work within their AL teams. The focus was on the internal dynamics of the AL team itself.

In this chapter, we focus on the functions served by AL in the context of complex, planned organizational change projects that address multiple issues affecting the entire organizational system. We describe how the theory, strategies, and processes of organization development and change (OD&C) can be combined with AL to add considerable value when included in such major change projects as mergers and acquisitions, global expansion, centralization or decentralization of business functions, downsizing, or the design and implementation of systemwide software platform systems (e.g., enterprise resource planning, customer relations management).

In these fundamental, often transformational change projects, neither OD&C nor AL is likely to be the primary approach used to plan and implement the changes desired by executive management. Rather, external subject matter expert advisors (SMEs) and technical expert consultants (techsperts) usually introduce the core strategies, structures, and technologies for designing the changes. Techsperts and SMEs are most likely to know (from experience) what must be done or to know how to learn what must be done to achieve the desired results. However, their approach is typically authoritative and directive—rather like the first techspert consultant, Frederick Taylor, at the turn of the 20th century—and their results often fall short of expectations. Even so, client system leaders require SMEs and techsperts to meet expectations in planning and managing complex system change projects.

OD&C as a field of practice emerged in 1959 and, since then, has demonstrated its value in crafting highly participative processes through which all involved and affected parties are actively involved in making decisions that would have an impact on them and their work life. The major consequence of high levels of participation is that involved parties experience an enhanced emotional investment in the organizational change effort that expresses itself as a deep commitment to actively support the change effort. As a result, organizational projects that utilize both techsperts and OD&C practitioners are far more effective in helping organizations to change than are those that utilize SMEs or techspert consultants alone.

In this chapter, we demonstrate that OD&C practices are greatly improved when augmented by AL. Consequently, techspert- or SME-directed organizational change projects can be further enhanced in partnership with OD&C practitioners and AL team coaches.

As noted in chapter 1, organizations across the globe have found it necessary to continuously adapt to multiple, often simultaneous, complex organizational changes. These changes are generally responses to both discontinuous threats and opportunities that occur in their external environments. Most of the threats and opportunities are unprecedented with respect to the organizations' past history and experience; many are radical. Public, private, nongovernmental organization (NGO), and nonprofit organizations all engage in planning and executing adaptive organizational changes.

The external events include the consequences of an increasingly global economy, technological innovations, shifting demographic trends among employees and customers, competitive pressures, off-shoring industrial production and high-tech development from post-industrialized to developing societies, mergers and acquisitions (they are really all acquisitions), vertical and horizontal strategic alliances, changing customer preferences and requirements, economic fluctuations, as well as such global, transnational threats as terrorism, geopolitical instability, natural disasters, threats of pandemics, climate change, and international crime. These external events occur in unpredictable combinations and permutations and create significant challenges (both threats and opportunities) for most organizations. Organizations cannot realistically deal with events like these one at a time—but they often expect to do just that.

To continuously adapt, organizations must accurately assess the threats and opportunities inherent in each external event and then, taking their own internal strengths and weaknesses into consideration, design and implement some combination of corrective and preventive strategic, technological, structural, and/or business process change plans. Most organizational change efforts, especially those guided by the techsperts described in chapter 1, primarily use single-loop learning (Argyris & Schön, 1978, 1996)—learning with the purpose of gaining efficiency in achieving the desired or expected results. Single-loop learning, if used exclusively, neglects the opportunity for organizational leaders and members to learn why and how the processes employed to make such changes work (or do not work).

The focus on the process of achieving results, double-loop learning (Argyris & Schön, 1978, 1996) is the primary source of organizational learning and the creation of intellectual capital. Double-loop learning enables people to examine and question the governing variables and assumptions that are embedded in a problem or change effort. Double-loop learning is, therefore, critical for creativity and innovative thinking. Whereas single-loop learning can create incremental improvements, double-loop learning focuses on results as well as novel thinking, changes in mental mindsets, and quantum shifts in performance.

Freedman (2006) noted that a third level of learning is possible during a change process. During triple-loop learning, people learn about themselves by reflecting on their experiences during the change effort (as discussed in chap. 2, this volume). That is, they learn how their beliefs, assumptions, attitudes, preoccupations, and preferences influence how they perceive what they believe is (and is not) pertinent for the change effort. Subsequently, the meanings people attribute to their perceptions influence what they think, how they feel, and what they do as they participate in the change effort.

Without triple-loop learning, organizational leaders, managers, and workers are unlikely to think about the future value of investing the time and effort required to learn about themselves as agents or leaders of change. Therefore, they are unlikely to learn how they, personally, contribute to either effective or unsuccessful efforts to implement fundamental complex organizational changes. Revans (1998) explicitly based AL on the traditional scientific method and applied this process to the "therapeutic" or action phase of studying technical and structural problems and opportunities in organizations. It is clear that Revans (1982a, 1998); Marquardt (1999, 2004); and Enderby, Phelan, and Birchall (1998), among others, understand this process in a manner that is very similar to OD&C practitioners and AL team coaches. Furthermore, theorists and practitioners seem to incorporate a three-tiered set of outcomes that is quite similar to those of OD&C and AL (see Exhibit 6.1). That is, they see it as essential that—in addition to achieving their change

EXHIBIT 6.1

Single-, Double-, and Triple-Loop Learning

Single-loop learning	Action Research method applied to creating and executing the steps taken in an effort to reach ambiguous goals (what action steps produced the expected, desired results; what did not work as expected; what innovative actions did we create)
Double-loop learning	Action Research method applied to the process of working collaboratively in planning and executing implementation plans (how did we work well together; how can we do better)
Triple-loop learning	Action Research method applied to reflection and self-awareness (did my perceptions, expectations, beliefs, opinions, preferences, assumptions, etc., help or hinder our work; what I learned about myself)

goal (single-loop learning)—AL team members are helped to focus and reflect on each phase of their applied scientific method to enhance their understanding of the process of change (double-loop learning) and their reflective capacities as leaders and as members of participating problem-solving teams (triple-loop learning). Thus, AL methodologies naturally create defined opportunities and the time for reflection required for single-, double-, and triple-loop learning for organizational members from all parts and levels of the organization.

The enduring, enhanced capacity of all organizational leaders and members to continue to learn how to autonomously plan and implement adaptive organizational change is the predictable consequence of combining the double- and triple-loop learning facilitated by AL and OD&C, with the single-loop learning promoted by techsperts (Freedman & Zackrison, 2001).

It is remarkable that Revans apparently created AL (circa 1945, according to Revans, 1982a) independent of the seminal contributions of the pioneers in the field of OD&C. Specifically, the compatibility of Revans's AL theory and methods with the Action Research method, a core methodology for OD&C that was created by Kurt Lewin (1946), is striking. This seems to be an example of serendipitous, simultaneous but independent development of harmonious theory and method in the same historical period. An example of this harmony is the similarity between Lewin's and Revans's admonitions: There can be "No action without research; no research without action" (Lewin, according to Marrow, 1972, p. 90), and "There can be no action without learning, and no learning without action" (Revans, 1998, p, 14).

Comparison of Action
Learning With OD&C

AL is complementary, not competitive, with most versions of OD&C theories, strategies, and methods (Cummings & Worley, 2005; French, Bell, & Zawacki, 2000; Jones & Brazzel, 2006; Rothwell, Sullivan, & McLean, 1995). As previously mentioned, the origins of AL are independent of those of OD&C (Marquardt, 1999, 2004; Revans, 1998). However, Revans's writings (e.g., 1998) make it clear that in 1978 he was aware of at least two of the OD&C pioneers, Chris Argyris and Ron Lippitt. Yet, it is odd that four major contemporary texts on OD&C (previously cited) fail to mention either Revans or AL.

AL and OD&C seem to have evolved along parallel paths, at least until recently. The purposes and values as well as theories and practice of both AL and OD&C are consistent and complementary.

PURPOSES

The primary purpose of both AL and OD&C is to enable the leaders and members of their client systems—and techspert consultants or SME advisors—to achieve the specific results that the organization wants or needs. In some cases the results or products of an AL process are recommendations for (a) solving a high-priority problem, (b) exploiting an opportunity (Marquardt, 1999, 2004), or (c) managing a persistent, unsolvable dilemma or paradox (Johnson, 1997). This is consistent with the diagnostic Action Research approach to OD&C (Marrow, 1972), which is only a partial application of OD&C theory and methods because it does not include implementation. However, in other cases, after executive management review and approval or the AL team's recommendations, AL teams may also be authorized to execute the implementation plans they developed to achieve established change goals. This is totally consistent with the participative Action Research approach to OD&C (Marrow, 1972). Both versions of Action Research exemplify the integration of single-, double-, and triple-loop learning. We discuss Action Research in some detail later in this chapter; for now, Action Research and OD&C should be viewed as roughly equivalent.

AL's second purpose is to develop the leadership, membership, or followership skills of organizational members. AL's third purpose is to enable team members to learn how to create and contribute to high-performing teams.

OD&C's second and third purposes seem to differ somewhat from those of AL, but these apparent differences may be a matter of semantics. OD&C's second purpose focuses on helping client system leaders and members to become increasingly self-reliant by enabling them to learn how to manage and facilitate complex system change processes by reflecting on their experiences as active participants (double-loop learning). This is consistent with AL's third purpose. OD&C's third purpose is to help client system members to learn about themselves as instruments of positive change (Levinson, 1993) and to develop and use their self-reflective awareness to illuminate how their assumptions, attitudes, values, beliefs, preoccupations, and interests influence their perceptions, thoughts, feelings, and actions (triple-loop learning). It is expected that enhanced self-awareness will translate into increasing interpersonal effectiveness. This seems to encompass AL's second purpose.

It is generally understood by OD&C scholar-practitioners that, in fulfilling their third purpose (enhanced self-reflective awareness and use of self), client system members develop their leadership and membership skills (AL's second purpose) as well as their capacity to develop high-performing teams (AL's third purpose). Also, AL enables team members to gain personal awareness and interpersonal competence through the feedback and resulting self-reflection that is stimulated by the AL team coach's questions (Marquardt, 1999, 2004). Therefore, although the language differs, the intended purposes of AL and OD&C appear to be remarkably similar.

VALUES

Although the AL literature discusses the impact of client organizations' culture and the values of organizational leaders on the effectiveness of an AL intervention, little if anything is explicitly mentioned about any intrinsic values of the practice of AL or of those who practice AL. Yet, it seems likely that AL theorists and practitioners would be in considerable agreement with the explicit OD&C values.[1]

Opinions vary about the specific values that OD&C scholar–practitioners should hold and demonstrate (Cummings & Worley, 2005; The Organization Development Institute, 2008). Yet, there is a fair amount of agreement that OD&C scholar-practitioners should acknowledge the fundamental importance of the following values both for themselves and for their field of practice:

1. *Inquiry and science*—applying the principles of Action Research (i.e., reiterative cycles of data-based action) at every phase of the OD&C consultation process to generate actionable knowledge that has value for the client system, scholar-practitioners, and the discipline of OD&C;

---

[1]According to Hofstede and Hofstede (2005), organizational culture is often confused with national culture. An organization's culture seems to consist of its prevailing organizational practices. An organization's practices are influenced by its host national culture, the values of the organization's founders, and the organization's core technology and its major business processes as well as its structure.

2. *Human potential, enablement and empowerment, growth, and excellence*—increasing self-determination and self-control by organizational members, one's own and others' increasing awareness of potential capacities, and recognizing one's power to actualize that potential;

3. *Freedom and responsibility*—people making self-enhancing, fully informed life choices and accepting responsibility for the consequences of their choices about how they choose to live their lives;

4. *Integrity in all relationships*—respecting the worth and fundamental rights of individuals, organizations, communities, societies, and other human systems; utilizing diversity in an inclusive manner and acknowledging the legitimacy of varied perspectives, values, interests, information, skills, roles, etc.;

5. *Collaborative orientation*—people working together to achieve results that have value for all involved parties;

6. *Authenticity and openness in all relationships*—with the intention of building and maintaining trust among all involved parties;

7. *Organizational effectiveness, efficiency, and alignment*—achieving optimal desired organizational results, at minimum cost, in ways that match persons' individual purposes with those of the subsystems of which they are parts, and with the larger system of which their subsystems are parts;

8. *Holistic, systemic view, and stakeholder orientation*—understanding human behavior from a whole system perspective; recognizing that different stakeholders have varying, competing interests in the system's operations and results; and valuing those different interests fairly and justly; and

9. *Broad and deep participation and transparency*—in system affairs, overt confrontation of issues leading to effective participatory problem solving, and involvement of all relevant parties in decision making.

FOCAL ISSUES: PROBLEMS, OPPORTUNITIES, AND DILEMMAS

Both AL and OD&C focus on organizational issues (i.e., problems to solve, opportunities to exploit, dilemmas to manage) that have the following characteristics (Cummings & Worley, 2005; Marquardt, 1999):

- They are real and seen as crucial and must be addressed.
- They must be issues that the AL team members really care about.
- When dealt with effectively, the results will make a visible, tangible, and meaningful organizational difference.
- They are complex and affect many different parts and levels of the organization.

- They are not puzzles that have known results and known solutions to achieve those results; rather they are problems with ambiguous goals and uncertain pathways that are not amenable to pre-existing expert solutions.
- Organizational leaders have not yet made decisions about their disposition; thus, leaders are open and amenable to others' ideas.
- They are organizational (psychosocial) and technical or structural rather than only technical or structural.
- They are within the capabilities and competencies of the AL team.
- The organization's leaders expect a tangible result (e.g., a recommendation for action—with or without a demonstration or pilot project—or the complete execution of an implementation plan and achievement of expected results) within a specific time frame.
- They must provide learning opportunities for the AL team members, the AL program, champions, sponsors, clients, and the larger host organization.

Participative OD&C Theory and Method

The core technology in OD&C is Action Research (Freedman, 2006). According to Cummings and Worley (2005), OD&C is "a systemwide application and transfer of behavioral science knowledge to the planned development, improvement, and reinforcement of the strategies, structures, and processes that lead to organizational effectiveness" (p. 1). The practical application of Action Research is characterized by high levels of involvement and participation of all parties (including stakeholders and constituents) who are, or are likely to be, affected by the planning or implementing of the complex system change. At this point in history, OD&C is a well-established discipline with clearly explicated values, theories, strategies, and methods (Cummings & Worley, 2005; French et al., 2000; Jones & Brazzel, 2006; Rothwell et al., 1995). However, some have raised questions about the future direction of the field of practice as it evolves (e.g., Bradford & Burke, 2005).

Action Research

Action Research is a reiterative cycle of (a) planning to take action to achieve some goal, (b) taking action, (c) assessing the effects of having taken action, (d) reflecting on the implications of those effects (e.g., what led to movement toward or away from the intended goal), (e) reevaluating and possibly modifying either the implementation plan or the goal or both, and (f) starting again at the beginning of the succeeding cycle by taking the next action step, and so forth (Freedman, 2006; Lewin, 1946).

Sometimes the Action Research method is confused with the phases of most kinds of consulting engagements. Benne, Bennis, and Chin (1969) reminded us that, at least in the United States, it was John Dewey who originally adapted the scientific method to accommodate systemic inquiry into societal and organizational issues. Although various authors define the phases of the process of consultation differently, we emphasize the following eight phases: (a) an explication of the strategic reasons for the organizational change, (b) a specification of the desired future state, (c) a detailed description of the current state, (d) an organizational diagnostic process, (e) a data feedback process resulting in identifying and setting change goals for high priority issues, (f) the development of implementation plans designed to achieve each of the change goals, (g) the execution of each of the implementation plans and careful monitoring of progress achieved and scanning for the emergence of (and coping with) predictable surprises—unexpected side effects or emerging nascent organizational obstacles—during the execution of each of the implementation plans, and (h) an assessment of the degree to which the desired future state has been realized through the achievement of the change goals.

Because no action plan is executed as originally intended, the Action Research method is properly applied within each of these consultation phases. Techspert consultants and SMEs typically conceive of implementation plans as linear rather than cyclical and reiterative (Freedman & Zackrison, 2001). Their implicit assumption seems to be that all involved parties will be cooperative and responsive, contributing whatever is needed without complaint. However, the inevitable reality is that organizational changes perturbate the psychosocial system, provoking considerable stress and anxiety and threatening established authority, prerogatives, and power relationships as well as the basis of people's sense of competence and self-esteem. Thus, multiple reiterative cycles of the Action Research method are often required to deal with these predictable surprises as they emerge and complete each of the consultation phases before proceeding to the next.

The effects of having taken action that are illuminated through the Action Research method and on which action researchers typically reflect include what AL team members, clients, sponsors, champions, project managers, and the larger organization may have learned about (a) what and how progress was made in the direction of the desired state, (b) emergent predictable surprises that interfere with or obstruct progress, (c) impacts of taking action on the operations of other interdependent groups and their dynamic interactions within the larger organizational system, (d) the operation of the larger organizational system and its dynamic relationships to its external stakeholders, and (e) impacts on the individuals and groups who sponsor, manage, and execute the planning and implementation of the organizational change and their interactions with one another (Freedman, 2006).

Each phase in the consulting process consists of a series of action steps that are to be executed, sequentially or in parallel. The Action Research method is applied to each action step within each phase of the consultation process, at least once but often more frequently for each action step. When an action step fails to yield the expected results, the Action Research cycle is repeated. The Action Research method facilitates reflection and enables implementers to modify the action step and improve the results. For example, in Phase 2 (entry and contracting), considerable recycling using the Action Research method with AL process skills may be necessary during the back-and-forth negotiations before coming to a mutually acceptable consulting agreement. As a function of applying this reiterative Action Research cycle, reflection opportunities are created that enable all involved parties to (a) contribute to achieving the desired result—that is, a mutually acceptable consulting agreement; (b) learn how to improve the process of negotiating consulting contracts; and (c) increase the self-reflective awareness of all involved parties (e.g., how their values, beliefs, attitudes, preferences, preoccupations, and vested interests influence their perceptions and, as a result, their thoughts, feelings, and actions), thus enabling all involved parties to learn how to use self-reflective awareness to enhance their capacity to use themselves as instruments during every phase of the consultation process.

Figure 6.1 provides a visual representation of the repetitive and reiterative process in Step 9 of the consultation process—executing the implementation plans. The reader will note that the trajectory of implementation activities is disrupted at various points by unexpected events—i.e., predictable surprises. When this occurs, the Action Research cycle begins again (evaluating what just happened, diagnosing the cause, devising a new plan). It is simply unrealistic to expect that implementation plans will be executed without a hitch. Unpleasant predictable surprises are bound to occur. The Action Research process provides a method for rapidly and successfully responding to the expected perturbations in the implementation process.

The Action Research method informs the practice of both AL and OD&C at all levels: team, project, subsystems and their interactions, the entire organization, and the organization–environment interface. OD&C practitioners employ the Action Research method at the macro or system level, whereas AL team coaches use the Action Research

FIGURE 6.1

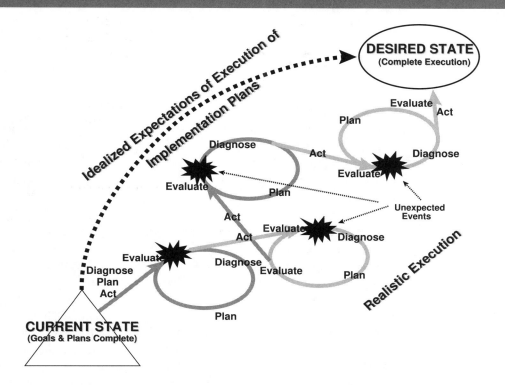

Visual presentation of the Action Research process in the implementation phase of the consultation process. Adapted from *The Complete Social Scientist: A Kurt Lewin Reader* (pp. 265–284), edited by M. Gold, 1948, Washington, DC: American Psychological Association. Copyright 1948 by the American Psychological Association.

method at the micro or team level. Both AL team coaches and OD&C practitioners ask good questions based on the Action Research method: How did you—the team or project management—know what actions to include in your plan? (Plan); Who had what responsibilities for executing the plan? What assumptions were you making? (Act); What was done well during implementation? What could be done better? (Evaluate Results); What happened as a result of taking action based upon the plan? How do you make sense out of what happened? What did you (the team or project) learn—about implementing plans, about direct and indirect impacts on stakeholders, and about yourselves as instruments or agents of change—from taking action? What did you learn about how your projects' stakeholders affected the execution of your plan? (Reflect); In what ways will you modify your goals and plans as a result of what you have learned thus far? What assumptions are you making? (Reevaluate Goals and Plans).

Sociotechnical System Theory

Reg Revans (1998) thought of "the enterprise as a system [composed] of systems" (p. 126). He believed that managers and executives must expand their awareness beyond the boundaries of their own subsystem to encompass the transactions and interactions among interdependent subsystems within the larger enterprise. Participation in AL teams helps participants to acquire a transorganizational, systemic perspective that enables them to recognize and consider how, for example, changes in one part or level of an enterprise can and will impact all other parts and levels of the enterprise.

Very early in its evolution, OD&C incorporated an organization-as-a-system orientation (von Bertalanffy, 1963) and its practical applications that are exemplified by the sociotechnical systems perspectives pioneered by such British and Scandinavian action researchers as Gyllenhamer (1977); Rice (1958); Thorsrud, Sorensen, and Gustavsen (1976); and Trist and Bamforth (1951). Depending on the situational context and circumstances, OD&C focused on some combination or permutation of the following levels of intervention: (a) the individual; (b) interpersonal relations; (c) group dynamics; (d) intergroup dynamics; (e) the total organization, including the interactions among the interdependent subsystems of which the total organization is composed; and (f) the interactions and transactions between the total organization and its relevant external stakeholders (e.g., suppliers, customers, investors, regulators, media).

Application of Action Learning to Complex Systems Change

As noted earlier, the external environments within which organizations must operate continue to change—constantly. These challenge and affect organizations in all sectors: public, private, nongovernmental, and nonprofit. Organizations must recognize and adapt to the context of their unique environments' particular demand characteristics. Invariably and inevitably, they must continuously reinvent themselves; they must learn what to change and how to change—quickly. The demand for change is not optional; it is essential for the organizations' survival. Thus, organizations must learn to invent and apply solutions to cope with ambiguous circumstances in which both the adaptive goals and the pathways to those goals are likely to be uncertain or ambiguous.

AL, integrated within a techspert-driven and OD&C-supported organizational change effort, enables system leaders and members to learn how to learn and to retain what is learned about planning and managing complex system changes.

Action Learning and Organizational Learning at Krones

While you read this book, you might have a bottle of water or juice or a soft drink next to you. Do you know how many machines are necessary to prepare the drink, clean the bottle, fill the drink in the bottle, label the bottle, ensure the quality, and pack the bottles in boxes? Krones, the market leader in this industry with nearly 10,000 employees worldwide, uses AL to provide value to their customers by ensuring high quality at a low cost.

Krones uses AL to effectively respond to the three major challenges faced by the bottling industry: (a) an increasing gap between the skills needed by Krones and the competency of their employment pool, (b) an increasing turnover of personnel, and (c) profit pressures to reduce costs. Plant managers responsible for operations of a filling plant are especially affected by these challenges and need to develop new leadership skills in order to remain effective in their positions.

The AL programs at Krones include two modules related to leadership and line efficiency. The content includes presentations, reflections on best practices, and AL sessions with an AL team coach. By using a mix of training approaches, Krones hopes to encourage both "right-brain" and "left-brain" thinking. A gap of 6 weeks between the modules allows the managers to apply the new knowledge.

Plant mangers from different bottlers like Coca Cola, Bitburger, and Heineken and from throughout Europe, Africa, South America, and Asia participated in the AL programs. The results have been very encouraging. Participants report that this learning experience is more relevant for them than their previous trainings. (See www.krones.com for a movie with interviews with participants.) Helio Portela, Krones's training manager, noted that the "Action Learning method contributes to the factual learning targets as well as develops great team dynamic between the participants from different, often competing companies. The shared best practices and exchange of tacit knowledge during the process of Action Learning maximized the training outcome."

AL with an AL team coach develops a structured environment which, in turn, creates a positive atmosphere. "The investment to train our trainers as AL team coaches certainly paid off," commented Dr. Joerg Puma, global director of the Krones Academy. "For me, Action Learning is the iPod of the learning methods for practical adult learning. Action Learning, although complex and powerful, has become very easy and comfortable to use at Krones."

Action Learning and the OD&C Consultative Process

As previously mentioned, although there are alternative versions of the consultative process, we conceive of the OD&C consultative process as comprising eight phases (Beckhard & Harris, 1987; Lippitt & Lippitt, 1986). We now elaborate on how AL, OD&C, and Action Research are applied to the eight phases of consultation.

1. AN EXPLICATION OF THE REASONS FOR THE ORGANIZATIONAL CHANGE

OD&C and relevant techspert consultants or SME advisors can help client system leaders understand why their organization is endangered unless it can cope with certain threats that have evolved in its external environment (e.g., new competition or economic downturns). Questions that are based on AL theory and methods and informed by OD&C strategies promote reflection on these threats and dangers. For example, one might ask: What are the risks if we continue business as usual? What are the risks if we implemented major changes? What valid information do we have about these risks? From what sources—and how recently—have we obtained this information?

Nor can the organization grow and thrive unless it can identify and exploit new opportunities (e.g., new global markets, the acquisition of a company possessing highly valued new technology, scarce expertise). One might ask: What are the substantive benefits to be gained from trying to take advantage of this opportunity? How can we determine whether the benefits will be greater than the costs of exploiting this opportunity?

Neither can the enterprise be managed effectively unless recurrent, operational dilemmas that have no permanent solutions are accurately identified and managed (Johnson, 1997). One might ask: How can we determine that we are addressing a dilemma that cannot be solved permanently but must be managed rather than a solvable problem?

Leaders must make it abundantly clear to all involved parties (e.g., employees, customers, suppliers, stockowners, other stakeholders) that evolving business requirements make major organizational changes essential, critical, urgent, and achievable. Perpetuating the status quo is a formula for ultimate failure. The requisite changes will be some mix of technological, structural, strategic, operational, business processes, talent management, knowledge management, cultural, relationships with suppliers and customers, and the like. The rationale should be sufficiently vivid and compelling to evoke widespread dissatisfaction with the status quo among organizational leaders, members, and stakeholders. Techspert consultants often refer to this rationale as "the burning platform." Bruch and Ghoshal (2003), however, present a convincing argument for evoking both dissatisfaction with the status quo (slay the dragon) as well as hope for achieving a desirable future (win the princess).

2. THE DESIRED FUTURE STATE

OD&C and, where appropriate, relevant techspert consultants or SME advisors can enable organizational leaders to create a believable, compelling vision of an achievable future that can deal with the threats, solve the problems, capitalize on the opportunities, and manage the dilemmas. This vision can provide all involved parties with a personally meaningful, hopeful, strategic direction in which they can invest their energy and capabilities. AL-type questions that can help include: Specifically, what will the world or environment in which we hope to operate look like in 5, 10, or 20 years? By what threats, opportunities, and dilemmas are we likely to be confronted? What are we trying to accomplish? What will it look like? Who will be impacted by achieving this result? In what ways will these people and groups be impacted? To what extent will these people or groups participate in planning and implementing this change effort?

3. THE CURRENT STATE

A comparison of the desired results with the organization's current state should be made. An organizational diagnosis will illuminate the current condition of the relevant elements of the client system and their dynamic interactions. OD&C practitioners and, where appropriate, relevant techspert consultants and organizational members collect and organize the data to prepare them for providing feedback to the members and leaders of the client system. Techspert consultants may provide what Revans (1998) called programmed information to help the AL teams determine what they should look for (and where to look). Either OD&C practitioners or AL team coaches may ask questions that can facilitate the process. These include the following: What kinds of information will be most useful for us? Who has this information? What data-gathering methods can we employ to obtain this information? How shall we organize the data we collect? What diagnostic model shall we use to help organize the data? Who will organize the data? AL team coaches may, as teams progress through the diagnostic process, ask questions to encourage reflection and learning. These include the following: What are we learning about the organizational diagnostic process? our organizations? our subsystems? our involved parties' political interests? interdependencies among systems? and ourselves? These questions would only be asked when relevant and when the AL team members have not raised them on their own initiative.

4. THE DATA FEEDBACK PROCESS

OD&C practitioners, AL team coaches and, where appropriate, relevant techspert consultants may help feed organized diagnostic data back to the organizational leaders and members who provided the data. AL team coaches would work directly with the project management, champions, sponsors, executives, and all of those people that are intended to receive the fed-back data. OD&C practitioners would facilitate the data feedback process, guiding leaders, members, and other involved parties through a process during which these parties review the organized diagnostic data to ensure that they recognize themselves and their organization in the data. OD&C practitioners can then assist client system members to identify and prioritize evident issues (i.e., problems, opportunities, dilemmas) that must be dealt with to realize the vision and purposes of the organizational change. OD&C practitioners assist leaders and members to agree on and set provisional change goals for from three to no more than five high-priority issues.

It is during the data feedback phase that AL theory and methods can be easily blended into the planned organizational change process. First, the project manager, authorized by executive management, forms a cadre of potential AL team members. In collaboration with line managers and AL team coaches, a sufficient number of high-potential organizational members are nominated, recruited, convened, oriented, and trained. The cadre members should be nominated, sponsored, and mentored by senior managers and executives who sit at least two levels above their current positions. (If and when they are promoted, cadre members would become the direct reports of their sponsors.)

The cadre members are formed into several four- to eight-person AL teams. There must be one AL team to deal with each of the selected high-priority issues. Each AL team either is asked to volunteer to take on one of the high-priority issues or is assigned to one of them. Appropriate questions for the OD&C practitioner or the AL team coach to ask during this phase include the following: To whom will we feed back our organized diagnostic data? Why these people? What are their individual interests regarding this change? How do we know they really care about these issues? Will they have the authority to act on the data that is fed back to them? From whom do we need support, including authorization, for this data feedback process? What are the communication preferences for processing complex information for the people who will be receiving the data? How can we help them to recognize themselves and their organization in the data—without evoking denial or other forms of resistance?

As progress is achieved during this data feedback process, AL team coaches may ask additional questions to encourage team members to reflect and learn from their unfolding experiences. These include the following: What are we learning about the data feedback process? About our organization, its political dynamics? our subsystems and their interactions? and about ourselves? Again, it is preferable for team members to ask these questions on a regular basis. Until they do, the questions should be asked, when appropriate, by the AL team coach.

A critical part of the data feedback process is setting goals. Each AL team establishes a provisional goal for its identified high-priority issue. (It is provisional because subsequent action taking may reveal information calling for a revision of the goal and/or its implementation plan.) AL team coaches might ask the following questions: How can we help the members of our audience to extract and prioritize the critical issues that their organization will face when trying to achieve the change goals? How can we help them to set specific, measurable, achievable, realistic, time-bound, economic, and relevant change goals? How can we help them to make informed decisions about the strategies to be employed in achieving these change goals? As the AL teams progress through their respective goal setting process, the AL team coach would also ask, what are we learning about the process of setting goals? our organizations? and ourselves?

5. DEVELOPING IMPLEMENTATION PLANS

OD&C practitioners manage the implementation of the designed planning process. AL team coaches work directly with the AL teams. Techspert consultants or SME advisors may provide programmed information as needed by the AL teams. Techsperts should probably not be permanent members of the AL teams because team members are likely to defer to their expert opinions rather than search for and discover their own answers to critical questions. Instead, techsperts should make themselves available as consultants to the AL teams and respond to the teams' technical questions.

Each AL team defines or redefines the scope of its issue, agrees to the goals set by legitimate authorities, or establishes a modified or new provisional change goal and seeks validation of the original or new scope and goal from both its champion and sponsor. The team then begins an in-depth exploration for information about its issue (a tightly focused microdiagnosis) that includes how the issue is perceived by all relevant involved parties and stakeholders, and their opinions and preferences for a means of dealing effectively with that focal issue. This will generate a partial list of potential action steps that are agreeable to the stakeholders. This process often entails a collaborative analysis of the issue resulting in clarification, specification, and agreement with the given issue's current and desired states.

For each high-priority issue for which their AL teams have assumed responsibility, OD&C practitioners or AL team coaches should consider asking four questions: What is the preferred desired state? What is the current state? Why is it important to achieve the desired state? Why is it difficult to achieve the desired state? As the AL team members brainstorm answers to these four questions, they will create a force field analysis (Freedman, 1987; Lewin, 1931, 1943, 1946, 1961); the answers to these questions could be written on poster boards to serve as an enduring, visible "memory" for the entire group.

The answers to the "Why important?" question yield a list of the driving forces that illuminates many of the most powerful motivating factors that impel the organization to undertake this change. The answers to the "Why difficult?" question yield a list of restraining forces that identifies and illuminates many obstacles and sources of resistance to the change. Most techspert consultants make an error by trying to increase the number or power of the driving forces. The preferred OD&C strategy is to focus on the restraining forces. By identifying actions that will eliminate or reduce the power of each of the primary restraining forces, force field analysis suggests plausible, viable actions for organizational change.

During the microdiagnosis and implementation planning phases, individual AL team members and subgroups carry out any AL team tasks, activities, and functions (e.g., collecting pertinent diagnostic information from stakeholders) for which they have accepted responsibility. These may include, for example, discovering the varied assumptions, perceptions, interests, needs, concerns, and preferences of all involved parties and stakeholders who may be affected by the organizational change relating to the AL team's focal issue.

AL teams generally convene once every 2 or 3 weeks with an AL team coach to discuss progress for their specific issue: actions taken, results achieved, difficulties encountered, analysis, reflection, and next steps. The AL team coach asks pertinent questions to enable team members to learn from their experiences, learn about themselves, learn how to improve their work as a participative problem-solving and decision-making team, and learn about transorganizational issues and how they impact—and are impacted by—all parts and levels of their organization. In between AL team meetings, in addition to carrying out their individual assignments and commitments, individual AL team members continue to fulfill their routine work responsibilities.

Whenever they reconvene, during the AL team meetings, members share what they have discovered and seek to understand, reflect on, and integrate that information into a new analysis of the issue. If team members do not raise the questions on their own OD&C practitioners or AL team coaches ask: How does this new information or new perspective change our understanding of the focal issue? our change goals? and/or our implementation plan? To encourage reflection and learning,

AL team coaches may ask: What are we learning about developing an implementation plan? about how our team operates? about the interdependencies of our organization's subsystems? about how changes may affect the political and economic interests of involved stakeholders? and about ourselves? When AL team members ask these questions on a routine basis, coaches can refrain from this line of inquiry.

The AL team must prepare and deliver its recommended goals and implementation plan to clients, sponsors, and organizational leaders for their review and approval. The presentation may include the results of a pilot project that has been undertaken to test the validity and usefulness of a team's evolving hypotheses about what might be helpful in achieving the team's objectives. The presentation allows AL team members to display and practice their presentation skills with their organizational leaders. These presentations give them unprecedented access to and visibility in the presence of their peers and organizational leaders.

Those vested with the requisite authority may decide to delay, modify, or move ahead with the recommended goals and plans. OD&C practitioners or the AL team coach may help the legitimate authorities to make informed decisions regarding these recommendations. Decision makers should be prepared to provide AL teams and stakeholders with detailed feedback explaining their decisions. OD&C practitioners or AL coaches should be asked to assist the decision-making group with their deliberations.

For each AL team and its particular issue, the outcome of this phase of the process will be an approved goal (description of the desired state), a viable strategy, a provisional implementation plan, requisite resources, active support from executive management, a champion, sponsors, and commitments for the active involvement and participation by all involved organizational subsystems and stakeholders. This will have been supported by each team's microdiagnosis and, possibly, by a relevant pilot project.

6. EXECUTING THE IMPLEMENTATION PLANS

OD&C practitioners assist project managers to manage the implementation process and its vicissitudes. AL coaches work directly with the AL teams and stakeholder groups that are affected by the execution of the implementation plans. Once authorized to move ahead into the implementation phase, AL teams may lead, participate, or contribute to the process of executing the implementation plans. AL teams continue to meet weekly or every other week with an AL team coach. With broad, complex change projects, members of AL teams may be dispersed; consequently, the weekly or biweekly meeting may be virtual, augmented by video- or teleconferencing, instant messaging, e-mail, and fax technologies.

Between AL team meetings, individuals and subgroups execute and monitor the direct and indirect effects of specific action steps that are elements of their overall implementation plan. When the AL team reconvenes, members share, reflect on, and integrate information about specific actions taken and their effects on the implementers themselves, the project management, champion, sponsors, stakeholders, organizational subsystems (and their interactions), and organizational leaders. Again, new information and perspectives may call for modifications in either the change goal and/or the implementation plans, not merely for a specific AL team but for all the other AL teams. This emphasizes the potential interdependencies among the AL teams and their work on their respective issues. That is, changes in one team's goal and implementation plan are likely to affect the other goals and plans. Interteam communication and coordination is essential.

During this phase, there will likely be three to five AL teams whose members are working part-time on the execution and full-time on their regular jobs. Close attention to the possibility of work overload and stress on AL team members is essential. OD&C practitioners and AL team coaches might ask: How are you feeling at this stage of your organizational change project? What tensions are you experiencing as you divide your time between your project responsibilities and your routine responsibilities? How are you handling these tensions? What results are you getting from your efforts to manage these tensions? Additional probing questions may reveal indicators of fatigue, overwork, and stress. It may be necessary to arrange for the project manager to intervene with AL team members' line managers to determine how to get temporary relief for AL team members from their routine responsibilities.

It is essential that the executive management team, project champion, sponsors of individual issues, project manager, and significant stakeholders share a common, realistic understanding of the technostructural and psychosocial dynamics and vicissitudes encountered during the implementation process. OD&C practitioners are particularly well suited to clarify and make explicit the decision makers' various mental models and assumptions that have been driving strategies and actions along with their potential advantages and disadvantages. They can predict, with considerable accuracy, the dynamics and vicissitudes of the implementation process and guide the project manager, staff, and team members in recognizing and managing emerging resistance to the planned organizational change (Burke, 2002; Freedman, 1997).

7. CAREFUL MONITORING OF PROGRESS ACHIEVED AND SCANNING FOR THE EMERGENCE OF PREDICTABLE SURPRISES

As the execution of the AL teams' implementation plans proceeds, particularly when three or more AL teams are operating in parallel, AL team members, clients, sponsors, and project managers should document each specific action step taken and the (expected and unexpected) consequences of having taken action for the operations of all involved parties. These consequences would include the impact that the execution of each team's tasks has on the other teams, on the organization's subsystems and their interactions, on the total organization, and on stakeholders.

It is essential for all parties to adopt an attitude of intense interest and curiosity pertaining to the inevitable emergence of predictable surprises (Freedman, 1997). Thus, all involved parties must scan both their internal and external environments for indications that any effort to change the organization either precipitates unexpected adverse side effects or perturbs and exacerbates preexisting nascent organizational issues that may have been benign and ignored prior to the initiation of the change effort.

Special Action Learning Teams

Proactive scanning and "scouting" (Holder & McKinney, 1993) is essential for early recognition and specification of unexpected, emerging implementation challenges. OD&C practitioners must encourage all involved parties to be alert for the occurrence of early indicators of these challenges. Predictable surprises are inevitable even though one may not be able to predict their exact nature, their causes and sources, when they will manifest themselves, how they will impact implementation, or whom they will affect. If team members do not raise questions on their own, OD&C practitioners and AL team coaches must be prepared to ask: What kinds of surprises did you run into during implementation? What impact did they have on the execution of the implementation plan? What early indicators did you notice that preceded the emergence of a predictable surprise? What have we learned about being prepared for the emergence of predictable surprises? How can we learn what other predictable surprises are being created as we execute our implementation plans?

By definition, most people are not prepared to recognize predictable surprises because they are unprecedented and discontinuous with historically routine operations. There are individual, cultural, and organizational barriers to prepare for their occurrence (Bazerman & Watkins, 2008). Established organizational problem-solving mechanisms are unlikely to be effective in efforts to deal with them. Innovative preventive or corrective actions are required, but people may not see the need until after they encounter their first major predictable surprise. Then, OD&C practitioners or AL team coaches might productively ask: What new problem identification and problem-solving mechanism should we create to deal with a specific emerging unprecedented predictable surprise? What have we learned about the nature and sources of predictable surprises? What can we do to prepare ourselves for the emergence of predictable surprises? AL team coaches might add such questions as: What have we learned about how predictable surprises affect our plans? our teams? our stakeholders? and our selves?

One structural way to prepare to manage emerging predictable surprises is to create a Special Action Learning Team (SALT) that is prepared to mobilize when the early indicators of a predictable surprise become evident. A SALT is composed of one or two members from each AL team, plus any relevant techsperts or SME advisors (who serve as on-call consultants). A SALT would operate concurrently with the established AL teams without disrupting their operations.

Project managers should give each SALT a firm schedule with a relatively short deadline to work against. The project manager should give SALTs carte blanche that authorizes their members to act as plenipotentiaries so they have access to all parts and levels of the organization as well as to stakeholders who may be affected by or contribute to the predictable surprise. OD&C practitioners and AL team coaches might ask: How can we be sure we have access to all possible, relevant sources of information pertaining to the predictable surprise?

As they proceed with their work, SALT members maintain contact with their respective AL teams, providing them with updates on the SALT's progress and obtaining guidance (and support) from them. The same kind of transactions would occur between the SALT members and their respective back-home organizational subsystem managers and members. This process of remaining open to and continuously scanning for possible emerging difficulties, specifying those challenges, and dealing with them uses the same reiterative Action Research cyclical process previously described. AL team coaches might ask: How shall we assess and analyze the effects of the predictable surprise on all involved parties?

Each side effect or nascent issue and what was done to cope with it should be documented and archived as part of the organizational learning process. OD&C practitioners or AL team coaches might ask: How can we capture, organize, and archive what we have learned so it can be retrieved when needed by future generations of organizational leaders and members?

Project Management

When several AL teams are operating concurrently, the organizational change effort should have a project management function that includes OD&C resources along with techspert consultants, SME advisors, and AL team coaches. Either OD&C practitioners or AL team coaches might ask: How can we deal with logistics; interfacing with the permanent organizational hierarchy; and ensure that the organizational learning system is properly designed, operated, and used?

AL theory and methods are also applicable when assessing progress or evaluating the results achieved through an organizational change initiative.

8. ASSESSING THE DEGREE TO WHICH THE DESIRED FUTURE STATE HAS BEEN REALIZED THROUGH THE ACHIEVEMENT OF THE CHANGE GOALS

Organizational leaders should have pertinent, objective, and credible evidence to determine the extent to which the organizational change effort has made acceptable progress or resulted in the achievement of the established change goals and the realization of its desired state. This, of course, calls for evaluation research to measure the specific dimensions that were expected to vary as a function of the planned organizational change. These should be specified when change goals are established and modified when change goals are modified. Evaluation must also identify the nature and the extent to which the organizational change process causes side effects and reveals nascent problems—and how the organization dealt with those side effects and nascent problems, what results (positive, negative, or no results) were produced by these efforts, and what was learned from these efforts.

Evaluation research requires specialized techsperts. Evaluations are often time- and labor-intensive. Many client organizations are unwilling to pay for such evaluations. Thus, a dilemma emerges that can be illuminated by asking: How can we be sure that an organizational change initiative is truly effective? We address program evaluation issues in more depth in chapter 10.

These eight phases of the OD&C consulting process are roughly equivalent to a practical application of the scientific method to real-world human and organizational issues. Rarely is there a clear delineation of any phase. Overlaps, regressions, fixations, and reiterations are common and should be expected. The succession of phases should not be thought of as a linear process. Rather, the completion of each phase is achieved through the reiterative cyclical application of the Action Research method.

FEEDBACK

What best keeps the overall organizational change effort aligned is transparency, best characterized by pervasive *feedback*: the constant timely exchange of pertinent, reliable, comprehensive information gathered and shared during every phase among all involved parties. Feedback mechanisms and channels must be created and maintained to connect all involved parties with one another during every phase of the organizational change effort. Feedback may be requested and provided in many formats and modalities (e.g., town hall meetings, e-mail, attitude and opinion questionnaires, staff meetings).

The challenge is to create and institutionalize a system and set of processes to gather pertinent feedback from all parts and levels of an organization and its external stakeholders, organize that data, feed the data back in real time to those who need it to keep the change process intact and moving, and archive the data in a manner that it can be accessed and used to continuously improve the process of the current organizational change initiatives.

Partnerships among AL team coaches, OD&C practitioners, techspert consultants, and SME advisors are extremely useful in assisting a client system's leaders to design, operate, institutionalize, and update such an organizational change system so it endures and is continuously useful. Such an organizational learning system (Argyris & Schön, 1978, 1996) requires that what is learned is retained and can be easily retrieved for the benefit of those who will be responsible for planning and implementing any future organizational change.

Reflection Questions

1. Consider a long-term complicated change initiative in a complex organization in which you are involved perhaps as a champion, sponsor, project manager, or OD&C practitioner. Where, with whom, when, and for what purposed might you introduce AL?

2. What are the benefits of enabling AL team members to develop an enhanced capacity for self-reflective awareness? What are the disadvantages?

3. How do the values underlying the practices of OD&C and AL support or compete with the underlying values held by most techsperts?

4. In their work with their teams, how do AL team coaches apply the principles and methods of Action Research?

5. During the planning and implementation of a significant organizational change effort, how might the AL team coach prepare champions, sponsors, project managers, planners, implementers, and stakeholders to anticipate and prepare themselves to cope with predictable surprises?

Embedding Action Learning in the Organization   7

A ction Learning (AL) is often an "easy sell" in organizations. In this era of lean organizations and tight budgets, AL has great appeal to senior management that has traditionally seen training and leadership development as overhead costs to be reduced to a minimum. Although it is difficult to establish the return on investment (ROI) for traditional leadership development programs, Human Resources can point to a tangible outcome or deliverable from AL that frequently has a direct, positive financial impact on profitability (see chap. 10, this volume, for a more in-depth discussion of the benefits of conducting ROI analyses for AL). Even if the actual learning is limited, at least the organization receives a solution developed by its most talented managers to an urgent and critical problem that it probably would not have received otherwise. In many instances, an ROI can be established for AL programs. In addition, AL programs do not require large investments for curriculum development. It is relatively easy, therefore, to sell AL to senior leaders who recognize the need to develop leadership talent but are suspicious of the promised indirect benefits of traditional leadership training programs. In AL, these decision makers perceive an investment with few downside risks.

Successful implementation of AL, however, can be deceptively difficult. AL is a powerful method for organizational development as well as leadership development. AL, therefore, must be seen as an organizational intervention involving complex systems change and not just as an innovative training program. As established in chapter 6, the principles and methods of organizational development and change need to be considered and applied in designing, planning, and implementing AL.

AL has downsides and drawbacks that may not be anticipated by the organization. In many cases, AL is the first time that an organization's most talented managers have a chance to work on strategic problems with other rising stars in the organization. It is important, therefore, that these future leaders have good experiences working with each other and have their initiative and creativity reinforced through implementation of their solutions when worthy. If careful attention is not paid to the process of embedding AL in the fabric of the organization by using sound organization development and change principles and methods, participants may emerge from an AL process feeling demotivated and demoralized, and the solution produced may be mediocre and of limited benefit to the organization. The downside risks of poorly implemented AL programs should be raised when senior management is tempted to cut corners in planning or executing these programs.

Action Learning as an Organizational Intervention

Many previous reviews of AL have mentioned the organization dimension of AL. Marquardt (1999, 2004) and Boshyk (2002) emphasized the need for senior management/executive support. Hill, Leonard, and Sokol (2006) gave this issue more attention and provided a practical framework for implementing AL as an organization development intervention. In the following section, we discuss the process of embedding AL in the organization. In many ways, this process parallels the phases in the organization development and change process identified by Beckhard and Harris (1987) and discussed in chapter 6.

SELLING ACTION LEARNING TO SENIOR LEADERSHIP

As noted earlier, selling AL may be the easiest part of the process. Senior decision makers intuitively understand how working on real and important problems builds leadership skills. Executives report that being held accountable for important business results or projects was more helpful in their efforts to develop leadership skills than taking courses/seminars, reading books, or listening to tapes (Corporate Leadership Council 2000/

Leadership Survey; Corporate Leadership Council, 2000). Top leaders, therefore, have firsthand experience with working on important high-profile projects to build leadership skills.

Approving or funding an AL program, however, is a necessary but not sufficient requirement for the program's success. Senior leaders may not understand the level of involvement necessary for a successful AL process. Senior leaders are accustomed to "writing the check," giving short kick-off presentations to demonstrate top management support, and presenting diplomas or certificates of completion for training or development programs. In most cases, however, they have little involvement in the design, planning, and execution of more traditional leadership development programs. It is not surprising, therefore, that they believe they will have a similar limited role with respect to AL programs.

In selling the program to senior leadership, it is important to describe AL as an important organizational intervention and not just as a classroom exercise. In fact, we suggest that the term *exercise* be avoided altogether because of the high likelihood that the process will be associated with the typical school class project. In contrast to school class projects, AL projects are not academic exercises in which the burden of work often falls on one or two team members.

Because AL is an organizational intervention, senior leaders are significant stakeholders. Consequently, they need to be highly involved in (a) identifying urgent and critical challenges, (b) approving the charters developed by the teams to address these challenges, (c) evaluating products or solutions, and (d) supporting materially as well as psychologically the implementation of worthy products or solutions.

Although senior leaders understand the importance of developing the leadership skills of their high-potential leaders, they may not have a good understanding of how AL works, and they may have an even more limited appreciation of the roles they need to play. Specifically, they may not understand the need for skilled team coaching and may believe that providing teams with problems to work on is sufficient. Although most senior leaders have worked with team facilitators, relatively few executives have experience with the AL process and, therefore, may see active coaching as inhibiting rather than facilitating learning. They may correctly believe that task facilitators encourage dependency by taking responsibility for the success of a project and therefore limit the opportunities for team members to take the initiative to explore new ways of creating and implementing organizational solutions.

One way to build understanding and support for AL is to offer a live demonstration of the method. For instance, an experienced AL coach can demonstrate the method at a planning retreat using an urgent issue that is on the agenda for discussion. When the leadership team members see how quickly the method helps their team be more creative and effective, they are likely to become enthusiastic supporters of the process. They are also likely to have a greater appreciation of the need for continued involvement of senior management throughout the process.

IDENTIFYING PROJECT CHALLENGES

Identifying good problems and challenges for AL teams to work on is probably the single most important step in implementing AL projects. In chapter 2, we stated that a good AL problem or challenge needed to be significant, urgent, have no easily identifiable solution, and be the responsibility of the team. If a team is given a problem or challenge with these characteristics, team members will learn valuable organizational leadership skills even with mediocre AL coaching. To be sure, team members will learn far less than they would with a skilled AL coach, but the challenge and accountability ensures that they will be invested in the project and will learn important lessons. On the other hand, even the most skilled AL coaching will not be effective in promoting learning if the problem or challenge is inappropriate, unachievable, of limited importance, or redundant. Care must also be taken to ensure that AL is the best strategy for addressing a problem. The reader should review the discussion related to Figure 2.1 to decide whether an AL strategy should be pursued.

In most cases, top management will have a significant role in selecting the problems or challenges for the projects. They have the best vantage point for identifying issues, problems, and challenges that will have the most strategic impact. They also have a better sense of how much impact a problem solution will have on the organization as a whole. Finally, they have the broad institutional perspective to know who else may be working on a particular problem or what efforts have already been made to address this challenge.

To minimize the time and effort required for this task and ensure that the topics are well defined and appropriate, the AL project manager (or someone skilled and knowledgeable about AL) can provide active consultation to top management throughout the problem or challenge identification process. The AL consultant can suggest a variety of frameworks or lenses such as the following to help them identify worthy problems or challenges:

- leverage a strength or strategic advantage,
- address a weakness,
- pursue strategic growth/opportunities,
- anticipate a threat,
- fill or develop needed talent,
- increase revenue generation (top-line growth), and
- improve operational efficiency.

In some situations, it is desirable to let the team itself or an individual team member define the problem or challenge. For instance, the team may be instructed to identify a problem or challenge whose solution will provide the biggest benefit to the organization. This instruction is based on the assumption that the people who are closer to the core operations or clients are the best judges of what is urgent and important. In AL teams with multiple problems, each team member is instructed to identify a problem in his or her normal work experience that is both urgent and significant. In both situations, the team's AL coach will need to ask insightful and probing questions to ensure that the problems or challenges chosen meet the criteria described earlier.

Alternatively, input from both senior management and team members can be obtained to ensure that both the organization and the team believe that the problem is both urgent and relevant (see the following example).

Choosing Meaningful Problems at the National Institutes of Health

A research institute at the National Institutes of Health (NIH) decided to include AL projects in a year-long leadership development program. The senior leadership had little difficulty identifying a number of strategic issues that were critical to ensuring that the institute maintain its leadership in the scientific community. An organizational survey also indicated a significant amount of discontent with the working environment. The complaints were too general, however, to generate specific and unambiguous goals for an AL team to work on. Senior leaders also wanted to ensure that the goals addressed root causes and not superficial symptoms of this discontent.

To uncover and identify the sources of the discontent and unhappiness, the AL project manager contracted with an external consultant specializing in corporate storytelling to run a half-day workshop with the participants of the leadership development program. The workshop had two purposes: (a) to teach participants how to use narratives and stories more effectively as leaders, and (b) to uncover latent but important problems by telling personally relevant and important stories.

The method was very simple and highly experiential. After demonstrating what makes for a good and impactful story, the consultant created three teams of six to seven individuals and instructed each participant within the team to tell a short and personal story (2 minutes maximum) about an event or incident that was very important to the participant. After the consultant critiqued the first stories and offered coaching on how to improve them, participants retold their stories within their groups. Each group then voted to identify the story that had the most significance and impact for them. The three participants who had created these stories then retold their stories to everyone in the workshop. The consultant then asked participants to share what meaning and impact any of the stories had for them. Each participant was encouraged to contribute in this discussion.

Following this discussion, participants were asked to stand, walk over to the person whose story or explanation had the most impact and meaning for them, and place an arm on that person's shoulder. This nonverbal exercise generated a sociogram (Moreno, 1951) or network of connections between participants on the basis of personal impact. This process created a number of intersections or "nodes" in which a single participant had a physical connection with two or more participants (i.e., participants had more than one hand on their shoulders). Workshop participants were then asked to provide explanations and meaning for the pattern of connections that were created through this nonverbal exercise.

These discussions led to the identification of several urgent and critical problems and challenges that were highly relevant to a large number of the participants. These problems and challenges were added to the list of strategic problems or challenges generated by senior management to create the final set of issues or topics for the AL teams.

POPULATING ACTION LEARNING TEAMS

Decisions to determine who should be members of an AL team can be based on simple factors such as availability of participants as well as on both short-term needs and long-term benefits for the organization. In most organizations, the membership in teams is determined by top management or the problem sponsor.

A number of factors should be considered in selecting members for AL teams. First, at least some of the members should have an understanding of the issue and the organization. While it is important that we not create a team of experts, it is also important that at least some of the team members have an understanding or, at least, some appreciation of the problem. Without someone with a basis understanding of the problem, the team will need a high level of involvement from the problem sponsor. In many situations extensive involvement in the team's work is not feasible (or desirable).

Second, the primary purpose of the program should be considered in determining team membership. Thus, if a team's purpose is to break down silos or to change the culture of the organization, its members are selected from throughout the vertical and or horizontal levels of the organization. If AL is seen as a way of developing high-potential leaders, then such individuals will be assigned to the organization. If the purpose is to build powerful, high-performing teams that will work with both AL and other organizational programs, then top management will focus on identifying members who may work together in future teams (e.g., Six Sigma teams).

There are several other factors to consider in assigning participants to teams and projects, including (a) the degree of personal interest, (b) the diversity of the team, and (c) the balancing of the number of participants in each team. The last consideration is important because the ideal size for an AL team is five to eight members. It is also desirable to leverage the natural interest participants have for the various problems or challenges. Finally, experience indicates that AL teams are most creative when the team's composition is diverse with respect to such factors as experience with the problem, organizational role and placement, age, gender, ethnicity, culture, and introversion/extroversion. Although it is not possible to create diversity on all relevant dimensions, care should be taken to make sure that there is not an obvious imbalance in the profile of a team on any of the most important dimensions (i.e., an all female or male profile, or an overly introverted or extroverted team profile). A team of strong introverts in an AL project can create some difficult challenges for the AL coach.

In the previous example at NIH teams were populated in the following way. Participants were asked to attend a poster session[1] at an evening kick-off event for the AL program. Booths were set up for each problem/challenge project. One or more subject matter experts who understood the problem manned the booths. These subject matter experts were often the project sponsors (see section on sponsor role in next section) who worked with the team and the AL coach to provide linkage between the team's work and the organization's needs and expectations. At the end of the poster session, each participant was asked to indicate his or her first, second, and third preferences for each of the problems or challenges.

The program managers created a first-cut roster by assigning all participants their first choice. It was apparent after this first sort that not all participants could get their first choice because there was a clear imbalance (particularly in numbers) along the dimensions discussed above. The program managers then created a second-cut roster by moving some participants to their second choice to create better balance and diversity. This process went through several iterations until a satisfactory balance was achieved. A small number of participants needed to be assigned to their third choice. This process creates some difficult trade-offs. In this situation, for instance, better balance and diversity was achieved at the expense of allowing participants to work on the projects that best captured their interest. This compromise generated some grumbling later in the process and created some challenges for the coaches who had to deal a few disaffected team members.

---

[1]Many of the participants regularly attended scientific conferences in which poster sessions were commonly used.

SPONSORS

AL team sponsors provide a valuable role in the embedding process and should not be confused with AL coaches. Sponsors play an important "linking pin" function throughout the life of the team. For instance, in the team population process previously described, sponsors can not only help describe the challenge to prospective team members but also articulate why senior leaders consider this problem to be urgent and important to the organization.

Sponsors are typically chosen for this role because (a) they have a personal or professional interest in a particular challenge, or (b) they have demonstrated or expressed an interest in developing the talent of future leaders. There are pros and cons of assigning a sponsor to a team that is working on a challenge that the sponsor has a particular interest or expertise in. On the positive side, sponsors can be a great help to the team in understanding the problem and its history and in creating a realistic charter. However, sponsors may become so invested in the challenge that they try to exert influence on the team, which would inhibit the development of a creative solution and interfere with personal and team learning opportunities. Sponsors should not be included in the ongoing work of the team. To be optimally useful to the team, sponsors need to maintain their neutral relationship on the boundary between the team and the larger organization. AL coaches may need to consult with sponsors outside of (and sometimes during) team working sessions to make sure that they stay within the role expectations for sponsors.

During the chartering process described in the next section, sponsors can help the team in the "scoping and scaling" process so that the resulting charter is not too ambitious or too limited. In essence, the sponsors bring a reality-testing capability often lacking in teams that have limited knowledge of and experience with the challenges, issues, history, or difficulty in achieving significant changes at a higher organizational level than team members typically deal with.

In the middle of the solution development process, the team may request a consultation with the sponsor to get useful feedback from a person who has both the team and the larger organizational perspective. During these consultations, the team can use the sponsor as a sounding board to get reactions to its emerging solutions or as a source of information about organizational priorities, stakeholder positions, or informational resources. It goes without saying that sponsors should not get involved in the actual problem-solving deliberations. Sponsors either answer questions developed by the team or ask questions to foster greater reflection and awareness on the part of the team. They do not provide their vision of what the solution should look like or state their opinion regarding their preferences for solutions prior to the team's work. Because sponsors typically have greater status in the organization than team members, their opinions will often have greater influence than those of the team members and will limit the amount of creativity that they express.

Sponsors also play a significant role in the solution presentation and implementation processes. Sponsors can be invited to role-play senior management when the team conducts a dress rehearsal for the team's presentation of its solution to senior management. In their role as linking pins, sponsors often have valuable insights into how senior leaders view issues, what their unstated priorities are, and how they will respond to various presentations strategies. If the team's solution gets a positive reaction from senior management and is selected for implementation, the sponsor can provide very useful guidance in helping the team develop a change management strategy for solution implementation. Again, sponsors serve as consultants to the implementation design process and should avoid taking a directive role in developing the implementation plan.

THE CHARTERING PROCESS

The problems that have been identified by senior management and participants as urgent need to be further refined by the team before teams can begin formal problem solving. Senior management typically defines problems at a fairly general and conceptual level. For instance, one AL team was assigned the challenge of developing new products that addressed "gaps" in customer demographics (e.g., the growing Hispanic and Asian populations in the United States). This is a very broad mandate and the reader can appreciate the concern that the team experienced in trying to define the scale and scope of this assignment.

The purpose of the chartering process is to develop a formal definition of the problem so that the team can begin its work. The team should consider the following parameters in developing the charter:

1. Time—How much time does the team have to work on this challenge?
2. Resources—What resources in terms of money, expertise, and access does the team have available for this challenge?
3. Parallel work—Who else in the organization is working on this challenge?
4. History—What has the organization done previously to address this challenge?
5. Extension—How broadly should the solutions apply through the organization?

The team's sponsor can give valuable assistance in developing the charter. Because of sponsors' role as linking pins between the team and the larger organization, they are often in the position to provide information about these parameters.

The final team charter is submitted to the organization for approval. In many cases, senior leadership evaluates charters and either approves them or provides recommendations for revisions. In other cases, a chartering approval board composed of program managers, sponsors, and representatives from senior management reviews the charter statements. This process gives teams the necessary feedback on whether their scope and scale is appropriate and their understanding of the challenge is consistent with the intent of the individuals who developed the problem statement. In any case, a reviewing body must approve the team's charter before the team can begin the problem solution development process. The team that hears team solution presentations can also use the charter to evaluate challenge solutions.

Although an approved charter is required at the beginning of a project, this does not mean that it cannot be revised later on. In some cases, the team will get new insights into or experiences with the problem that will require modification of the charter. When this happens, the revised charter will need to be approved through a review process similar to the one used initially to review charters.

SENIOR MANAGEMENT INVOLVEMENT

Senior leaders often believe that their involvement in the AL process is limited to authorizing funding, providing ideas for projects, giving 15-minute kick-off addresses, and listening to problem solution presentations. These are reasonable expectations, and people involved in planning and implementing AL programs need to recognize that executives invest a significant amount of time. Nevertheless, senior leaders need to understand the importance of their consistent involvement throughout the life of AL projects.

At the start of projects, senior management needs to be proactive in offering support, input, and advice in helping teams understand the importance of the challenges they have been assigned. Their assistance is also vital in helping the team understand senior management's expectations regarding the solution. This input will help the team understand the appropriate scope and scale for the project.

Involving Senior Management at Chrysler LLC

A number of senior executives were invited to the kick-off session for a large multigroup leadership development program using AL at Chrysler. During a 2-hour exercise, these executives rotated between the AL teams, spending 10 minutes with each team to allow members to ask questions about the challenge that had been assigned to them. By the end of the exercise, each team had gained a comprehensive understanding of the challenge as well as an appreciation of how the challenge was related to or impacted a wide spectrum of business units and functions within the corporation. As a side benefit, future leaders of the corporation had an opportunity to meet senior leaders of the organization whom they would have been unlikely to meet in normal business activities.

In the middle phase of AL projects, senior management will interface with team sponsors as they serve as linking pins between the team and the organization's leadership. Because sponsors generally have greater status in the organization than team members, they often have better access to the power centers of the organization.

After a team presents its solution, senior management needs to spend some political capital to support projects in the budget allocation process. The impact on future AL projects will be devastating if worthy solutions to urgent challenges and problems seem ignored by the organization when funding for implementation is required. Senior leadership needs to put its money where its mouth is to demonstrate its commitment to ensure that the team's creative efforts are more than program exercises.

When worthy solutions are funded for implementation, senior management can be invaluable as resources in giving input regarding the change management process. Senior managers have the experience and battle scars from previous efforts at organizational change and can help teams to avoid many of the hidden pitfalls and landmines that threaten the success of solution implementation.

Embedding Action Learning at Nationwide
Ursula Nation, Senior Consultant, Learning and Development

Nationwide, based in Columbus, Ohio, is one of the largest diversified insurance and financial services organizations in the world, with more than $161 billion in assets. Nationwide ranks #108 on the *Fortune 500* list. The company provides a full range of insurance and financial services, including auto, motorcycle, boat, homeowners, life, farm, and commercial insurance; administrative services; annuities; mortgages; mutual funds; pensions; and long-term savings plans.

Leaders in Action is a leadership program for midlevel managers at Nationwide. Eighty people at the assistant vice president/ director level are accepted into the program every year. The program consists of three core components: classroom learning, personal assessments, and an AL team assignment.

Each AL team consists of eight or nine members, an executive sponsor, and a team coach. All the assigned team project topics are approved by Nationwide's CEO and his team members. The teams have about 5 months to complete their projects in tandem with their "day jobs." At the end of the program, each team creatively presents its recommendation, findings, or results to about 160 top leaders at Nationwide, including the CEO and his team.

Since 2005, we have had several successful AL team results. The most successful has been the creation of a new company called Nationwide Better Health. Here is an excerpt from the Nationwide Better Health Web site: "The story of Nationwide

Better Health begins within Nationwide itself, where a group of individuals were contemplating several health care trends that were negatively affecting employers, as well as employees. . . . Nationwide's big idea was simple: bring all the pieces of a health and productivity solution under one roof by leveraging its own best practice programs as well as those of its partners. Finally, employers would be able to deal with one partner, one eligibility file, one reporting structure and one outcome." Two AL team members are currently serving on the senior leadership team for Nationwide Better Health.

Other AL team successes include,

1. A corporate-wide point of view on organizational change called Change Leadership was rolled out to the entire organization beginning May, 2008. This includes an adopted philosophy, a "How to be a Successful Change Consultant" training for HR reps, as well as tools and classroom training for leaders who are executing a major organizational change.
2. A "discount" on insurance and financial services products for Nationwide associates. This was particularly successful because it had been talked about internally for 20 years and this team had a breakthrough on how to get it done. The team's presentation included little "elephants in the room" (i.e., obvious issues not addressed) in the audience and the opening line, "Today, we're going to address the elephant in the room."

Program Design Considerations

CO-COACHING

An excellent way to ensure that AL gets embedded in the organization is to use co-coaching. In this model, an internal coach (often from the human resources, training, or organization development functions) is paired with a trained and experienced external AL coach.[2] This model has a number of advantages. First, few organizations have trained and experienced AL coaches at the beginning of projects. Adequate training of coaches can take 5 to 6 days at a minimum. A day or two of training is usually sufficient, however, to prepare internal coaches to work with an experienced and trained external AL coach.

Second, internal coaches are more aware of and sensitive to the culture, history, and "minefields" of the organization. They can not only

---

[2]The World Institute for Action Learning provides intensive training in the principles in techniques detailed in this book for coaching, designing, and managing Action Learning programs. Personnel Decisions International also offers AL consultation and services.

ask very useful questions to get at these aspects of the problem or challenge but also keep the external coach from prematurely attacking "sacred cows" or wandering, unknowingly, into organizational minefields, quicksand, or whirlpools. Even though AL coaches need to challenge assumptions and encourage team members to take risks in the way they approach problems, coaches also need to be aware of context when considering these issues so that they understand what they are walking into and can carefully plan their interventions. By focusing on the contextual issues and by providing "color commentary," internal coaches allow external coaches to concentrate on what they do best—focus on learning process issues in the team.

Internal coaches are often available to attend AL meetings when the external coach is not. The availability of the coaches can be a real problem. It is difficult enough to find available blocks of time when team members, who are often overcommitted, can meet. It may be even more difficult to find times when external coaches, who may not be based near the client organization, can also attend. We believe that it is very important to have a trained coach available for all AL meetings; having a coach who is internal to the organization gives the team a great deal more flexibility in scheduling meetings.

ACTION LEARNING SCHEDULES

As noted in chapter 2, there are two basic approaches to scheduling AL programs: spaced and massed. Each design has its strengths and limitations.

Spaced Designs

The spaced format is probably the more popular of the two approaches. Typically, spaced designs are planned to run over several months (3 to 4 months is quite popular) with 2- to 3-hour team meetings spaced every 2 to 3 weeks. These programs generally begin with a kick-off program of 1 to 2 days that includes team sponsors and representatives from senior management. Presentations to senior management conclude the programs unless a team receives authorization to continue on into the implementation of the solution.

Teams face several major challenges in spaced designs. First, scheduling meetings with all team members and coaches can be quite difficult, especially when team members and coaches are not co-located. It is becoming increasingly difficult to find 2- to 3-hour blocks of time when everyone can attend given the busy schedules of highly successful high-potential managers. Even though their bosses have authorized their attendance in these programs, team members may be pulled out of meetings to deal with crises and high-priority projects. As a result, the scheduling process in spaced designs can take up an inordinate amount of the team's time.

A second challenge is maintaining morale over the life of the project. The typical pattern is for the team to start out with great enthusiasm and energy. After several months, however, attendance becomes more sporadic as team members are pulled away by other responsibilities and the process moves from brainstorming into the nitty-gritty of solution design. In recognition of this problem, many programs plan "re-energizer" sessions to be held off-site with sponsors and representatives from senior management.

Because of these difficulties, spaced designs should only be undertaken when the program has solid support from the organization and senior management recognizes the importance of its sustained involvement in the process. These programs also require the use of seasoned AL coaches who have a good understanding of the life cycles of task teams (see chap. 5, this volume) and can focus their interventions and questions on the issues of commitment and sustaining energy and morale.

Massed Designs

AL projects may also be completed during one continuous time period: one 3-hour session if a crisis needs to be handled or 2 consecutive days or even up to 2 consecutive weeks. The General Electric (GE) Work-Out Program (Davids, Aspler, & McIvor, 2002; Tourloukis, 2002) is an excellent example of a massed design approach. The typical GE Work-Out process is a 2-week leadership development program designed to prepare high-potential leaders for the increasingly complex challenges they will face in future assignments. Participants are given orientations to AL and their team assignments on the first evening of the program. Although they are aware of their project assignments, teams do not actually start the AL projects until the next week. During the 1st week of the program, participants are enrolled in more traditional classroom work that provides information and technical training that is pertinent to advanced leadership positions in GE.

At the start of the 2nd week, participants spend a day gathering data that will be necessary to work on the challenge or problem assigned to the group. GE provides airline tickets and other travel resources to support these efforts. The teams reassemble on Tuesday and spend the next 3 days developing a solution and preparing for the presentation of their solution to senior management in the client organizations that sponsor the projects. The last day of the program is devoted to these presentations as well as to activities and exercises that help capture the learnings from the 2-week program.

The massed design approach has some important advantages as well as some limitations. One significant strength of this approach is that it greatly simplifies the scheduling process. Because these programs are usually held off-site, teams can operate at full-strength for the week, and participants are physically separated from their regular jobs and therefore less likely to be pulled into their regular everyday work. Mobile phones and e-mail can pull participants back into their regular work environment, but these distractions can be more easily managed in a massed design program held off-site.

A second major advantage of the massed approach is that it uses coaching resources very efficiently. In spaced designs, coaches are used in blocks of 2 to 3 hours separated by several weeks. If external coaches are employed, they typically need to bill at half- or full-day rates in order to compensate for travel time. Having to coordinate the team's meeting schedule with busy consultant schedules also adds another layer of complexity and complication. Because of these factors, massed programs are usually much easier to schedule, and the final cost is lower than in spaced programs.

One drawback of massed programs is the flip side of the advantages previously noted. The massed approach is not as realistic as the spaced model. As a result, teams do not have to grapple with real-life issues of how to conduct projects in which team members, usually from multiple functions or business units, can only meet periodically over a period of months. Good coaching can help teams recognize these challenges and develop strategies and practices for mitigating and limiting scheduling and morale difficulties.

TECHNOLOGY AND VIRTUAL TEAMS

Virtual teaming is standard practice in most contemporary organizations. The incredible advances in communication (e.g., mobile phones and other wireless hand-held communication devices such as the BlackBerry, the Internet and related technologies such as e-mail) allow teams to meet routinely and communicate virtually even though they are in different cities and time zones. It was inevitable that these technologies and methods would be included in AL practices. Although virtual teaming provides many advantages and benefits, the increased interpersonal distance and separation creates significant complications for effective team performance (Freedman & Leonard, 2002; Lipnack & Stamps, 1997). Compared with teams meeting face to face, virtual teams take considerably longer to become cohesive, creative, and high performing. One major factor that contributes to this difference is the lack of visual cues (which can be mitigated by using video-conferencing) in virtual teaming. Team members do not see facial expressions and other nonverbal cues or whether people are actively attending, multitasking, or even in the room with the telephone. It is difficult to build trust and rapport under these conditions. If team members are attending from their work desk or client sites, they often are not capable of applying their full attention to the AL problem or process.

Some virtual teaming is probably unavoidable when using a spaced design. AL coaches, however, should be sensitive to the consequences of virtual teaming; they should ask questions that require team members to consider the impact of distance attendance and invent practices and methods to limit the downside effects. Coaches should also be responsive to any significant use of teleconferencing in AL sessions. Marked increases can signal morale problems or increases in the demands that the organization is making on team members. Coaches need to ask probing questions to get the team to reflect on this phenomenon. Through appropriate questioning, the coach can encourage team members to confront each other when commitment flags. The coach may also need to consult with team sponsors and senior management to make sure that the organizations (especially bosses of participants) fully support the AL process.

Reflection Questions

1. What would be the major obstacles in embedding AL into your organization?
2. How would you overcome those obstacles?
3. How could you get senior leadership in your organization to support AL programs?
4. What steps would you take to ensure that senior management provides urgent, important, and complex problems to the AL teams?
5. What criteria would you use if you were populating an AL team?
6. How could AL improve the speed and quality of Six Sigma programs?
7. What are key strategies in obtaining and retaining AL champions?
8. More and more groups work virtually. How could you incorporate the six dimensions and two ground rules of AL when groups meet virtually?

Integrating Action Learning Within Larger Developmental Programs

ncreasingly, Action Learning (AL) programming is being included in larger comprehensive leadership and management development programs. The emphasis on participant involvement in real organizational problems provides a nice balance with other experiential learning programming as well as with more formal content presentation. When an AL component is added to a leadership or management development program, participants are also provided the opportunity to apply the theory and concepts that were presented in previous lectures and content presentations.

An AL component also provides the participant with a more robust learning experience. As discussed in chapter 1, Hicks and Peterson (1999) described the following five elements that provide the five necessary and sufficient conditions or requirements for the success of any developmental program:

- insight—knowing what to develop,
- motivation—motivating people to invest the necessary time and energy in their development,
- capability development—gaining necessary skills and knowledge,
- real-world practice—giving people the opportunities to practice newly learned skills in real-world settings, and

> ▪ accountability—giving people the incentive to apply newly developed skills at work.

These authors conceived these processes to be sequentially organized and to contain the active ingredients that determine the amount of development that actually results from an organization's developmental programming. Each element addresses a different requirement and is a potential "pinch point" for development. For instance, even with a very effective training component to develop specific skills, if there is little incentive to demonstrate the skill (low accountability) or little opportunity to practice the skills in a real-world setting, then there will probably be limited improvement in actual on-the-job performance.

Adding a robust AL program to a larger leadership development program provides the real-world practice and accountability as well as the skill development, motivation, and insight that ensure that the skills learned in the larger leadership development program are actually transferred to the workplace. AL provides the missing pieces to the "transfer of training" problem that has challenged training and development programs for decades (Broad & Newstrom, 1992).

Proper Placement of Action Learning Within Larger Leadership Development Designs

Hicks and Peterson's developmental model (1999) discussed in chapter 1 provides guidance in determining the most effective placement of the various components of a comprehensive leadership development program.

INSIGHT

Leadership development programs typically include a 360-degree feedback survey to provide specific and detailed insight to the participants regarding their current leadership capabilities. This information is most helpful at the start of the program when it can be used to develop a gap analysis that provides the basis for an individual development plan (IDP). Of course, insight is promoted in other components of the program, but these tend not to be phase specific. AL in particular, with its emphasis on critical reflection, is highly effective in promoting insights at the personal, team, and organizational level.

MOTIVATION

Motivation is often assumed to be present at the start of leadership development programs because of the elite and exclusive status of these programs. This assumption is not always valid, however. In many bureaucratically organized programs, leadership development programs are seen as a necessary part of the process for career development. Because these programs are required for career advancement, participants often invest only the minimum level of energy and resources to "get their ticket punched."

In results-driven and technology organizations, in contrast, managers are often promoted and selected for leadership development programs on the basis of their ability to achieve immediate, short-term results and their technical knowledge (Leonard, 2003). Individuals promoted on this basis may be reluctant to invest in longer term development, especially when the curriculum does not provide a clear line of sight for advancement or emphasizes the "soft" management skills that have not been necessary in their career to date.

AL provides motivation to fully invest in the program in several ways:

1. Because AL involves participants in problems that are urgent and critical to success, participants believe that their efforts will have a direct impact on the success of the company.
2. By engaging senior management meaningfully in the program, participants perceive a direct linkage between their efforts and their career prospects. Nothing motivates a group of ambitious and practical managers as much as knowing that the CEO or other senior managers will be personally reviewing and evaluating their work.

CAPABILITY DEVELOPMENT

Virtually all leadership development programs are accompanied by a leadership competency model that identifies the leadership skills and behaviors that will be the keys to the future success of the organization and its leaders. As noted in chapters 4 and 10, AL can be used successfully to develop a broad range of leadership skills, either alone or as part of a larger and more comprehensive leadership development program.

AL's emphasis on the use of questions and critical reflection promotes insight that is critical for creative and innovative behavior. The inclusion of a specialized learning coach also accelerates learning and minimizes the use of habitual and ineffective behavior as well as unsystematic trial-and-error, problem-solving strategies.

Like other experientially based learning approaches, AL emphasizes learning through action. The key advantage that AL has over other experiential learning approaches is that participants work on meaningful and urgent problems rather than on exercises and simulations. Although exercises and simulations can be engaging and entertaining, translation of the learning to real organizational problems can be difficult. In addition, some participants attach less importance to these approaches, seeing them as merely games or exercises. Furthermore, participants in AL programs learn theory inductively as the challenges emerge, rather than from predesigned and deductively inspired learning points to be provided whether or not the issue or challenge actually is relevant to the participants' experiences.

REAL-WORLD PRACTICE

AL has significant advantages in its ability to provide real-world practice. Classroom training designs have always struggled to provide participants with adequate practice opportunities. To this end, most traditional classroom programs include role-playing and homework assignments. Although these strategies provide some practice opportunities, they are not quite real world; they simulate the real world but they are only approximations.

AL, on the other hand, immerses participants in an urgent and critical problem that is facing the organization, their team, or them personally. This is not a game, and the stakes are real. The biggest challenge is not that participants will find the problem artificial or unrealistic but that they will find it too realistic and compelling and become engrossed in the problem without stopping periodically to reflect, examine, invent, develop, and change. The key role of the coach is to prevent participants and the team from going on "autopilot" and approaching the problem the way they always have without learning, growing, or achieving new insights.

ACCOUNTABILITY

AL is especially strong in the ability to deliver accountability. Accountability is built into the model by virtue of the requirement for the problem to be urgent and by the reality that each team solution will be reviewed and evaluated by senior management, preferably the CEO. We typically think of accountability from the negative standpoint—what will happen if the team does not perform well. That sort of accountability is certainly relevant in AL. Nobody wants to look bad in front of the boss. Positive accountability, however, is also a key factor in AL. The positive impact of having an AL project selected for implementation by the senior management is not lost on participants!

No other leadership development methodology delivers as much accountability as AL. The resistance of regular work units and participants' bosses to change has been a huge obstacle to transferring learning in the classroom to the work floor. What boss is willing to challenge the value of AL methodology when it has demonstrated its value by being selected by senior management for implementation for a mission-critical problem?

Table 1.1 compares AL with other popular leadership development approaches with estimates of the degree to which each approach satisfies the five requirements for development identified by Hicks and Peterson (1999). This analysis demonstrates that AL, along with personal coaching, is the most complete leadership development methodology with Hicks and Peterson's factors and is therefore most likely to deliver the development that is promised and expected.

To illustrate how AL can be integrated with larger developmental programs, several examples of leadership development programs with AL included are offered. Both examples demonstrate how the principles described by Hicks and Peterson (1999) can be applied to create a robust leadership development experience that satisfies all five requirements of the developmental sequence.

Example 1: The National Institutes of Health

One of the institutes within the National Institutes of Health (NIH)[1] became concerned that the leaders and managers lacked the leadership skills necessary to keep the organization at the forefront of bio-medical science. To address this concern, the institute contracted with a management consulting firm to develop a leadership development program for scientists with high potential for leadership and management within the institute. The charter for this program was to

- develop scientists who can lead science, not just be better managers of science projects;
- increase collaboration between scientists and programs, not just produce better project teams; and
- develop scientist-leaders and programs that are more flexible, creative, and adaptive, not just more proficient in the areas of their specialization.

LEADERSHIP DEVELOPMENT PROGRAM DESIGN

Each class consisted of 25 people who participated in each element of the leadership development program as a cohort. Although participants

---

[1] This case is a continuation of the case first presented in chapter 7.

were nominated for inclusion in the program, each participant attended an orientation program describing all phases of the program before personally enrolling.

The leadership development program had the following components:

- An organizational survey of the entire organization—All permanent employees were invited to take a 122-item organizational survey that assessed organizational functioning in 21 dimensions.[2] Data from this survey were used by the institute's senior leadership team to identify important organizational problems for AL teams to tackle.
- 360-degree feedback survey—A comprehensive anonymous survey of participants' leadership and management skills by bosses, peers, subordinates, clients, and the participants themselves was conducted.
- Training Modules—Three training modules were developed that were aligned with the institute's vision for leadership: Personal Leadership, Teamwork/Creativity, and Strategic Leadership.
- Personal Coaching—Voluntary personal coaching programs were offered to participants to help them apply the learnings from the leadership development program to their particular jobs and circumstances.
- AL Projects—Participants were organized into six AL teams to provide solutions to important institute problems. The process for selecting problems and assembling the teams is discussed in more detail later in this chapter.
- Follow-up 360-degree feedback survey—A follow-up 360-degree feedback survey was conducted for each participant. This abbreviated survey of bosses, peers, subordinates, and clients was based on behaviors linked to the participant's IDP (no more than 10 behaviors assessed) or the institute's priority leadership behaviors (10 items selected by the institute as being critical to the organization's mission).

Figure 8.1 provides a flow diagram for the institute's leadership development program.

---

[2] The 21 dimensions included strategy, planning and goal-setting, leadership, innovation and risk taking, anticipating and adapting to change, absence of obstacles, commitment to the whole team, handling conflict, consistency and fairness, respecting and supporting others, sharing learnings and ideas, working with other groups, accountability, facilitating structure, informing, making decisions, managing results, recruiting and staffing, training and development, financial resources, and physical resources.

FIGURE 8.1

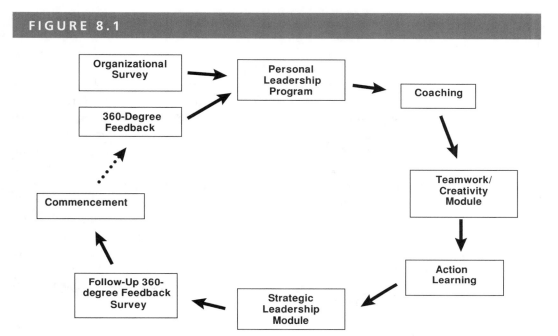

Flow diagram for the institute's Leadership Development Program. Text taken from "Leadership Development as an Intervention for Organizational Transformation: A Case Study," by H. S. Leonard and M. Goff, 2003, *Consulting Psychology Journal: Practice and Research, 55,* 58–67. Copyright 2003 by the American Psychological Association.

THE ACTION LEARNING COMPONENT

As previously noted, including AL in a leadership development program improves the effectiveness of the program. Other elements of a leadership development program can also be used to strengthen the AL component. For instance, results from the organizational survey of the institute conducted at the start of the program provided data that pointed to significant and important organizational problems. For instance, the organizational survey indicated serious problems in the way that the institute communicated with its employees. Employees reported that the "grapevine" was more reliable and accurate than formal communications channels. This problem resulted in a lack of trust in the leadership in the institute and a perception of favoritism in decision making by senior leaders. As a result of this information, an AL team was given the problem of developing better and more transparent internal communication processes.

Other development methodologies can be combined with AL quite effectively. An example of using an experiential learning methodology to identify problems that have personal importance to participants was presented in chapter 7 (p. 159). In addition to helping identify good AL problems, this workshop at NIH also developed communications skills that would be useful during the AL program.

The AL projects were placed between the Teamwork and Creativity module and the Strategic Leadership module quite purposefully. Although the AL process teaches many useful skills for teams to behave more creatively, the AL process works best when participants already have some knowledge about teams and creativity before they enter the process. In the Teamwork and Creativity module, participants learned many basic teamwork and creativity-enhancing skills (e.g., communication, decision making, brainstorming) that would be helpful in their AL projects. The team leadership skills that were developed in the AL programs were applied later in the Strategic Leadership module. In this module, participants faced the challenges of senior leaders in a 3-day organizational simulation. In this sequence of program elements, the leadership skills necessary for later in the program are developed in earlier program components.

PROGRAM OUTCOMES

The impact and value of this program was measured at all four levels of Kirkpatrick's (1998) training evaluation model.[3]

Level 1—Participant Reactions

As is typical in most training evaluations, participants rated major aspects of a program component at its completion—what they liked, what could be improved, the competence of the training staff, and so forth. This information was used in planning and executing the next program component. In addition, focus groups were conducted with a subgroup of participants who volunteered at the end of the entire program to provide unstructured feedback with respect to the following issues: (a) what they believed was valuable about the program, and (b) how they believed they would have behaved differently at work as a result of the program (this question is also relevant to Kirpatrick's Level 3 assessment).

---

[3] Please refer to chapter 10 for a more detailed discussion of the merits and drawbacks of using Kirkpatrick's four-level model for evaluating training programs. A primary complaint leveled at the Kirkpatrick approach is that the four-step model does not provide, examine, or assess the necessary intervening variables that affect outcomes and that would be necessary to build a robust model for program evaluation (Holton, 1996).

Level 2—Participant Learning

A 360-degree style feedback survey (see a fuller description of this instrument in chap. 11, p. 268) was conducted at the conclusion of the program. Self-ratings of improvement on leadership skills identified as priority learning goals at the start of the program provided data on how much participants believed they had learned as a result of this program.

Level 3—Participants' Application of What They Learned to the Workplace

Supervisor, peer/colleague, and subordinate ratings on the 360-degree instrument previously described provided measures of how much change in workplace behavior was noticed by those who worked with the participants over the period of the program (refer to chap. 11, p. 268, for more details on the advantages of this analytical strategy).

Level 4—Organizational Results

The institute was also interested in the impact of this program on the functioning of the organization as a whole. To assess the organization-wide impact, a survey tapping 22 basic dimensions was administered online to all members of the institute, not just to participants in the leadership development program (see chap. 11, p. 268, for more details on these dimensions). Pre- and postanalyses of these data were conducted to evaluate the overall impact of the leadership development program on the institute's functioning (see chap. 11, p. 268, for more details on the results of this analysis).

Although this evaluation strategy was developed to assess the impact of the entire leadership development program and was not specifically focused on the AL component, it would work equally well if used to evaluate a stand-alone AL program or an individual AL component in a larger developmental program.

Example 2: Chrysler LLC

In recent years, Chrysler LLC[4] has seen its competitive position be eroded not only in North American but also globally. Chrysler has had difficulty keeping up with the fast pace of globalization over this period. Corporate

---

[4] This case is a continuation of the case first presented in chapter 7.

leadership has taken a number of strategic steps in recent years to improve sales and profitability in a very competitive industry: increased investments in new products, acquisitions of companies in other markets, and new advertising campaigns. In spite of these actions, Chrysler has continued to lose market share.

Chrysler has a long history of innovation, and many of its product lines command intense loyalty. That being said, Chrysler's traditional customer base was shrinking, and the current and new products had little appeal to the market segments that were rapidly increasing. It was clear that revenues and even profitability would stagnate or decline unless the company made many changes in the way it was doing business.

In senior leadership's view, the strategic shifts in the marketplace were both significant and long lasting. To compete, Chrysler needed to become more agile and transform itself fundamentally. This process of transformation would involve a significant commitment on the part of employees at all levels as well as an aligned and collaborative leadership mind-set at all levels. Chrysler needed to become a rapid-learning organization (Marquardt, 2002) to survive the turbulent times of today and thrive on the opportunities presented by tomorrow. Accordingly, the Corporate Training group began to focus on creating a high-impact leadership development system.

ADVANCED LEADERSHIP DEVELOPMENT PROGRAM

The Advanced Leadership Development Program (ALDP) developed by the Corporate Training group included assessment, coaching, and skill-building workshops as well as AL. One main driver for including AL was that it would encourage managers to ask more questions and to challenge accepted assumptions in every facet of their work. In addition to teaching practical problem-solving and teaming skills, AL would help to change the mind-set with respect to learning and change. The program goals reflected this intention. As a result of this program, participants would gain the following:

- improved individual leadership competence,
- enhanced capacity to work together with other leaders to solve complex business problems, and
- skills for building a resilient high-performance work environment.

In addition to the three goals, through ALDP program managers aimed to change the way people worked together. Participants were expected to demonstrate the following:

1. Radical collaboration—Success in the program required participants to break-down bureaucracy to gain insights and perspectives on their business challenges.
2. Break-through thinking—Participants were encouraged to take risks and look at long-standing assumptions in completely different and creative ways.
3. Entrepreneurialism—Each team was fully responsible for achieving its own results, building and delivering a compelling recommendation, a solid business case, and an implementation plan to top management on an important strategic issue.

AL projects were given prominence in the ALDP. The AL program was set up before decisions were made on where to place other developmental components such as 360-degree feedback and specific training modules. Other ALDP components were seen as supporting to the central developmental process, AL. This pedagogic strategy was different from the one employed at NIH in the previous example. In the NIH program, AL was a key part in the sequence of development that culminated in the demonstration of leadership skills in a high-fidelity organizational simulation. In contrast, in Chrysler's program, participants directly demonstrated new leadership skills in developing solutions to some of the organization's most pressing strategic problems.

The differences in the way AL was used in the two leadership development programs reflected differences in the goals and objectives. In the NIH program, the priority was on developing the "soft skills" of leadership and management. Program participants were already competing well in the highly competitive arena of personal scientific achievement. On the one hand, the ability to work collaboratively in a common direction was a less well-developed skill for this group. On the other hand, Chrysler's managers had good teaming skills but were less likely to think creatively by challenging assumptions or considering changes in the current operational strategies and tactics. For this group, making AL the keystone of the ALDP made sense. Figure 8.2 provides a flow diagram for Chrysler's ALDP.

The various components of the Chrysler ALDP are described in the following sections.

Nomination and Individual Developmental Planning

Approximately 90 midlevel managers identified by their managers as "top talent" were nominated for this program. Nominations were based on both their current and past performance and their supervisor's estimate of their potential for further advancement as leaders within the company. Supervisors and nominated managers discussed how the ALDP would fit

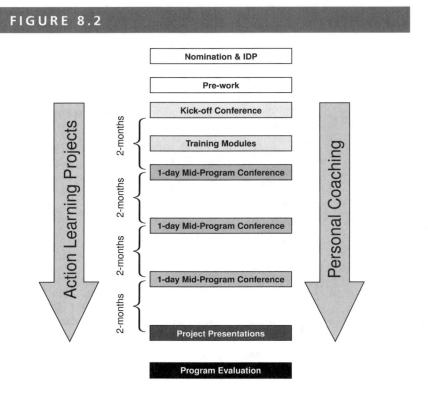

FIGURE 8.2

Flow diagram for Chrysler Advanced Leadership Development Program. IDP = individual development program.

into the managers' career plans and their individual development goals. Managers who accepted[5] were then assigned to 1 of 12 AL teams.

Pre-Work

Prior to the program's initiation, managers completed pertinent reading assignments and a self-assessment as part of a 360-degree feedback process. Participants also had their first meeting with their personal coach. During this meeting, an initial personal leadership development plan was drafted. The AL process was initiated with a brief teleconference, in essence, a "virtual meeting." During this meeting, the AL coach was introduced and the team's topic was discussed (team members already knew the general topic).

_____

[5] Virtually all managers nominated for the ALDP accepted because of the status and prospects for more rapid advancement as managers within Chrysler.

Kick-Off Conference

All participants took part in a 2-day, off-site conference to formally kick off both the AL and the personal coaching programs. The 2-day conference had three major priorities. First, participants and teams began the important task of scoping their individual development plans and their AL projects. As noted in chapter 7, AL topics often come with limited definition as to scale and scope. During this process, AL teams must first come to agreement not only on what they understand to be the problem but also on what is practical and doable given the time and resources available.

A second priority of the kick-off process was the alignment of individual and team goals. In meetings with personal coaches, participants identify two or three personal skills or competencies that they would like to develop during the ALDP. The AL team coaches reinforced these goals by asking participants what they learned during the AL process in relation to their leadership development agenda.

A third priority of the kick-off process was to demonstrate support for the program from senior leadership. Senior leaders displayed support not only through the traditional kick-off addresses but also by being available to individual AL teams to answer questions about the topic. Using a structured process, 15 of the company's senior executives rotated between the projects, giving each team 10 minutes to question them about the intent of senior leadership in developing the problem statement for their specific problem assignment and providing their perspective on the importance of the problem, expectations regarding team solutions, and possible resources elsewhere in the company.

Using the information gained from their meetings with senior leaders, teams were able to complete the process of defining the problem as well as project goals—what the teams believed would be both valuable to the company as well as feasible. At the end of the kick-off process, teams presented their newly drafted project charter to the other teams using a "sharing and comparing" process. While several team members presented their project charter and initial project plan, the rest of the team visited other teams (also manned by several team members) to share perspectives and ideas. In the follow-up team meetings, the team members who had presented their project work to other teams shared reactions and suggestions from other teams. Team members who had visited other teams brought back information about linkages with other topics as well as new problem-solving approaches. This cross-fertilization helped to expand perspectives and leveraged the creativity and problem-solving skills in the larger learning community.

The kick-off process was concluded with a meeting between the AL team and the team sponsor (see chap. 7, p. 162, for a fuller description of the team sponsor role). During this initial meeting, the team briefed the sponsor on what had transpired during the conference, the emerging charter, and received information from the sponsor regarding solution planning. The team and sponsor also discussed the appropriate role and involvement of the sponsor.

Training Modules

In the 2 months following the kick-off conference, each participant chose and attended one of seven 2- or 3-day training programs. The focus of each program was related to a subtheme of the leadership program: building value, strategy, continuous process improvement, coaching, career transition, personal development, and innovation. After attending the modules, participants shared their experiences and learnings with other team members. Because participants chose programs on the basis of their personal learning goals, each program had participants from a number of AL teams. The diversity of module attendance facilitated "cross-pollination" of ideas and promoted a broader interaction between future leaders of the company. The building of enduring relationships on the basis of real work has been identified as a major benefit of AL (Leonard & Goff, 2003).

Personal Coaching

Personal coaching was provided to all participants to ensure the continued alignment of participants' individual development with AL. Personal coaching allowed participants to explore personal issues that emerged as they interacted with other AL team members "off-line." Because the AL coaches did not facilitate team process and did not do any individual or team coaching, personal coaches allowed participants to explore and address personal issues that emerged from the unstructured (by the coach) team process.

Action Learning Projects

With a team charter developed, the AL teams worked over the next 7 months to develop a solution to the problem provided to them. Teams scheduled and managed their own meetings and obtained their own resources. The AL coaches confined their activities to asking good questions that took advantage of opportunities to learn how to be more a more effective team member, team, and organization.

Each team had two AL coaches: an external coach from one of several consulting firms who had specific expertise in AL and an internal coach who was a member of the organization with some training in AL. Although not required, it was strongly recommended that at least one of the AL coaches be present (in person or via video- or teleconference) for all meetings.

Mid-Program Conferences

Three off-site, 1-day mid-program conferences were conducted, spaced roughly 2 months apart. Program managers anticipated that an AL program that took place over 7 months would require several milestone events to maintain the focus, energy, and momentum of the AL work. These events also offered opportunities for sharing and collaboration across the 15 groups as well as for demonstrations of continued support from senior leadership. These conferences included plenary presentations by senior executives, "sharing and comparing" events, meetings with project sponsors, and AL work sessions.

Project Presentations

Roughly 7 months after project initiation, each team presented its problem solution to a panel that included the CEO as well as a majority of his direct reports. Executive panel members were provided a simple document to record their questions and observations. Teams' presentations were evaluated according to the extent to which the solution

- identified potential obstacles and risks,
- identified resources required to implement the ideas,
- demonstrated leadership behaviors,
- delivered a solid presentation,
- earned my confidence and trust, and
- gained my support for their proposal.

Each team was allowed 30 minutes for its presentation, and then the executive team had 15 minutes for a question-and-answer session. All 12 teams made strong presentations. Several of the presentations had come together in the final week before the actual presentation, but the effort was evident. There was also variation in the presentations: Some teams had supplemental briefing books to capture the research they could not work into their presentation. One team had posters; another had sample devices that it recommended. Some teams had more elaborate cost/benefits analyses, whereas others focused more on the possibilities within a proposed course of action. Each team had one or two members making the primary presentation and all team members answering questions.

During the presentations, most teams discussed what they had learned in the process of the AL project and the ALDP overall. In several cases, there were follow-up questions from the executive panel as well. Following are some of the questions asked by the executive panel:

- What did you learn about organization strategy/finance in this project?
- What is the cost of not acting? Can you put a price on it?
- What might be the impact on employees?
- How might "X" change your recommendations or priorities?
- What would we tell investors while we are making this extensive change?
- What are some of the best practices across the industry?
- You are not experts in this area. What impact did this have on the team's work?
- What has kept us, the company, from making progress on this in the past?

After each team completed its presentation, the executive panel met briefly to discuss reactions and identify a member of the panel to take action on the recommendations. A coach recorded feedback and general reactions in this session. These notes were then integrated into a more complete feedback process led by the selected panel member. After presenting, each team adjourned to a "team" room with its AL team coach. An after-action review session was conducted at that time; prior to the end of the after-action review, the executive panel member selected to move the project forward entered the team briefing room and provided initial executive reactions. A follow-up meeting designed to provide an opportunity for more feedback and follow-up actions were planned at that time.

Program Evaluation

The ALDP described in this case study was groundbreaking for the organization. Conducted during a truly momentous and stressful time in the life of the company, the inventiveness, collegiality, and mutual support of learning that was demonstrated throughout was inspiring. Because this program was not yet concluded at the time of writing of this book, the program evaluation process had not been completed. Chrysler planned to gather evaluation data for the following five key metrics:

- increase in observable leadership behaviors;
- increase in performance in core work;
- number of innovative ideas designed, developed, presented, and approved to implement or not;
- value (revenues or savings) generated per project presented and eventually implemented; and
- percentage of participants retained over the years.

Action Learning in the Classroom

Increasingly, universities, colleges, and even secondary schools are including AL components as part of their curriculum. Beginning in the early 1990s, a number of universities in the United States (e.g., George Washington University, James Madison University, Columbia University, American University, Roger Williams University), in other countries such as the United Kingdom (e.g., Lancaster University, University of Salford, Coventry University), and in Australia (e.g., Australia Cross University, National University of Australia, University of Queensland, University of Ballarat) began offering specialized AL programs in conjunction with professional graduate programs. In the past decade, universities in a number of countries such as Singapore (University of SIM) and the Netherlands (Business School Netherlands—see case example that follows) have begun offering AL as a core academic program, much like writing and math, to their undergraduate and graduate students. These traditional educational organizations have recognized the unique ability of AL to develop highly valued leadership competencies such as critical thinking and creativity, collaborative problem solving, communications, planning, and interpersonal skills.

Leadership Development Via Action Learning Projects at Business School Netherlands
Herman van Niekerk

Business School Netherlands (BSN) offers executive management development and MBA programs, all of which are based and assessed on AL principles. The school offers both open and in-company programs, and has achieved remarkable results with both these programs. Managers come from countries such as South Africa, Rwanda, Nigeria, the Netherlands, and Germany and from companies ranging from local government and manufacturing, to the financial and insurance industries, including Old Mutual (insurance), Absa (finance), UTi (transport), Timken (manufacturing), and Shell (energy).

The students/leaders are assessed on an AL project in which they have to identify a management challenge in a specific discipline, such as strategy or operations management. They conduct their own literature research and then meet in small groups of four to nine to discuss their challenges with one another and to obtain different insights and perspectives. Students conduct empirical research, analyze the results, and generate different alternatives on the basis of action-learning, decision-making criteria. The AL project must include the recommendation of a specific option supported by a detailed implementation plan on how the students will take action on their decisions. During their studies, they maintain a learning logbook in which their personal learning experiences are captured. As part of their final dissertation, students submit an evaluation of their own personal learning in which they reflect on their study.

Results from a recent research project involving over 130 MBA leaders from different countries determined that AL made a significant contribution to the development of individual managers. More than 90% of the respondents indicated that AL improved their critical thinking skills and ability to ask relevant questions. Almost 89% indicated that through this approach to learning they improved their problem-solving techniques. Nearly 75% responded that AL helped them to improve and foster creativity and innovation, whereas nearly 70% indicated that it contributed greatly to establishing a learning culture in the organization. A remarkable 92% concluded that AL contributed significantly to their development as leaders. This research project showed that AL has the ability to transcend national cultures and can be applied in many diverse business environments.

Reflection Questions

1. Consider the leadership development process in your organization. Evaluate this process using the development pipeline (Hicks & Peterson, 1999):
   - Insight—Do people understand their own strengths and weaknesses as leaders? Do they know what to develop?
   - Motivation—Are people motivated to develop their leadership abilities? Are people willing to invest the time and energy it takes?
   - Capabilities—Does the program provide people with the skills and knowledge they need?
   - Real-world practice—Do people have opportunities to apply their capabilities at work?
   - Accountability—Does the program provide incentives for people to internalize their new capabilities to actually improve performance and results?
2. Given this analysis, what changes or additions would you recommend for this process?
3. What are the advantages and disadvantages of including an AL component in a larger leadership development program?

4. What must coaches and managers of AL do to ensure that the team believes it will be held accountable for its work in a meaningful way?
5. It is often difficult to incorporate real accountability in training programs. How can you use some of the principles of AL to increase accountability in other training programs?

Application of Action Learning Principles in Other Developmental Processes

9

A s noted in chapter 3, the demonstrated power of Action Learning (AL) is based on the method's unique capacity to interweave principles and processes that form the foundation from a wide array of disciplines such as psychology, sociology, education, organizational change and development, and management. The focus and simplicity of the AL process bring the "active ingredients" of these disciplines and sciences together synergistically as few other problem-solving and developmental approaches can.

In a complementary fashion, this chapter discusses how the principles, core values, and methods of AL can be used in activities in which problem solving; learning; and individual, team, and organizational development are important, if not primary, goals. In fact, many people who are exposed to the principles and power of AL naturally find themselves using many of the skills learned through their practice of active learning in many other parts of their lives. For instance, managers make a point of leaving a few minutes at the end of meetings to capture learnings and review what worked, what could have been improved, and what they would do differently in the future. Coaches search for really good questions rather than trying to give really good advice. Executives make organizational learning as big a priority as maximizing quarterly performance.

Action Learning as a General Strategy for Improving Creativity and Problem Solving as Well as Promoting Growth and Development

AL principles can be effectively used in many situations in which a formal AL process would not be appropriate. Recall from chapter 2 that AL is the method of choice when the goals are clear and specific but the solution's methods are uncertain or ambiguous. Although it would be unwise and inappropriate to give an AL team a goal that is vague and undefined (cf. Figure 2.1), AL principles and methods could be used in a meeting with senior leaders to identify AL goals. In another example, an executive coach may use AL principles and methods to generate probing questions that will facilitate creativity and personal development rather than dependency on the coach.

As noted in Table 9.1, AL principles and methods can be used in a number of different roles: AL coach, team/organizational leader, team/task facilitator, consultant/coach. In each of these roles, some or all of the following six basic components of AL may be used.

1. *A problem.* To use AL principles, there must be an important problem that needs to be solved.
2. *An AL group or team.* AL principles can be used with any problem-focused group or team. They can also be used in one-on-one, problem-solving activities such as coaching.
3. *Insightful questioning and reflective listening.* This is probably the most critical component of any process using AL principles. The core active ingredient of any AL-inspired process is the emphasis on asking great questions before asserting a point of view. Although there may not be as strict an adherence to the principle of "statements only in response to questions," there is a strong emphasis on leading with questions whenever possible. In addition to making a priority of asking questions rather than making statements, AL-inspired processes encourage reflection and sense-making dialogue (Bohm, 1996; Weick, 1995).
4. *Taking action on the problem.* This is another principle of AL that can be applied in almost any AL-inspired process. Simply exploring an issue and making recommendations for a solution is not enough. For meaningful learning to occur, teams, groups, and individuals need to complete the cycle of learning suggested by Kolb (1984; see Figure 2.2).

TABLE 9.1

Application of Action Learning in Other Roles

	Action Learning coach	Team/ organizational leader	Team/task facilitator	Consultant/ coach
Importance of problem	An important problem	An important problem	An important problem	An important problem
Focus of application	Action Learning group or team	A team or organization	A team or group	A client
Centrality of asking questions	Statements only in response to questions	Emphasize/ encourage asking good questions	Emphasize/ encourage asking good questions	Emphasize asking good questions
Taking action on problem	Taking action on the problem	Taking action on the problem	Taking action on the problem	Taking action on the problem
Learning goal	A commitment to learning	A commitment to learning	A commitment to learning	A commitment to learning
Expertise of coach	A trained Action Learning coach	Knowledge of Action Learning principles and appropriate mind-set	Knowledge of Action Learning principles and appropriate mind-set	Knowledge of Action Learning principles and appropriate mind-set

5. *A commitment to learning.* Whereas application of AL principles invariably results in more creative and effective solutions, commitment to capturing and remembering what was learned allows teams, groups, and individuals to transfer these learnings to new situations in the future. A commitment to learning provides the integrative matrix of activities necessary for developing a learning organization (Marquardt, 2000).

6. *An AL coach.* Although experience in coaching AL teams would be very helpful, an individual does not need to have this experience to apply AL principles to solving problems and facilitating learning and development. As long as an individual has sufficient understanding of the active ingredients of AL and possesses, and the requisite mind-set of reflection and curiosity, he or she will be able to effectively apply the principles of AL to a variety of situations that require problem solving and learning.

Table 9.1 shows that the core elements of (a) needing an important problem, (b) taking action as a requirement, and (c) making a commitment to learning as well as solution development remain constant for all roles that are inspired by AL. The major differences in practice are (a) the target client (individuals and organizations as well as teams or groups), (b) the degree of emphasis on asking questions rather than making statements, and (c) the level of training and experience in AL of the coach/facilitator/consultant/leader. The remainder of this chapter provides more discussion of the use of AL principles and methods in the roles described above.

Panasonic's Journey With Action Learning and Questions
Jasmine Liew
Panasonic Regional Training Center, Panasonic Asia Pacific Pte Ltd

AL has been quickly and successfully implemented at Panasonic because it matches well with the following four components of the Basic Business Philosophy (BBP) of Panasonic's Founder, Konosuke Matsushita.

1. Courtesy and Humility
    Mr. Matsushita practiced and encouraged the skill of listening to one another with respect. To strengthen cordial work relationships, modesty and respect should be shown for the rights and needs of others. These virtues of courtesy and humility correspond closely to the two ground rules of AL: (a) statements should be made only in response to questions, and (b) the AL coach intervenes whenever there is a learning opportunity. Everyone in the team is therefore treated with equal respect as they have equal opportunity to share by asking or responding to questions.
2. Cooperation and Team Spirit and Collective Wisdom
    Mr. Matsushita had a penchant for asking questions and learning from others to create better alternatives for effective problem solving and decision making. He believed that wise leaders could not solve problems on the basis of their own personal experiences and perspectives. Instead, Mr. Matsushita believed that people who ask good questions are more valuable than those who simply spout knowledge.
    In our AL programs at Panasonic, by asking questions, leaders can gain more respect from others as this will reflect their desire to understand what their members know or think. Individuals feel appreciated, motivated, and gratified when they are given the opportunity to share their ideas and experiences with interested parties. Moreover, questions provide a fountain of collective information as a leader listens and taps the wealth of the collective wisdom and experiences that lie within the team.
    AL encourages collective wisdom. It fosters a climate of understanding, an openness to different ideas, and the humility and willingness to interact and learn within a diverse team, seeking solutions to a common issue. The BBP encourages "cooperation and team spirit." With this in mind, Panasonic teams can expect to develop better solutions and to elevate

their learning as an individual and as a team. This also enhances the team dynamics and builds effective and cohesive problem-solving teams.

3. Sunao Mind

The *sunao mind* is a Japanese phrase that means understanding the truth without bias or self-interest. One is willing to hear different perspectives and have an open mind. Panasonic employees are to practice sunao mind when they engage in conversations. With an open mind, they are able to listen and empathize with the other person's point of view, look at things as they are from an objective and nonbiased perspective, and thus have a concrete paradigm of the actual situation/issue under discussion.

In Panasonic's AL teams, there is framing and reframing of the problem, and every team member must be objective, have an open mind, and be unbiased. Through questions, the problem can be framed and reframed as the group practices sunao mind in accepting others' interpretation of the perceived problem. With greater clarity of the real problem, a more effective action or decision thus emerges from the team to help in solving the problem.

4. Adaptability and Untiring Effort for Improvement

Panasonic employees are to adapt our thinking and behavior to meet the ever-changing conditions of the business environment. Continuous learning, relearning, and unlearning are the foundations of AL. The impact of learning through questions unfolds as members share their views when responding to the questions raised by other members. Members have to adapt to changes quickly due to the dynamic forces of questions, leading members to frame and reframe the contents, when the need arises.

AL serves as an effective learning technique for the manifestation of BBP and assists employees to further appreciate and apply the BBP in their day-to-day work and decision-making processes. The birth of "BBP and Action Learning" as a key human resources development activity in the Panasonic Regional Training Center took place in January 2008. Since then, a series of training programs incorporating AL have been successfully launched, including AL application as a component of all of our seminars for high-potential candidates.

AL has enriched the learning activities and human resource development efforts in the Panasonic Regional Training Center. The alignment of BBP with AL is a further testimony of Mr. Matsushita's thoughts on "people before products." As Panasonic develops state-of-the-art products and services, we also develop "thinking employees" and "thinking leaders." Panasonic's Management Philosophy and AL promote self-development and development of others in the team. Collective wisdom within the AL team allows Panasonic staff to further benefit in terms of their personal development. AL will continue to develop their leadership skills to be in line with Panasonic's mission, values and actions.

Using Action Learning as a Team/Organizational Leader

Team/organizational leaders have many opportunities to apply AL principles and methods. In fact, any leader who is committed to building a learning organization (Marquardt, 2002) should consider using AL principles and methods in any organizational event that involves more than one person in a problem-solving task. Leaders who aspire to create a true learning organization will look at every organizational event as an opportunity to develop individual organizational members, teams, and organizational units as well as a process for achieving an organizational goal.

The leader's attitudes about problem solving and development are critical to this process. He or she must believe that the best solutions to the challenges facing the organization will emerge from problem-solving and decision-making processes that include the thinking and judgment of others besides themselves. They must firmly believe that teams with diverse membership in terms of experience, background, knowledge, and expertise have the power and the ability to solve complex problems. In short, leaders who want to facilitate the highest performance from their team/organization must "trust the process" as much as they trust their own judgment to come up with the best solutions.

A second leadership attitude that is critical to creating a learning organization is curiosity. Curiosity encourages leaders to ask whether the current procedures are the most appropriate. Curiosity motivates leaders to "think outside of the box" in considering how to approach a problem. Curiosity helps leaders experience unexpected and untoward events and setbacks as learning opportunities rather than failures. Curiosity inspires a reaction of "isn't that interesting" rather than "isn't that awful" when things do not go as desired or planned (Zander & Zander, 2002).

If leaders truly believe in the power of "we" and approach a problem or goal with a mind-set of curiosity, then they are ready to consider whether and to what degree to apply the principles and methods of AL.

In considering whether to use some or all of the AL principles and methods to address an issue, leaders should consider whether formal AL is the best approach to take. The leader needs to determine whether the goal is sufficiently understood and developed to undertake AL. The leader should also consider whether other tried-and-true methods or protocols are available for the kinds of problems the team or organization needs to face. Is it necessary to reinvent the wheel? For instance, well-established and proven problem-solving methodologies such as Six Sigma are available for addressing quality issues. AL also does not replace the need for leaders to develop strong team facilitation skills (cf. Schwarz, 2002).

Here are some situations in which a leader might consider using AL principles and methods.

TEAM MEETINGS

During meetings, the leader can model good questioning behavior (Marquardt, 2005) by beginning the discussion of issues by asking good questions that encourage problem definition and exploration and that foster dialogue rather than premature debate. The leader may also encourage team members to lead with questions rather than by asserting their opinion. At the end of each meeting, the leader can devote 5 to 10 minutes to ask the team to reflect on questions such as (a) What contributed to success/what worked well/what did we like? (b) In what areas could the team improve/what activities should we discontinue/what didn't we like? (c) What did we learn/what would we do differently next time? and (d) What did we learn that can be transferred or translated to other problems/issues that the team or organization is facing?

STRATEGIC PLANNING MEETINGS

Leaders may decide to integrate AL principles and methodologies with other structuring strategies. Strategic planning meetings have two characteristics that make the use of a pure AL methodology impractical. First, time is more limited than is normally the case in AL projects. Second, many separate problems are usually embedded in the larger umbrella problem of creating a strategic plan. Because of these characteristics, the facilitator usually will choose a more directive style (cf. Schwarz, 2002) than would be appropriate for an AL coach. Superimposing another structure (such as a balanced scorecard) over the process while using an AL inquiry process (Carson, 2006) combines some of the benefits of both approaches while meeting the challenges of time and multiple agenda items. Regardless of how directive the facilitator decides to be, the emphasis would be on leading with questions rather than forcefully asserting positions. Also, at the end of the meeting, the facilitator would be able to devote time to capturing learnings as described in the previous section.

ONE-ON-ONE MEETINGS WITH SUBORDINATES

In getting updates from subordinates, leaders frequently begin by asking questions. The more that these questions reflect a problem-solving and curiosity-driven style, the less likely the employee is to respond defensively or aggressively. If the leader makes an effort to ask great questions that drill down to uncover root causes of problems, subordinates will feel less of a need to explain themselves or justify their actions. If the leader asks good questions and listens patiently, employees will come to believe that the leader wants to understand rather than blame them for problems and difficulties.

When the purpose of the meeting is to coach an employee, the AL principle of leading with questions is usually more effective than opening the discussion with the leader's analysis of the problem and interpretation of the employee's intent or motivation. If the purpose of the session is to conduct an annual review of the employee's performance, the supervisor can create a developmental rather than strictly feedback culture by asking questions that focus on what the employee learned over the year, what successes the employee wants to build up, what changes the employee intends to make, and what personal goals the employee has established for the coming year.

INDIVIDUAL WORK

Even in situations in which no one else is present, the leader can increase the level of creativity in his or her work by adopting the mind-set of AL and developing questions that are relevant to the problem: What is not known? Who has the information needed? What can I learn from this situation? How can I apply what I have learned to other situations? and more. Taking an inventory of what is not known or what information and resources are needed promotes new ways of thinking about problems. Many of the creativity-enhancing methods developed over the years are based on the principle that asking questions that encourage people to look at problems from unusual angles (Gordon, 1961) increases innovative thinking. Whitney and Giovagnoli (1997) developed 75 "cage-rattling questions" to stimulate new ideas at work. Ray and Myers's (1986) discussion of creativity in business has a chapter titled, "Ask Dumb Questions." These examples demonstrate that the principle of leading with questions applies to individuals as well as to groups or teams.

Leadership and Action Learning at Hewlett-Packard

The Hewlett-Packard Company, commonly referred to as HP, is an information technology corporation specializing in personal computers, notebook computers, servers, printers, digital cameras, calculators, network management software, among other technology related products. Headquartered in Palo Alto, California, HP has a global presence in the fields of computing, printing, and digital imaging and also provides software and services. In 2007 the revenue was $104 billion, making HP the first IT company in history to report revenues exceeding $100 billion.

In 2005 Personnel Decisions International (PDI) partnered with HP to create a leadership development process called The

Winning Edge. There were 66 participants in 16 teams and eight PDI AL coaches. Participants attended a plenary launch session, formed a team, created feedback contracts, identified an initial issue, and began the search for an organizational sponsor. Participants met two to three times per month.

Participants reported numerous benefits in the AL leadership program including:

- much better understanding of the complete value of our portfolio,
- ability to practice collaboration essentials and authentic conversations,
- increased competence in working in global environment with different cultures and points of view, and
- experience in working with and managing virtual teams.

The process was seen as highly successful and valuable and continues to be an important part of the organization's high-potential development process.

Using Action Learning as a Team/Task Facilitator

The primary goal for groups meeting as project teams, task forces, committees, or strategy leadership teams is to accomplish a designated task or set of tasks. Team/task facilitators, therefore, usually feel a strong sense of responsibility and obligation for goal accomplishment. Because they are being held accountable for making sure that the group/team/committee efficiently delivers a superior product, facilitators usually feel that they need to be more directive than would be appropriate as an AL coach. They are usually willing to sacrifice some opportunities for team members to learn in order to achieve a quality product as efficiently as possible.

Moreover, in many situations a methodology already exists for achieving the desired results in a predictable and efficient manner. Six Sigma (Breyfogle, 1999) and task facilitation (Schwarz, 2002) are excellent examples of methodologies that the task/team can use to accomplish a desired goal. These situations correspond to Quadrant A in Figure 2.1—situations in which the desired goals are specific and pathways to the solution are known and acceptable. Because the skills for these methodologies take time and effort to develop, why apply a rigorous AL procedure when a well-practiced alternative procedure already exists?

Even though a different team methodology is being used, however, the application of the principles, values, and practices of AL will improve the resulting products. It goes without saying that the mind-sets that are foundational to AL (curiosity and trust in the capabilities of the group and the process) will also improve the problem-solving capabilities of any group/team/committee. Likewise, emphasizing the AL principles of leading with questions whenever possible, challenging assumptions, and encouraging reflection will also invariably improve the problem-solving capabilities of any group/team/committee.

It is also worth noting that asking good, probing questions, challenging assumptions, and holding to strict ground rules for team behavior lies at the foundation of effective and skilled team facilitation (Schwarz, 2002).

Using Action Learning as a Coach

Using AL principles and methods in coaching will be natural for some coaches but foreign and even controversial for others. Coaches who come from the teaching, counseling, and helping professions will find the principles, values, and practices of AL to be largely consistent with those that they found useful in their primary professions or roles. Since the time of Socrates (Robinson, 1953), pedagogy has identified the asking of questions, the challenging of assumptions, and the encouragement of reflection to be highly effective methods for encouraging learning and for developing students' curiosity and enthusiasm for learning.

In counseling, Rodgers (1961) demonstrated the importance of encouraging clients to take responsibility for their own learning and growth rather than following the direction or prescription of the counselor or therapist. He also emphasized the inherent capabilities of humans to develop and be creative. Because of these innate capabilities, Rodgers encouraged counselors to using mirroring communications (e.g., "I hear you saying that what happened today made you feel angry") to encourage reflection and self-study.

Kurt Lewin, father of Action Research, famously noted that "learning is more effective when it is an active rather than a passive process" (Wagner, 2006, para. 10). This principle no doubt was the basis for his statement: "no action without research; no research without action" (Marrow, 1969, p. 193). The importance of action in theory building was further identified when Lewin remarked, "If you want truly to understand something, try to change it" (Wagner, 2006, para. 3). Because these principles are at the core of applied social and organizational psychology, many coaches find the emphasis on learning through action to be a natural fit.

Coaches who received their training in business schools or whose coaching models are former business executives or athletic coaches, however, may find the nondirective style of AL coaching that emphasizes the importance of facilitating learning rather than imparting expertise uncomfortable. Many business coaches have hired coaches and consultants earlier in their careers who behaved in an expert role by providing direct advice and opinion. For these coaches, the ground rule requiring statements only in response to questions and the dual focus on learning as well as task accomplishment may seem unusual if not inappropriate. Other coaches with prior management experience may agree with the basic ground rules in principle but may find it difficult to suppress the "bias to action" and the urge to take charge that was the basis for much personal success earlier in their career.

Seasoned coaches, however, are aware of the value of asking good questions. They are also aware of the trap of being seen as the source of the most important knowledge and information. Peterson and Hicks (1996) noted that one of the biggest misconceptions about coaching is that it is primarily concerned with giving feedback and advice. Because coaches cannot be constantly available now or in the future, Peterson and Hicks believed that a primary goal of coaching is to help people learn for themselves.

Coaches who perceive their role as helping people learn for themselves will naturally adopt the attitudes that are used in AL: (a) a belief in the capacity of their clients to solve problems themselves, (b) curiosity, and (c) a belief in the fundamental value of leading with questions rather than dispensing advice. To ensure that their clients incorporate important lessons rather than just follow their recommendations, these coaches build in time at the end of coaching sessions to reflect on what happened so that they can not only understand the reasons for success or sources of failure or problems but also make plans to alter their behavior in the future.

Reflection Questions

1. How applicable would the principles of AL be to improving the performance of your staff meetings? What modifications would you need to make to use AL in this situation?
2. Would you consider using AL at your next strategic planning session? What modifications would you need to make to use AL in this setting?
3. Think of the last feedback meeting you had with someone. How could the effectiveness of that meeting be improved by using AL strategies and principles?
4. What are the advantages and drawbacks to using a directive, task facilitator style when coaching an AL team?
5. What similarities do you see between effective individual coaching and AL? What adjustments do you need to make when using AL in individual coaching situations?

BEST PRACTICES FROM THE PRESENT TO THE FUTURE

The Evidence for the Effectiveness of Action Learning

10

A ction Learning (AL) has developed largely through systematic and empirically based experimentation. Revans (1980) offered some basic ideas about how to promote learning and creativity, but the method we now call AL evolved over decades of practice during which team members were encouraged to ask basic questions such as the following: (a) What is the nature of the problem? (b) What are we trying to accomplish? (c) What assumptions are we working under? (d) How do we know if things are improving? (e) What actions/behaviors achieve our desired results? (f) What actions/behaviors hamper our efforts? and (g) How can we be sure that progress is caused by a particular strategy, act, or behavior on our part? These questions, of course, are at the base of any scientific inquiry. In a sense, therefore, the examination and assessment of evidence has always been the sine qua non for effective AL practice.

We purposely chose to organize this chapter around a broader review of the evidence for the effectiveness of AL rather than solely around formal outcomes research for AL. Advances in clinical practices are invariably linked to a broader examination of evidence rather than the results of formally designed research studies.

Evidence-Based Practice

Recently, there has been considerable interest in establishing principles that ensure that the practices in clinical fields such as medicine, nursing, social work, clinical psychology, and psychotherapy are based on empirical evidence for the efficacy of the various procedures and treatments used (Carr & McNulty, 2006; Evidence-Based Working Group, 1992; Freeman & Power, 2007; Gambrill, 2003; Norcross, Beutler, & Levant, 2006; Sackett et al., 1996). The basic principle applied in evidence-based practice is that some evidence is better than other evidence—that is, evidence obtained from properly designed studies using randomization of subject assignment, using control groups and placebos and double-blind measurement of results, and using properly applied statistical analyses is better support for effective practice than evidence from subjective testimonials or even expert opinion.

The U.S. Preventative Task Force (Harris et al., 2001) uses the following classification of *evidence:*

- Level I: Evidence obtained from at least one properly designed, randomized, and controlled trial;
- Level II-1: Evidence obtained from well-designed and controlled trials without randomization;
- Level II-2: Evidence obtained from well-designed cohort or case-controlled analytic studies, preferably from more than one center or research group;
- Level II-3: Evidence obtained from multiple time series with or without intervention (e.g., longitudinal analysis for establishing causal relationships and forecasting). Dramatic results in uncontrolled trials might also be regarded as this type of evidence; and
- Level III: Opinions of respected authorities, based on clinical experience, descriptive studies, or reports of expert committees.

Level I studies, randomized clinical (or controlled) trials, are often considered the "gold standard" in establishing cause and effect relationships (Norcross et al., 2006, p. 9). The vast majority of applied research studies do not reach this aspirational goal. It is no surprise, therefore, that most of the evidence for the effectiveness of AL would be classified as Level II-2, Level II-3, or Level III. The real-life, the in situ nature of AL practice makes it difficult to carefully control or manipulate independent variables, to randomly assign subjects to treatment groups or create comparable control groups, and to develop double-blind dependent variable measurement procedures. In most cases, the only feasible research designs are quasi-experimental (Campbell & Stanley, 1966), limiting the ability to draw strong inferential conclusions from the results.

The majority of studies examining the effectiveness of AL are field studies that report differences or changes in learning or skill demonstration as a result of participation in AL designs that are part of management or leadership development programs sponsored by private and nonprofit organizations. In many cases, the data have been gathered primarily to justify the expense of the program rather than to promote scientific knowledge about AL. As a result, compromises in design or procedure are adopted that would not be acceptable in more scholarly research.

The importance and power of studies that fail to meet the stringent standards required for Level 1 evidence should not be discounted, dismissed, or ignored. Despite the limitations and design flaws that result, these studies add to the evidence available to evaluate the effectiveness of AL. In the aggregate, these studies can be powerful—just as the power of the single, relatively slow and weak personal computer is leveraged and greatly amplified when combined with other personal computers in a parallel computing network. Indeed, the enormous computer network used by Google to support its sophisticated search process is based on the lowly personal computer connected in parallel with other slow, simple, and cheap PCs rather than on more powerful server-grade computers, much less the "big iron" computers previously preferred in corporate settings.

It is likely that the effectiveness of AL will be established only when enough data gathered through Level II-3 designs have been reported to enable meta-analyses[1] to estimate the effect of AL on dependent variables such as individual, team, and organizational learning, and the value of the resultant solutions. The accumulation of evidence gathered in these less-than-ideal circumstances will add to or detract from the confidence that practitioners have in the efficacy of AL.

---

[1]Meta-analysis combines the result of several studies that address a set of related research hypotheses. By pooling studies, the various biases and errors of measurement caused by flaws or limitations in experimental design (e.g., small sample size, restriction in range of the dependent variable) can be corrected so that a meaningful estimate of the effect size of the independent variables can be made. The effect size of a variable is commonly indexed by dividing the differences in means of a variable (usually, but not always, the dependent variable) by a measure dispersion (usually the standard deviation of the variable in question). Glass, McGaw, and Smith (1981) and Schmidt and Hunter (1977) are several classic references for meta-analysis that lay out most of the important principles and assumptions employed in meta-analysis.

Evaluation of Training and Development Programs

Kirkpatrick's (1998) four-level model for training evaluation has been used extensively to assess the outcomes of training and development (T&D) programs for the past 20 to 30 years.

Level 1—Participant reactions to the training. Evaluations at this level ask participants or students what they think or feel about the training program. Evaluations at this level are easily obtained and have been termed "happy face" evaluations because they primarily assess how well participants liked the training program.

Level 2—Participant learning. In evaluations at this level, participants are assessed to establish how much they learned from the program. In many cases, participants are asked to make a self-assessment of how much they learned about the process or issue that is the focus of the training. The information or knowledge that is to be provided in the training is usually identified in the learning goals established by the curriculum developers. Less frequently, participants are tested using assessment tools keyed to the predetermined learning goals to get an objective measure of how much the participants learned as a result of the program.

Level 3—Participant application of what they learned to the workplace. Evaluations at this level look for evidence that the training program actually resulted in improvements in the behaviors identified in the learning goals. Commonly, organizations use 360-degree survey feedback assessment tools (data obtained from the participant, their bosses, subordinates, and peers or colleagues) to establish whether people working with participants notice any changes in behavior that could be associated with the training goals. Evaluations at this level are much more difficult to obtain because the desired behaviors are usually expressed in the workplace. Classroom simulations are, at best, only approximations of the conditions that participants will experience in the real world. The difficulty in translating training from the classroom to the time and situation during which it will be needed in the workplace has been a long-standing issue in designing effective training programs. Evaluation models that assess behavioral outcomes in situ are therefore more compelling and more difficult to develop.

Level 4—Organizational results. Ultimately, organizations would like to determine whether any program, training or otherwise, has a positive impact on its strategic goals. One of the great difficulties in assessing training or development programs for impact is that the link between training and organizational results is not very direct. Although improving the skills and optimizing the talents of organizational members contribute to profitability and mission success, there are other factors, many of which are more powerful, that determine organizational success. In addition, it is usually impossible to develop a well-designed study (e.g., with randomized assignment of subjects, control groups) to test the impact on the strategic goals of the organization of any particular training program.

A number of problems have been noted with the Kirkpatrick model for evaluating the results (Tamkin, Yarnall, & Kerrin, 2002). Primary among the complaints is that the four-step model does not provide the necessary intervening variables that affect outcomes and that would be necessary to build a robust model for program evaluation (Holton, 1996). Holton argued that the Kirkpatrick model is really a taxonomy of programmatic outcomes that, although useful as gross metrics for making organizational decisions, is not adequate for developing and testing the kinds and levels of hypotheses that would allow a true evaluation of whether and how an organizational intervention is effective.

Although we agree with this critique of the Kirkpatrick four-level model, we cannot ignore that most organizations and many researchers have used and continue to use this model to evaluate the effectiveness of training programs. Although we might prefer a more robust model of evaluation, as Holton (1996) and Phillips (1997) recommended, much of the evidence for AL has been reported using this model. In other references to the Kirkpatrick model, we try to make connections back to the evidence-based practice model to indicate how strong the evidence is in terms of making causal inferences. As Holton (1996) noted, however, even when causal relationships are established, the Kirkpatrick model still leaves the reader in the dark regarding the intervening variables at work to create the somewhat superficial effects measured by the Kirkpatrick model. Although the human resources (HR) function commonly uses the Kirkpatrick model to evaluate effect, line business managers prefer return-on-investment (ROI) analyses to estimate the value of any particular program or decision that the organization invests in. Because ROI analysis is the lingua franca for business, senior leadership frequently asks the HR and training functions to provide an ROI analysis for training and development. Because one of the outputs of AL is a business or organizational solution, AL is one of the few T&D initiatives for which an ROI can reasonably be estimated.

Conclusion-Oriented Versus Decision-Oriented Inquiry

Cronbach and Suppes (1969) introduced a useful distinction between traditional scholarly research and program evaluation. In most cases, the purpose of scholarly research is to draw conclusions with respect to research hypotheses. In recent years, exploratory research has increasingly been conducted by researchers attempting to increase scientific knowledge regarding the relationships between independent and dependent variables. In either case, the aim of the research is to identify and ultimately confirm or disconfirm hypotheses. In contrast, the primary aim of program evaluation is to provide evidence that can be used to make decisions about whether the program is worth continuing or what parts of the program work well or need modification. This certainly is the primary aim of most organizations when they conduct program evaluations.

These same programs are also seen as opportunities to test, or at least explore, hypotheses that would be included in a traditional research study. The mixed, and sometimes crossed, purposes of the program evaluation process usually introduce compromises that create weaknesses in any subsequent analyses designed to confirm hypotheses. For instance, organizations seeking to establish the value of a particular program may not see the value or even desire random assignment of participants or see the point in creating a control group. A number of the studies reported here faced these challenges; the evaluation designs reflected the reality that the evaluation process was primarily designed to help the organization make decisions rather than draw conclusions.[2]

Quantitative Versus Qualitative Models for Data Collection

Traditionally, researchers have insisted on using quantitative analysis for serious research. Because many of the variables (particularly independent variables) are not directly observable, psychology and the behavioral sciences have developed appropriate methodologies for creating scales to convert continuous as well as discrete variable data into quantitative scales. Many of the studies reported here provide at least some quantita-

---

[2]It is interesting to note that the AL process itself reflects these mixed motives. The questions that the coach asks sometimes are aimed at generating reflection about the on-going process with the purpose of encouraging team members to test their hypotheses about what is going on while at other times the questions are aimed at making decisions about the value of individual, team, and organizational behavior so that team members can decide which behaviors to increase, to continue, and to stop or reduce.

tive data. A subset of these studies provide inferential (i.e., *t* tests) as well as descriptive (i.e., means, standard deviations, Pearson correlation coefficients) analysis of the data.

The difficulty in providing or developing quantitative scales for phenomenological data has made qualitative analysis of data more popular. With the availability of better methodology for treating qualitative data (Patton, 1990, 2002), a number of studies, even dissertations, rely heavily upon qualitative data analysis. As qualitative analysis methodology improves and becomes more sophisticated, we expect this trend to continue to increase in the future.

Confirmatory Versus Exploratory Research Designs

Confirmatory research designs use the scientific method to confirm or disconfirm hypotheses about the relationships between independent and dependent variables. When the differences between treatment conditions are large enough, the null hypothesis (i.e., that no relationship exists between variables) can be rejected, and the alternative experimental hypothesis can be confirmed. Very powerful tests of inference (e.g., *t* tests, analysis of variance, chi-square) have been developed to establish that the chances of differences this large or larger occurring by chance are within acceptable limits (generally, less than 5 times out of 100).

Using confirmatory research designs is the only acceptable method for establishing causality (i.e., demonstrating that variations in a particular independent variable reliably cause changes in a particular dependent variable). Although researchers would like to design studies that establish causality, the methodological requirements are usually quite high in the behavioral sciences. It is generally not feasible or practical to design field studies that randomly assign subjects, use double-blind measurement procedures, or include control groups. It is often possible, however, to design quasi-experimental research designs (Campbell & Stanley, 1966) that yield quantitative data and use inferential statistics but lack one or more requisites for a classic experimental design. These results can be interpreted as implying but not as demonstrating causality. Although one carefully designed experimental design can demonstrate causality (Level 1 in evidence-based practice protocol), it may take a number of quasi-experimental studies demonstrating similar directional results to demonstrate that a causal link exists between variables.

Exploratory research designs, in contrast, do not develop hypotheses to be tested. Rather, researchers using an exploratory design identify the variables that seem to be structurally related in a phenomenon, but they do not make hypotheses about the relationships between these variables. Instead, researchers search for patterns through graphical, statistical, or logical inference to identify hypotheses that can later be tested through confirmatory research designs. Because of the relative lack of prior research, a number of studies examining the governing or independent variables in the AL process use exploratory research designs.

Classification of Research Designs

The reported research studies related to AL that provide a primary analysis of research data (as opposed to a literature review of results) have been sorted into the four cells of a matrix created by classifying research according to the qualitative/quantitative data analysis and confirmatory/exploratory research design distinctions (see Figure 10.1).

QUANTITATIVE/CONFIRMATORY DESIGNS

These studies collect quantitative data that are used to test relevant hypotheses. In addition to scholarly research generated by academic researchers and student dissertations, many studies using the Kirkpatrick outcomes assessment approach (1998) are included in this category. The research questions tend to be more concrete and basic, but they are nonetheless hypotheses to be tested:

FIGURE 10.1

	Confirmatory	Exploratory
Quantitative	5	9
Qualitative	2	7

Frequency of research designs for reviewed research studies

- Was the program successful in achieving the learning goals?
- Was new learning translated into improved behavior on the job?
- Did the program have a significant impact on achieving strategic goals?

In some cases, the results are analyzed using statistical tests of inference, but in other cases only descriptive statistics are presented as confirmatory evidence. Studies of this sort were considered confirmatory not because they presented experimental hypotheses to be tested but because they posed specific questions about the process for participants to evaluate. Although studies lacking inferential testing can only provide weak evidence for confirmation of hypotheses, the resulting data can provide support for studies reporting more conclusive results.

QUANTITATIVE/EXPLORATORY DESIGNS

Studies of this type collect data about variables that a priori would appear to have some significance for the phenomenon being studied. The variables to be studied are usually suggested by earlier research or the opinions of experts or skilled practitioners. Researchers frequently provide surveys and/or psychological/behavioral inventories for participants and organizational stakeholders to complete regarding the process being studied. Researchers use these data to identify relationships, patterns, and associations that can be tested in subsequent research.

QUALITATIVE/CONFIRMATORY DESIGNS

Qualitative/confirmatory studies use nonmetric, qualitative data to test hypotheses. Although designs of this sort are conceptually possible, they are difficult to conduct. Hypothesis testing has some basic requirements that are hard to attain with qualitative data: agreement on the definitions of key independent and dependent variables, reliability of measurement and the validity of key measures, a limited number of statistical procedures for qualitative data, and the difficulty in developing double-blind data reduction and management. These are formidable obstacles, and only a few studies reported here use this data analytic model.

QUALITATIVE/EXPLORATORY DESIGNS

Most qualitative/exploratory designs are case studies that analyze and organize behavioral data (often verbal transcripts of participant or interviews during and after a program or event), creating themes or categories. The themes or categories that are generated are often compared with theoretical models to develop possible explanations for the observed behavior. In a few cases, quantitative/confirmatory designs report additional qualitative data based on open-ended course comments and evaluations that are used to generate hypotheses and suggestions for future research.

Figure 10.1 presents the observed frequencies for the four methodological designs described above. Please note that some studies ($n = 16$) were included in two categories if they had both a confirmatory and exploratory focus in reporting results.

The fact that the majority of the studies are exploratory rather than confirmatory reflects the fact that AL practice was developed based on experimentation (i.e., what works, what does not work, how can performance be improved). By encouraging teams and individuals to observe and reflect upon the effects of behavior, incremental adjustments and modifications of practice and practice principles were instituted to improve performance. In this process, theory evolved more on the basis of observation of cause and effect in practice than as a result of rigorous testing of principles before modifying practice. As in many practice-based disciplines, researchers are now trying to understand the governing variables that account for the observed large practice effect.

The Research Questions

The studies reviewed in this section address four major research questions.

1. *Does AL increase individual, team, and organizational learning and performance?* This question requires a confirmatory design with the null hypothesis being that changes in learning and performance levels can be attributed to chance variation alone. Assessment of improvement in learning corresponds to Level 2 in Kirkpatrick's model (1998). Assessment of performance would correspond to Level 3 in the Kirkpatrick model. Two reference standards are possible. Does AL improve learning and performance compared with no training or treatment? Does AL improve learning and performance more effectively than alternative T&D approaches? Only one study reported here (Jennings, 2002) addressed the effectiveness of AL in relation to alternative developmental approaches. There was limited use of inferential statistics to establish whether improvements in learning or performance are large enough to reject the null hypothesis that the observed effect was due to chance variation. Several studies concluded that their predictions were supported without providing tests of significance. These would obviously be considered weak confirmatory designs.

2. *What changes in learning and performance are observed as a result of an AL experience?* Studies addressing this question are exploratory

designs because the authors do not hypothesize in advance what the nature of these changes will be.

3. *How does AL work? What governing variables determine how well AL works?* Most of these studies use exploratory research designs reflecting a lack of prior consensus on what the most important independent variables are and how they are related to performance improvement. Several studies address this question as a secondary analysis after confirmatory analyses of other hypotheses.

4. *What are the significant success factors for conducting successful AL programs?* This question does not fit neatly into Kirkpatrick's classification system because it focuses on the necessary conditions for success rather than on the outcomes of a training process. This question reveals the weakness in the Kirkpatrick classification system: the lack of attention to intervening variables. The Kirkpatrick model is geared toward answering the questions related to how successful a program is in terms of enjoyment, learning, behavior change, and results. Analysis of critical success factors, on the other hand, asks the question: What factors are most important in determining whether a program is successful or not?[3]

Two important questions were not addressed by the reviewed research.

1. *Do increases in learning, changes in attitudes, and improvement in skills have a significant impact on organizational results?* This question corresponds to Level 4 in Kirkpatrick's model (1998). As noted earlier, measuring the outcomes of training programs in terms of organizational performance has always been difficult. The business metric that addresses results most directly is ROI. Although calculation of ROI is quite feasible for AL projects, no studies were found that provided estimates of the ROI. The studies reported here had difficulty demonstrating a link between increases in individual, team, and organizational learning and performance and business or organizational results. Conducting ROI studies for AL will go a long way toward demonstrating the value of AL to organizational leadership.

---

[3]A statistical analogy for this distinction might be the difference between multiple regression analysis and discriminant function analysis. Multiple regression analysis describes the relationship of a set of predictor variables to a criterion variable. The output of this process provides indices that represent the independent contribution of each variable to prediction (e.g., β-weights). Discriminant function analysis, on the other hand, reverses the logic of multiple regression analysis by assessing how important each predictor variable is in determining whether a subject or event falls into several categories. In discriminant function analysis, the β-weight reflects the importance of any specific variable to proper classification of a subject or event.

2. *What are the sizes of the learning and performance effects that can be attributed to AL?* Note the subtle but important distinction from question 1. Here the issue is not whether the differences are statistically significant. Significance is often as much a function of the size of the sample as the size of the effect.[4] Rather, the question here is whether the size of the effect is sufficiently large to justify the usage of the procedure. There are several statistical ways to estimate effect size: (a) The size of the effect can be computed as a comparison of treatment differences with a measure of dispersion such as standard deviations[4], or (b) The size of the effect can be estimated as the percentage of total variation in the dependent variable accounted for by the independent variable(s) (η^2). Meta-analysis is an excellent method for estimating the effect size for a particular process or procedure and regression analysis can provide useful estimates of the percentage of variance that can be attributed to a particular variable. Unfortunately, too few studies have been conducted that yield data that can be used to estimate effect size through either procedure.

ROI can also be used to estimate effect size. Businesses use the ratio of the amount of financial return in relation to the investment required as an index to determine whether investment in a particular product, process, or initiative reaches a certain level ("hurdle" in business lingo) and is, therefore, worthwhile. Cost/benefit ratios also provide a measure of effect size.

Many of the research studies described in the following section have serious methodological weaknesses. Just as in meta-analysis, however, the measurement errors across studies tend to be uncorrelated so that broad trends become apparent when enough studies, however flawed, are reported.

---

[4]The interested reader is referred to the classic text on the treatment of effect sizes rather than chance variation. Cohen (1988) introduced the concept of power analysis to determine whether a research design has sufficient "power" to detect a difference between treatments when a real difference between treatments exists in the larger population. Most tests of inference provide protection against Type I errors—drawing a false conclusion that a treatment difference exists when it really does not in the larger population. Power analysis examines Type II risk—the probability of a false conclusion when a treatment difference does exist in the larger population. A key determinant of power is the size of the treatment sample. When the sample size is too small, even a fairly large effect size will not result in a disconfirmation of the null hypothesis. A key concept in power analysis is the *effect size,* as indexed by the size of the treatment differences in relation measures of dispersion such as standard deviations. Cohen suggested that a small effect size is one in which the size of the treatment effect/standard deviations of the variables were equal to .10. Medium effect sizes were suggested to be about .30 and large effect sizes .50 or larger. It is important to understand that effect size is not synonymous with significance level. Results with effect sizes of .10, .30, and .50 can all be significant at the same level of significance depending solely on the size of the sample used in the study.

EVIDENCE

Question 1: Does Action Learning Increase Learning and Performance?

Leadership

Raudenbush, Marquardt, and Walls (2003), using a quantitative/confirmatory design, reported improvement in 9 out of 10 leadership competencies using a pre–post assessment design in conjunction with a 12-month AL program that was part of a leadership development program for senior managers in a large federal agency. A 360-degree survey instrument was used to measure changes in behavior over the course of the program. Unfortunately, because of a small sample size, no tests of inference were conducted to determine whether these differences reached acceptable levels of significance. The two competencies displaying the largest increases on the 360-degree survey were conflict management and continual learning.

S. H. Kim (2003), using quantitative/confirmatory design, did not get full support for his prediction that an AL process would produce increased transformational leadership behavior. Participants, enrolled in a leadership development program within a multinational high tech/telecommunications corporation in Asia and Australia, completed a leadership behavior and characteristics inventory, The Leadership Profile (Sashkin, Rosenbach, & Sashkin, 1998), before and after an AL program. Contrary to predictions, participant self-ratings for four transformational leadership behaviors (communication leadership, credible leadership, caring leadership, and creativity) showed a decrease (two, credible leadership and caring leadership, showed a significant decrease) over the course of the AL program. Kim did report increases in two of the four transformational leadership characteristics scales—follower-centered and visionary leadership (although he reports no tests of significance for the increases in these two subscales).

Although Kim believed that these results provided only weak support for his overall hypothesis that AL improves the transformational leadership skills of participants, these results are consistent with our proposal that AL improves collaborative or shared leadership skills. Transformational leadership is still a hierarchical model of leadership, emphasizing the behavior of the leader and considering followers only in relation to the leader's influence or impact on them. Although transformational leaders make a greater effort to engage subordinates psychologically, it is still a top-down model. AL, in contrast, emphasizes bottom-up leadership. Effective leaders in systems in which shared leadership is emphasized learn when and how to follow as well as when and how to lead. If AL promotes collaborative or shared leadership, then it should not be surprising that transformational leadership behavior becomes less prominent. Furthermore, one would expect that an AL experience would promote an environment that values follower-centered and visionary leadership.

Jennings (2002) compared the effectiveness of three leadership development strategies:

- The case method—Cases were developed to help students to gain a better understanding of situations, concepts, and techniques. Some cases involved making organizational diagnoses and recommendations for action.
- Simulation of a new business venture—The scope of the task included identifying a business opportunity; researching markets; defining the product/service offering and a competitive strategy; defining the resources, systems, and organizational requirements; developing financial reports; and identification of principles risks and contingencies.
- A consultancy project—Students acted in a consultancy role by developing a proposal for a product or process innovation of strategic importance to the company. These AL teams were self-organizing and did not include a trained AL coach or organizational sponsor.

All three of the methods are experiential, requiring students to actively participate in analysis and solution generation. A major difference between the case study and simulation approaches in comparison with the consultancy project approach was that the learning goals and curriculum framework were predetermined in the case study and simulation programs whereas learnings from the consultancy project program were inductively derived and determined by the students.

Jennings reported that the simulation model was more successful in developing leadership skills than the case study method that, in turn, was more effective than the project consultancy method. The results from this study demonstrated that simply putting people into teams and giving them an important problem is not the most effective way to develop leadership. Without some structuring process, participants will likely use the leadership skills they already possess, skills that have been reinforced and that are responsible for their current success, rather than take risks to broaden their perspective or leadership behavior repertoire. Simulations and case studies are generally structured to challenge current assumptions and ideas and usually include questions that encourage reflection. Engaging people in difficult problems without a learning coach does not provide this structure. The fact that these problems are not routine and have no known solution often increases participant stress, resulting in more cautious and less risky solutions.

Conflict Management

Hii (2000) conducted a quantitative/confirmatory analysis of case study data of 36 Malaysian managers participating in an AL program. Hii predicted that managers would learn more effective ways to handle conflict as the result of an AL experience. Although Hii used a quasi-experimental design, he was able to build in a control group into his design. He administered the Rahim Organizational Conflict Inventory II (ROCI-II) (1983) to participants before and after the AL project. The ROCI-II is modeled after the Thomas-Kilmann Conflict Mode Instrument (1974) and provides a profile of an individual's behavior preferences for managing interpersonal conflict. Hii reported that, as predicted, participants demonstrated an increase in the preference for integrative solutions (i.e., win/win solutions that reflect both concern for self-interests and concern for the interests of others). Again, these results are consistent with our proposal that AL fosters collaboration and shared leadership.

Question 2: What Changes in Learning and Performance Are Observed as a Result of an Action Learning Experience?

Leadership

Lee (2005) gathered both quantitative and qualitative data at four data points for 16 participants in four AL teams (sets) designed to develop leadership skills in managers in a Korean multinational corporation. Lee used a leadership model, visionary leadership theory (VLT; Sashkin, 1998; Sashkin & Sashkin, 2003), that was equivalent to the model used by Kim (2003).[5] Lee used the definitions from VLT to develop 10 questions that assessed participant perceptions of improvement on each of the leadership scales. Each participant was asked to complete the VLT questionnaire four times over the course of the AL program—three times during the 6½ weeks of the AL program and again 3 weeks after completion of the AL project. Nine of the 16 participants also agreed to be interviewed regarding their experiences in the AL project 3 weeks after the completion of the AL project.

At each survey point, participants were asked, using the VLT questionnaire, to rate the degree of improvement in relation to the 10 leadership behaviors and characteristics since the last sampling point (or the start of the program in the case of the first survey). In this way, Lee obtained longitudinal evidence of leadership changes within an AL experience. Participants reported consistent improvement (ratings of *to a*

---

[5]The VLT-derived questionnaire incorporates the same aspects of behavior and personal characteristics related to transactional and transformational leadership behaviors and characteristics that were used by Y. Kim (2003).

little extent or better) in all 10 leadership elements across the four survey points. Lee reported mean improvement ratings for 9 of 10 leadership elements in the range between *to some extent* and *to a great extent* at the third sampling point (at the end of the AL project). Significantly, the improvements in leadership were retained 3 weeks after the end of the AL project (in fact, improvement ratings increased for four of the elements—reward, communication, confident, and follower-centered leadership).[6]

The leadership elements receiving the highest ratings at the end of the AL project and 3 weeks later were communication (3.88, 4.00), follower-centered (3.56, 3.88), reward (3.56, 3.69), confident (3.44, 3.56), and caring (3.75, 3.56) leadership. The participants rated their improvement using the following definitions of these leadership elements:

- communications leadership—communicating information and opinions so that they are easily understood and can be acted upon, and listening to what others say;
- follower-centered leadership—delegating responsibility and discretion to others in work activities, and trusting others to solve problems and make decisions without getting prior approval;
- reward leadership—providing praise, recognition, or reward for good performance and significant achievements;
- confident leadership—possessing and demonstrating self-confidence; and
- caring leadership—demonstrating respect, concern, and care for others.

We believe that most readers would recognize these behaviors as being fundamental for developing collaboration and establishing shared leadership. The reader will also likely perceive a balance between the four fundamental leadership styles identified by Pearce et al. (2003). Exhibit 10.1 compares the leadership elements employed by Kim (S. H. Kim, 2003) using the Sashkin and Sashkin (2003) leadership dimensions and the leadership style model proposed by Pierce et al. (2003).

It is also interesting to note that participants gave the lowest improvement rating to creative leadership (2.94, 2.75). This finding would seem to run counter to expectations because a purported strength of AL is that the process develops creative solutions. Closer inspection of the definition that participants were using to rate improvement in this leadership element provides a possible explanation for this counter-intuitive finding. *Creative leadership* was defined as "creating opportunities for others to

---

[6]These data are in stark contrast to the experience of most participants in training programs. A joke among training professionals is that the half-life of a management training program is 3 hours—about the time it takes the system to send the clear message that the new methods or ideas are not "how we do things around here!"

EXHIBIT 10.1

Leadership Style in Relation to Leadership Element

Leadership style (Pearce et al., 2003)	Leadership element (Sashkin & Sashkin, 2003)
Directive leadership	Confident and communications leadership
Transactional leadership	Reward and communications leadership
Transformational leadership	Communications, confident, caring, and follower-centered leadership
Enabling leadership	Follower-centered, caring, and communications leadership

learn from and take risks." Participants may have seen the problem itself as providing learning opportunities rather than anything they were doing themselves.

Raudenbush et al. (2003) collected qualitative data through telephone interviews after the AL program described earlier. Results from the interviews indicated that the participants believed that their skills grew in the eight leadership competencies stressed in the program (interpersonal skills, team building, decisiveness, conflict management, continual learning, oral communications, creativity and innovation, and integrity and honesty). The three skills identified most in the interviews as improving most were communicating, team building, and conflict management. Participants gained a greater appreciation for how important communication is for leadership—asking questions and providing feedback, clarification, calmness, and patience. Participants also learned the importance of focusing on common concerns and mutual support, and how asking questions to understand the views and positions of others can be a more effective conflict resolution strategy than straightforward confrontation.

The qualitative data obtained by Raudenbush et al. (2003) are largely consistent with the results reported in the later study by Lee (2005). Although a broad spectrum of leadership skills were developed, communication, interpersonal, and conflict resolution skills were most improved through the AL process.

Acker-Hocevar, Pisapia, and Coukos-Semmel (2002) provided case data on six AL projects conducted with 30 doctoral education students. In this qualitative/exploratory design, the authors reviewed learning journals, team process survey reports, evaluations by staff and clients, and focus group interviews. Using coding, sorting, and analytical methodology recommended by Patton (1990) for qualitative data, the authors reported the following outcomes:

- AL reinforces the development of basic leadership skills;
- AL builds basic leadership skills in a safe environment;
- AL reinforces managerial, transformational, political, and professional aspects of leadership; and

▪ AL allows participants to understand themselves as developing leaders.

This study is a good example of research that would fall somewhere between Level II-3 and Level III in the Harris et al. (2001) classification of evidence—well short of the standards desired for rigorous research. Yet, these data do provide some evidence that AL is an effective methodology for developing leadership. In addition, these data support our contention that AL develops a broad spectrum of leadership skills, including transactional and transformational leadership.

In another Level II-3/III (Harris et al., 2001) qualitative/exploratory design, Weinstein (1997) reported data from 69 individuals who participated in AL. Results indicated that participants learned how to become better managers—how to build better relationships with staff, how to motivate staff, as well as how to delegate. They also improved their consulting, facilitating, communications, and networking skills.

Coaching Skills

Choi (2005) used both quantitative/exploratory and qualitative/exploratory approaches to examine the impact of AL on the skills considered critical to effective coaching: relationship building, setting and communicating clear expectations, observational skills, analytical skills, listening skills, questioning skills, feedback skills, and creating a supportive environment. The data from this study were collected from surveys and interviews completed with 19 upper middle-level managers in a Korean financial company. Although no tests of inference were conducted, Choi reported improvement in all eight coaching skills. Skills displaying the highest degree of improvement were listening, creating a supportive environment, questioning, and relationship building. Furthermore, Choi reported that each of the six elements of AL identified by Marquardt (2004) contributed to improvements in these coaching skills.

Question 3: How Does Action Learning Work? What Governing Variables Determine How Well Action Learning Works?

The Governing Variables

Following the AL program described earlier, Lee (2005) conducted interviews with a subset ($n = 9$) of the total sample, who provided additional qualitative data on the "active ingredients" in the participant learning process. Lee asked participants to identify the aspects or activities that they believed had the biggest impact on changes in leadership behavior or ability. These interviews were conducted 3 weeks after the conclusion of the projects.

As can be seen in Figure 10.2, participants attribute almost half of the development of leadership capability to the questioning/reflection process that is the core of the AL method. Another 40% of the development of leadership capabilities was attributed to the specific activities the team took (21%) and the ability of the team to work collectively rather than individually (19%).

Lee (2005) also asked interview participants to identify aspects and activities of the AL program that had little impact in changing leadership behavior or ability. Four themes were identified in relation to this question: high workload, time limitations, the makeup of the group, and insufficient AL team coaching skills.

Raudenbush et al. (2003) interviewed participants 12 months after the completion of an AL program to identify which aspects of the process had been most effective in developing their leadership skills. Participants identified the following AL processes as contributing the most to improvement in their leadership skills:

- by learning from each other,
- by taking action,

FIGURE 10.2

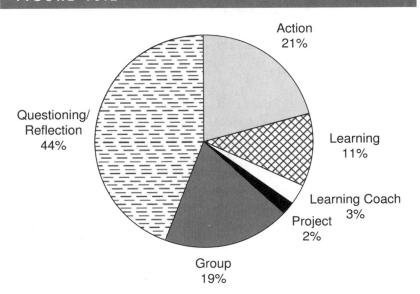

Contribution to leadership development by aspect of action learning process

- by asking questions,
- by listening, and
- by observing.

The data obtained by Raudenbush et al. (2003) are largely consistent with the list of facilitative processes generated by the participants reported in Lee's (2005) research.

In an earlier study, Butterfield (1999), using a qualitative/exploratory design, analyzed documents and interview data from 17 U.S.-based, first-line supervisors in a multinational financial services firm who participated in AL projects for the purposes of leadership development. Butterfield interviewed participants using a critical incidents approach (What were the events or behaviors during the program that led to personal learning?) 4 months after the AL program ended and a year later (only 10 of the 17 were available or agreed to be reinterviewed). The predominant learning modality reported by participants was thought-provoking questioning. Of the pool of participants interviewed 4 months after the program ended, 94% identified questioning as being a primary learning facilitator. A year later, participants had generalized the ability to ask good questions to solve a wide variety of problems in their lives. Half of the participants interviewed a year later believed that they had improved or reinforced their questioning skills. Participants identified the following questions as being particularly useful:

- What would happen (if you tried . . .)?
- Now what?
- So what?
- Who cares and why do they care?
- What is getting in the way (of solving the problem)?
- Have you thought about . . .?

One interesting finding was that although participants could not accurately recall what the AL process was a year later, they were able to be very specific about what they learned. This finding suggests that the approach to learning and solving problems learned in the AL process becomes integrated into continuous everyday learning and problem-solving behavior rather than being used as a specific external process or tool.

Four months after the program ended, 71% of participants identified the diversity of the participants as a critical learning factor. Feeling a personal sense of well-being (70%) and having a safe environment to work (53%) were also recognized as significant factors facilitating learning at this time.

A significant percentage of the participants (71%) indicated that the AL process also had an important impact on the development of their management style. Participants indicated that as managers they would emphasize the asking of thought-provoking questions, collaborating, seeking feedback, and seeking the input of stakeholders and peer managers.

Van Schuyver (2004) interviewed 22 masters' degree students who had participated in AL programs sponsored jointly by Virginia Commonwealth and Georgia State Universities. In this qualitative/exploratory design, Van Schuyver asked participants what they had learned in the five phases of AL that he believed were common to all AL programs: start-up, during AL sessions, during adjunctive class meetings, during meetings with the project client or sponsors, and during the solution presentation and program closing process.

Open-ended questions were asked to determine what, if any, learning had occurred in each of the five phases. Van Schuyver (2004) reported that all participants learned during the programs (these ratings appeared quite subjective—the definition of learning appears to have been left to each participant to determine for herself or himself), and that learning occurred in all five phases of AL identified. Most participants identified the questioning process as a major source of learning. Participants also reported metalearning (i.e., learning how to learn) as well as learning specific to the problem or to the problem-solving process.

The Coaching Role

Only 3% of participants in Lee's research (2000) mentioned the coach as a facilitative element for learning. However, there is considerable evidence that having a learning coaching is useful for gaining the full benefit of AL (Choi, 2005; Jennings, 2002; J. Kim, 2007; M. Kim, 2002; Park, 2004). The reader should also keep in mind Butterfield's (1999) finding that participants have some difficulty remembering the actual process of AL while internalizing the skills used in AL. Participants, therefore, may identify the questioning process as being the key element in AL rather than the learning coach's role in promoting questioning.

O'Neal (1999) used a qualitative/exploratory design to examine the role of the learning coach (O'Neal used the term *learning advisor*). O'Neil interviewed 23 experienced AL coaches: 6 from the United States, 13 from the United Kingdom, and 4 from Sweden. Using software to identify themes in participant responses, O'Neil reported findings relevant to the following questions:

- What skills and knowledge do learning advisors think they use?
  - process consultation skills; *not* an expert on problem or issue
  - consultation skills
  - knowledge of systems theory
- What characteristics do learning advisors need to have?
  - insightfulness
  - sensitivity

- empathy
- curiosity
- willingness to examine oneself critically
- ability to question oneself and admit uncertainty and errors
- How do learning advisors decide when they will intervene?
  - intuition/hunches, recognition of familiar patterns
  - verbal and nonverbal input
  - internal feelings/emotional reactions
  - the group's process and task work—perceived problems with the group process, reacting to group's efforts to engage the learning advisor as task facilitator
- How do learning advisors decide what kinds of interventions to make?
  - learning opportunities
  - shifts or gaps in group or problem-solving process
- What mental models do learning advisors use?
  - Kolb Learning Cycle (1984)
  - Honey-Mumford learning style (1995)
  - Action Science and ladder of inference (Argyris, Putnam, & Smith, 1985; Argyris & Schön, 1978)
  - Group development and group problem-solving models
  - Dialogue (Bohm, 1996)
  - Belbin roles (1993)
  - Tavistock model of group dynamics (Bion, 1961)
  - Gestalt theory
- What kind of interventions does a learning advisor make?
  - contracting roles and confidentiality
  - questioning
  - programmed knowledge and just-in-time learning
  - encouraging participants to give help and feedback
  - helping group deal with emotions
  - making work more explicit and concrete
  - transfer of learning
  - enable learning
  - challenge the group
  - model learning advisor skills
- How does the espoused theory of learning advisors compare to the actual theory in use? (Argyris & Schön, 1978)
  - Learning advisors' espoused theories, and in some cases their actual practices, are affected by how they believe learning takes place in AL and by their mental models or metaphors for practice.
  - Learning advisors using mental models are more likely to have theories in use that match their espoused theories of practice.

O'Neil's findings reflect similarities and contrasts in the practice of AL coaches in the United States and Europe just prior to 2000. Although most, if not all, coaches recognize the primacy of questioning and critical reflection and focus their interventions on process rather than content or product, some disagreement remains over how permissible it is for learning coaches to take on task facilitation or training roles.[7] It is our position that learning coaches can work most effectively by asking questions only and having confidence that the team's reflections will allow it to develop effective solutions. Although there may be some exceptions to this principle (see chap. 5, this volume), we believe that virtually all learning and task objectives can be met by following the ground rule that "statements can only follow questions." We have seen too many learning coaches inhibit learning when tempted (or seduced) into taking on a task facilitation role rather than challenging the team to solve its own problems by asking the right questions.

Learning Styles

De Haan and de Ridder (2006) examined the impact of AL on the four learning styles described by Kolb (1984): divergent, assimilative, accommodative, and convergent. These authors had a diverse group of 126 professionals and managers from 39 mostly European organizations who had participated in AL programs complete a 32-item questionnaire with four scales based on the Kolb learning style model (divergent, assimilative, accommodative, and convergent[8]). For instance, one of the questions used to assess the assimilating style asks respondents to rate the degree of their agreement to the statement, "In AL, I learn to link things to knowledge I have gained before." Nearly 75% of respondents had completed the questionnaire from 3 months to 2 years after participating in AL.

Highest ratings were obtained for items in the divergent scale: receiving valuable feedback, concentrating on the crux of the issue at hand, and using methods that resulted in an in-depth exploration of the issues. The average respondent ratings were between *yes* and *definitely yes* (3.51, 3.45, 3.54) for these items. Respondents only disagreed (i.e., ratings of *definitely*

---

[7]For instance, Rimanoczy (1999) recommended that learning coaches take a more active and directive role at times. She indicated that the learning coach should take the lead in making observations; asking questions; paraphrasing; building links between discussion points; providing feedback, concepts, and tools; and highlighting learning moments.

[8]The authors report acceptable internal reliabilities (coefficient alpha > .60) for three of the four scales (divergent, assimilative, and convergent). The lower reliability for the accommodative style was attributed to the small number of items in that scale ($n = 2$). It should be noted, however, that only the scale with more than three items was the divergent style scale ($n = 8$). On the basis of a small number of items in three of the scales, it is remarkable that the author achieved internal reliabilities as high as reported.

no = 1 and *no* = 2) with 5 items; gaining greater insights into the strong points of my functioning (2.94—divergent scale); following new routes in my work (2.80—converging scale), improving interactions with clients/customers/managers (2.58—accommodating scale), changing the way I work (2.56—converging scale).

On the basis of these results, the authors reported support for the hypothesis that AL strengthened the divergent and assimilating capabilities more than the converging and accommodating capabilities of participants. The authors did not provide any details regarding the use of learning coaches for the AL programs assessed. It is likely that participants had a variety of coaching experiences; some programs probably had no trained learning coaches, others probably used coaches who took on a task facilitator role, whereas others probably employed coaching consistent with our approach.

In any case, the results of this study underscore the importance of having someone (preferably a trained learning coach) who will pay attention to and ask application questions: What did you learn about yourself as well as about the problem? How can these learnings be applied to your work? and so forth. Otherwise, it is likely that participants will simply apply old ideas and methods more efficiently, limiting the opportunities to learn more about themselves or to apply new learnings in the work and personal lives.

Self-Efficacy and Learning

Counter to their expectations, de Haan and de Ridder (2006) also reported no difference in ratings between those who self-enrolled and those who were enrolled by the organization. Yet, additional comments to open-ended questions indicated that participants felt personally responsible for their learning. They looked to each other rather than to an external facilitator for feedback, challenge, and support. These results indicate that the AL process itself is engaging and motivating and that it is not necessary for participants to have a high degree of interest and motivation prior to the project in order for it to be a valuable learning experience. These characteristics give the AL team coach the freedom to intervene primarily when he or she recognizes a learning opportunity rather than to facilitate, protect, or motivate the team.

Co-located Versus Web-Connected Teams

The teams for most AL programs have been co-located (i.e., working face-to-face in the same location and time zone). Because global organizations routinely use virtual teams using video- and teleconferencing in conjunction with Internet-based groupware applications to connect team members, it was only natural that virtual AL methodologies would be developed. It is likely that most AL programs in global organizations conduct meetings in which some or all participants are using some technology to connect and communicate with each other from dispersed locations and time zones.

Waddill (2001), using a qualitative/exploratory design, interviewed 12 participants who participated in what the author termed *Action e-Learning.* The volunteer participants, senior government managers in offices across the United States and graduates of a university-graduate management leadership program, were assigned[9] to one of three AL teams. The teams "met" over a 5-week period with questions and responses posted on a university-managed learning management system.[10] Each participant used the team to help him or her deal with a "live" and urgent business problem. During each week-long discussion period, participants asked questions about their issue in the first half of the week and posted responses to the questions of the other team members in the second half of the week. At the beginning of the following week, each participant had the option of reframing his or her problem on the basis of the responses and feedback to their questions of the previous week. Waddill played the dual role of researcher and learning coach[11] and asked learning-focused questions using Marquardt's (2004) coaching model when appropriate.

Although this ingenious design controlled many of the important independent variables, it was a somewhat contrived process; most AL teams meeting in different locations and time zones use video- and teleconferencing to create a more continuous and contiguous flow of communication. The Waddill design is really a cross between AL and Delphi Process (Delbecq, Van de Ven, & Gustafson, 1975).

Waddill (2006) used the Kirkpatrick evaluation model (1998) to organize the interview data with participants:

1. Level 1—Participant Reaction: 10 of the 12 participants believed that the learning goals of the course had been achieved (the two participants who responded negatively dropped out of the course before its termination). Most negative responses were related to the technology; the learning management system was optimized for standard coursework, not AL.
2. Level 2—Participant Learning: All 12 participants reported that they had learned something about the problem or AL during the program.

---

[9]An effort was made to balance gender and personality types.

[10]Blackboard Learning Management System.

[11]It is not clear what efforts Waddill made to control for potential of rater bias created by assuming this dual role.

3. Level 3—Behavior: Waddill reported that an analysis of the written transcript of questions and responses indicated that they had taken significant action as a result of the AL process. In addition, 8 of the 10 participants who completed the program reported that they had taken action to solve the problem as a result of the program. Those who took action reported receiving a positive response to their efforts.

4. Level 4—Results: Waddill did not have access to organizational performance data and, therefore, was unable to observe, much less assess, any organizational results.

Waddill also reported a surprising and unexpected finding: Participants did not report that a sense of community developed as a result of the online interaction as predicted by Murphy and Cifuentes (2001). This result may be an artifact of the somewhat contrived nature of the online interaction. AL, using video- or teleconference communication, may be more successful in building an online community.

Despite the lack of a double-blind data analysis process and the rather subjective evaluations of the participants, Waddill's data serve as a starting point for a more rigorous analysis of the AL using an e-learning or virtual team format.

Question 4: What Are the Significant Success Factors for Conducting Successful Action Learning Programs?

Knox (2000), using a qualitative/exploratory design, interviewed 30 participants selected to represent a cross-section sample from 1,700 participants enrolled in an executive development program at a Fortune 10 company over a span of 3 years. Knox used the Kirkpatrick evaluation model (1998) to develop specific questions for these interviews. The author used qualitative research strategies suggested by Patton (1990) to organize the data into six themes representing success factors for conducting successful AL programs:

- Setting the context—Make sure that participants understand how the problem the team is working on is related to strategic organizational goals or challenges.
- Timely sanctioning—Make sure that the problem scope and scale described in the team's charter is sanctioned by the organization in a timely manner.
- Involvement of key decision makers—Make sure that the decision makers/stakeholders relevant to the problem are involved in the AL process. Without involvement of these decision makers/stakeholders, even good solutions are unlikely to get implemented.
- Follow-up plan—Make sure that an accountability plan for implementing the solution is developed. Individual team members need

to accept responsibility for implementation and should be accordingly rewarded for contributing to solution implementation.

- Enriching team presentations—In addition to presenting a solution to the organization, make time for the team to meet and reflect on what happened, what went well and was successful, what could be improved, and what follow-on action steps need to be taken.
- Leveraging leadership resources—Because teams included members from different businesses and business units, it is important to develop a plan to promote collaboration, communication, and knowledge sharing between AL team leaders to facilitate inter-company partnering across a decentralized and segmented global organization.

J. Kim (2007) provided accounts of a number of studies conducted in Korea to explore significant success factors for AL. M. Kim (2002), using a survey, interview, and observation data collection process for 132 new managers who participated in AL reported the following critical success factors:

- having participants who are self-directed working in a voluntary learning culture,
- having a diverse team,
- having an experienced facilitator, and
- thoroughly implementing the AL solution and reflecting on action.

Y. Kim (2003) interviewed 55 participants randomly sampled from AL programs in a Korean company and added several other success factors: the support of responsible managers, establishing appropriate goals, and having a company culture that supports AL.

Roh (2003) took a closer look at the team processes by reanalyzing videotapes and interview data for eight managers in two teams in one company.

- *Questioning:* "Why" questions were reported to be more useful than "what" questions. It was also perceived to be useful for the coach to ask questions regarding values and beliefs or that encouraged looking at problems and issues from new perspectives.
- *Action:* Practical action was perceived as more useful than theoretical proposals. Also, the team that proposes the solution should be the team that is tasked to implement it.
- *Reflection:* Roh described three kinds of useful reflections:
  - objective reflections that emphasize analytical and logical discussions that test the validity of ideas,
  - subjective reflections that provide personal meaning and interpretation of individual differences, and
  - intersubjective reflections that encourage considering issues from different perspectives or frameworks.

Park (2004) used three rounds of a Delphi Process (cf. Delbecq et al., 1975) with 13 experts on AL to identify critical success factors. Park used the following schema to organize these expert opinions:

1. Analysis and facilitating conditions
   - having the support of top management
   - establishing clear objectives
   - gaining consensus on the need for leadership programming
   - getting the support of the local organizations sending participants
2. Program development
   - having skilled facilitators
   - carefully selected participants
   - aligning the curriculum goals with the program
   - having a systematic process for selecting topics or problems
   - having an AL manual
3. Program management
   - fostering an environment of continuous learning
   - maintaining top management involvement
   - getting support for adopting team solutions in the organization
   - reviewing activity and work
   - managing team activity
4. Evaluation and review
   - presenting solutions to top management
   - recognizing top performers as future leaders
   - aligning training performance with personnel management
   - building evaluation and feedback processes to improve future programs
   - assessing the effects of the program

The evidence from these studies would probably be considered Level III in an evidence-based practice framework (Harris et al., 2001). However, the results do provide some guidance for practitioners who are designing AL programs.

J. Kim (2007) has provided the most comprehensive and statistically sophisticated study of significant success factors for AL in Korean companies. Using a quantitative/exploratory design, Kim reported data from 288 participants who completed an online survey of their AL experiences.[12] The 53 items in the survey questionnaire were based upon possible success factors identified through (a) a literature review that identified conceptual domains, and (b) in-depth, semistructured interviews with 13 AL participants nominated by the 17 companies in which the AL programs were conducted. A provisional list of 93 items was reduced to the final 53 items that were then organized into 16 success factor dimensions by an

---

[12]This represented a 22.1% response (1,304 were invited to complete the survey).

expert panel of four individuals who were skilled and knowledgeable regarding AL. Through this process, Kim was able to identify success factors perceived by scholars and outside experts as well as by initially naive participants who had directly experienced the AL process. The 288 participants who completed this survey were asked to rate their degree of agreement (on a 6-point Likert scale ranging from 1 = *strongly disagree* to 6 = *strongly agree*) with items such as "The learning coach knew when s/he needed to intervene in a team meeting." Means and rank order of means for the 16 Success Factor Dimensions are given in Table 10.1.

It should be noted that three of the four highest rated success factors (orientation, launching the AL program, and problem selection) are related to the set-up and launching of the AL program. Also of interest was the low ranking given two factors often considered critical to AL success: involvement of top management and program design. The low ranking for top management involvement is surprising to us and not in line with our experience. Nor is this finding consistent with the opinions of AL experts (presumably Korean) reported by Park (2004) or of Knox's (2000) participants who worked in a large North American-based global organization. Is it possible that this factor has a large cultural loading? Would this rating be as low with a North American or European sample? The three items keyed to this success factor (top management involvement) are (a) top management participated in the AL program, (b) top management supported the AL program, and (c) top management had high expectations of the results of the AL program. Kim does not report means and standard deviations for individual items so it is not possible to see whether all three items had low ratings or the degree of agreement on the ratings.

It is possible that a more hierarchical structure in Korean companies makes visible and tangible top management support for AL programs less important than in North American or European-based companies in which leading through the use of influence has more impact than leading through the use of authority (Cohen & Bradford, 1991; Helsing, Geragherty, & Napolitano, 2003). More research needs to be done on this factor to determine whether these surprising findings are an artifact of Kim's survey or whether other factors, such as cultural differences, explain these discrepancies in data and opinion.

In addition to the descriptive analysis reported above, Kim also conducted an exploratory factor analysis using the correlation matrix between these 53 items.[13] The resulting factor structure[14] contained two

---

[13]The ratio of variables to sample size just met the minimum level of 5 subjects/variable (item) recommended by Gorsuch (1983).

[14]The initial solution was derived using a noniterative principal axis factoring process. The final solution was refined through use of a screening test, parallel analysis, percentage of variance, and intuitive factor interpretability (Brown, 2006; Thompson, 2004; Yang, 2005). The best fit, simple structure required an oblique rotation because the two resulting factors were moderately correlated ($r = 56$).

TABLE 10.1

Means and Rank Order of Means for the 16 Success Factors

Rank	Category	Items	Mean	Sample item
1	Orientation	1	4.80	Opportunity to ask questions.
2	Team meeting	8	4.65	There was regular reflection time to enhance learning.
3	Launching the program	3	4.60	The objectives of the program were well aligned with the goals of the organization.
4	Problem selection	4	4.55	The problem was very important to the organization.
5	Participant competency	5	4.53	Participants felt responsible for the accomplishments of the program.
6	Coach role	3	4.52	The coach had abundant experience in Action Learning.
6	Data collection	3	4.52	Collected data were analyzed comprehensively.
8	Strategic alignment	4	4.48	The objectives of the program were well aligned with the goals of the organization.
9	Other stakeholder help	2	4.47	The sponsor had commitment to provide support for the success of the program.
10	Presentation	3	4.46	The solutions were presented to top management.
11	Organization's supporting structure	5	4.42	The organization shared its goals with all members.
12	Implementation	1	4.31	After sponsor's decision, the solutions were implemented with monitoring processes.
12	Evaluation	2	4.31	Measurable evaluation criteria were used in the review process of solutions.
14	Program preparation	3	4.26	A guidebook for the Action Learning program was developed for participants.
15	Top management involvement	3	4.14	Top management had high expectations of the results of the Action Learning program.
16	Program design	3	4.06	Critical design decisions, such as hiring a learning coach, ways of forming teams, program period, separation from job, individual tasks, and so forth, were made according to the objectives of the Action Learning program.

Data from *Action Learning Factors Perceived by Action Learning Participants in Companies in South Korea*, by J. Kim, 2007, unpublished doctoral dissertation, University of Minnesota.

major clusters of success factors: (a) team processes, and (b) organizational support systems.

In addition to rating the 53 potential success factor items, participants were also asked to provide their perception of impact of the AL programs along four dimensions: problem solving, individual learning, team development, and organizational change. Although both of the success factors described were significantly related to a summed measure of the impact of the AL programs, the team processes factor had a much larger loading on the impact measure ($\beta = .58$, $p < .001$) than the organizational support systems factor ($\beta = .27$, $p < .001$). In addition, both factors together explained nearly 40% of the variability in the impact measure (adjusted $R^2 = .63$, $p < .001$).

SUMMARY OF RESEARCH FINDINGS FOR ACTION LEARNING

For the purposes of this summary, research questions 1 and 2 (Does AL increase learning and performance? What changes in learning and performance are observed as a result of an AL experience?) have been consolidated into one research question: What impact does AL have upon individual, team, and organizational learning and performance? Although these two questions are different (the first question requires a confirmatory design whereas the second question often results in an exploratory design), the thrust or focus of the two questions is quite similar—the impact of AL. Because most end-users of AL are most interested in the broader impact question, we believe that this consolidation is both justified and results in a simpler summary of the research results.

What Impact Does Action Learning Have Upon Individual, Team, and Organizational Learning and Performance?

While we await more substantial evidence (ideally Level I, Level II-1, or Level II-2; Harris et al., 2001), the evidence supports the following hypotheses:

- AL develops broad executive and managerial leadership skills,
- AL is particularly effective in developing collaborative/shared leadership skills,
- AL improves the ability of managers to develop integrative, win/win solutions in conflict situations, and
- AL improves manager coaching skills.

How Does Action Learning Work? What Are the Governing Variables That Determine How Well Action Learning Works?

The following elements or factors were consistently identified as the governing variables or active ingredients in AL:

- questioning—this was most commonly identified factor by far,
- taking action,
- learning from each other,
- listening,

- diversity of team membership,
- feelings of confidence and well-being,
- safe environment, and
- coach.

What Are the Significant Success Factors for Conducting Successful Action Learning Programs?

The following summary uses the two-factor structure identified by J. Kim (2007). The distinction between team and organizational-level processes not only makes intuitive sense to us but also provides a useful structure for summarizing the research findings in relation to this question.

1. Team-Level Processes
   - skilled coaching
   - diversity and behavior of team members
   - self-directed team process
   - effective team presentations
   - review of team process
2. Organization-Level Processes
   - ensuring implementation of solutions
   - orientation—communicating alignment and importance of problem
   - problem selection
   - support of top decision makers
   - leveraging resources—communication and collaboration across the organization

Priority Research Needs

Although the research reported here provides useful evidence for the "hows" and "whys" in relation to AL, some glaring gaps in our knowledge about AL still exist:

- A definitive Level 1 (Harris et al., 2001) study that demonstrates that AL produces significant improvements in both performance and learning. This design should be a true experimental design with random assignment of subjects and double-blind assessment of results, and should include a control group. Optimally, this design should include comparisons with other leadership development methods. The experimental analysis should also include evaluation of the effect size as well as significance (Cohen, 1988) of the AL main effect.

■ A rigorous analysis of the ROI for several AL programs to address Level 4 in Kirkpatrick's (1998) assessment of training programs. Data from these analyses would be extremely useful to those promoting AL as the process of choice to hard-nosed business leaders who are more likely to be swayed by familiar business metrics rather than by sophisticated statistical analyses.

RECOMMENDED DESIGNS

We believe that it is currently practical and feasible to conduct research to fill the gaps identified above. We have included several sample designs to assist practitioners in partnering with researchers who may not be as familiar with AL so that rigorous research that qualifies as either Level 1 evidence (Harris et al., 2001) in an evidence-based practice schema or Level 4 in Kirkpatrick's (1998) assessment system can be conducted.

A Test of the Significance and Effect Size of Action Learning

Students enrolled in graduate-level business programs (e.g., MBA or, even better, Executive MBA or professional development programs because they tend to be populated by working senior managers and executives) can be recruited to participate in a study of team problem solving. Students can be randomly assigned to experimental conditions (which, in any case, is desired to improve the diversity of the team). Each team can be given the sample problem, and raters, using a double-blind procedure,[15] would evaluate the quality and creativity of the solutions each team developed. Experimenters can also vary the length of time that each team has to produce solutions to the common problem.

The set of dependent variables should include measures of team performance and individual, team, and organizational learning. Analysis of results should include tests of statistical significant (e.g., analysis of variance, analysis of covariance, multiple regression; Cohen, Cohen, West, & Aiken, 1983) as well as the effect sizes of the experimental variables (Cohen, 1988).

Researchers should also be aware of some of the pitfalls of pre–post experimental designs (Linn & Slinde, 1977) when constructing/choosing dependent variables. Wherever possible, researchers should choose measures of absolute change (e.g., ratings of the quality or creativity of a solution) or perceived degree of change (e.g., asking raters to evaluate

---

[15]Subjects do not know which condition they are in and raters do not know which condition they are assessing when analyzing independent (process) and dependent (criterion) variables.

any changes they perceive with respect to a common reference point, e.g., a point just before the experiment started) rather than using a measure of difference between pre- and postassessment of the variables in question (Goff, 1998). These procedures will help researchers avoid common pre–post measurement pitfalls and will increase the power of the design and the probability that the study will yield significant results when a significant difference due to the independent variable(s) (e.g., AL) actually exists in the real world (i.e., avoiding a Type II experimental error).

In addition to including a control group (e.g., a collection of students who did not participate in an AL program over that period), it is also desirable to create other experimental conditions that represent competing leadership development methodologies such as traditional classroom training and classes using the case study method or simulations, as well as self-managed AL (without trained learning coaches).

We believe that research programs containing the above characteristics and elements are quite practical and feasible and would go a long way toward establishing the requisite scientific evidence that, as we believe, AL is the most effective leadership development methodology available today.

Estimating the ROI for Action Learning Programs

As noted earlier, AL is unique in allowing organizations to establish the value of a program in relation to the investment. This is because AL produces specific "products" whose value can be estimated using well-accepted business analyses (i.e., ROI). As opposed to other leadership development methodologies, researchers do not have to prove that the AL program has a causal impact on global business results. Establishing this link with other programs has been very difficult to do; as a result, HR and training and development professionals have typically felt on the defensive when trying to justify the value of costly leadership development programs.

ROI is the ratio of the money gained or lost on an investment relative to the amount of capital invested. In order to calculate ROI, it is necessary to estimate the value of the solution to the organization. This process is generally beyond the capabilities of most AL professionals but is a standard procedure for finance professionals. In some cases, this procedure is direct and straightforward as in the case of the development of a product or service that can be sold to customers. In the case of innovations in the sales or marketing process, one can derive an estimate of the increases in sales revenue that can be attributed to the change. Developing an estimate of the value of innovations in organizational process or policy is a little more complex. In these cases, the value can be derived by estimating the savings in labor, supplies, time, waste, and so on, attributable to the innovation. Some marketing solutions require an estimate of the additional revenue derived by clients acquired as a result of the changes in a procedure such as marketing or sales activities. Enlisting the assistance of the finance function in this process will usually yield some good ideas for establishing the value of the solution.

The estimated value of the solution is then compared with (or divided by) the costs for the program. The sources and estimates of costs have probably already been identified in earlier budgets and proposals submitted to senior management prior to authorization of the program. The actual costs, therefore, can be collected and summed to establish the cost basis for the program.

Finance professionals will argue that this ratio is too simple and that the cost of capital needs to be considered as well as the start-up and operating cost outlays identified in a typical budget. The cost of capital includes the cost of equity (roughly, opportunity costs) as well as the cost of debt. The sum of the costs of equity and debt is termed the *discount rate* or *hurdle rate* (the return on the investment that must be achieved to pay debt costs in addition to surpassing the return that could be achieved by investing in other projects with similar returns and level of risk). Most finance functions should be able to provide researchers with the discount rate for a company at any given time. The net benefit of an investment adjusted for capital costs is termed the *present value* of the benefit.

The ROI for a program adjusted for the cost of capital can be calculated using the following formula:

$$\text{ROI} = \left(\sum_{t=1}^{n} \text{NB}^t \Big/ (1 + \text{d})^t \right) \Big/ \text{C}_0$$

Where
> t = the time periods of the program (usually in years)
> n = the total number of time periods
> d = the discount rate
> NB^t = the net benefit of AL solutions for a given time period
> C_0 = the initial cost of the program

In other words, ROI is equal to the accumulated present value of a solution over a certain period of time divided by the initial costs. The following example will illustrate this calculation. Company A develops an AL program with set-up costs of $25,000. At the end of 3 years, the company would like to calculate the ROI for the project to see if it is worth continuing. The value of program solutions was calculated by the finance department to be $50,000 for Year 1; $250,000 for Year 2; and $75,000 for Year 3. Let's assume that the yearly operating cost for the program is $25,000. Let's also assume that the discount rate or cost of capital over this period remains a constant 10%. The calculation of the RIO for this program would look like this:

$$ROI = \left(\left(\left(50{,}000 - 25{,}000\right)/\left(1 + .1\right)\right)^{1}\right) + \left(\left(250{,}000 - 25{,}000\right)/\left(1 + .1\right)^{2}\right)$$
$$+ \left(\left(75{,}000 - 25{,}000\right)/\left(1 + 1\right)^{3}\right)/25{,}000$$
$$ROI = \left(\left(25{,}000/1.1\right) + \left(225{,}000/1.21\right) + \left(50{,}000/1.33\right)\right)/25{,}000$$
$$= 9.85 \text{ or } 985\%$$

An ROI of 985% means that this project provided almost ten times the value of its initial, operating, and capital costs. This is a number that senior management understands and can use to make consequential decisions.

With a little help from the finance function, calculation of an ROI should be possible for most programs as long as the prototype solution produced by an AL team is actually put into use in the organization.

The ability to calculate an ROI is another important reason why the organization as well as the AL coaches should insist that teams produce some sort of working prototype rather than merely a set of recommendations. Recommendations without action cannot be evaluated for value. Evidence of substantial ROI will have much more impact on key decision makers than the typical outcomes measures such as Kirkpatrick (1998) can ever muster!

Reflection Questions

1. How satisfied are you with the evidence that is reported in the literature regarding
   - the effectiveness of AL,
   - the changes in performance and behavior brought about by AL,
   - how AL works, and
   - the success factors for AL?
2. If you had the resources to conduct additional research, which research questions would you pursue?
3. What applied or theoretical research would be helpful to you to promote AL in your organization or practice?
4. What would be the most effective way to approach senior leadership in your or a client organization in order to gain their support for applied or theoretical research on AL?
5. How can you join with other interested parties to jointly support AL research?

Best Practices in Planning and Implementing Action Learning Programs

11

I n chapter 7 we discussed the process of embedding Action Learning (AL) within the client organization so that the program becomes part of a larger organizational change process. We argued that AL can be a highly effective organization change intervention if structured and implemented using sound organizational development and change (OD&C) principles.

In this chapter we present a practical 10-step model for planning and implementing AL programs that incorporates the principles discussed earlier in the book. In the following sections, after a brief summary of the goals and activities in each step, we provide case examples that represent best practices for planning and implementing this phase of an AL program. In some cases, we present negative examples of how a best practice or key success factor was ignored and note the consequences.

Step 1—Initial Client Contact, Goal-Setting, and Contract Development

The need for AL can develop in several ways. Increasingly, organizations have heard great things about AL (e.g., *Business Week;* Byres, 2005) and approach internal human resources (HR), training and development (T&D) departments, or external T&D or OD&C consultants with a specific request for AL. In other cases, a client may approach these same parties for recommendations for the best way to develop leadership skills or to develop plans to solve important and strategic problems.

In either case, when the HR, T&D, or OD&C practitioners determine that AL is the best strategy (cf. Figure 2.1), the following issues need to be addressed with the client:[1]

- identification of strategic needs;
- desired "future state" (Beckhard & Harris, 1987) for the client—definition of what success would look like;
- educating/demonstrating the effectiveness and value of AL;
- client constraints—budget, time, history;
- negotiation and development of contract for the program; and
- development of a dispute resolution process.

Several case examples and best practice examples are offered here to illustrate how the AL practitioner can address some of these issues.

NATIONAL INSTITUTES OF HEALTH

One of the institutes of the National Institutes of Health (NIH)[2] contracted with a consulting firm to provide a leadership development program for the senior leaders and managers in the organization. The organization saw this program as organizational renewal and change intervention to develop the leadership skills necessary to maintain and improve the institute's performance as well as its reputation among competitors in the world of elite global health research organizations.

The proposal offered by the consulting firm demonstrated how AL was the most effective and efficient way to develop the specific skills required in a unique organizational environment in which world-class scientists were also expected to demonstrate effective leadership and management skills. In addition, leaders and managers in this team-

---

[1]Block (2000) provided an excellent model for addressing these contracting issues with clients.

[2]Other aspects of the program are discussed in chapter 7.

based organization were expected to create an environment that promoted collaboration and team creativity in a competitive organizational culture that historically rewarded individual creativity and achievement, sometimes at the expense of team and organizational success.

The institute accepted the consulting firm's proposal to include AL projects as part of a larger leadership development program that included other more traditional leadership development components. The institute was persuaded that AL added lateral/collaborative and team creativity/innovation leadership skills that complemented the hierarchical/top-down leadership skills developed in other program components.

SAMSUNG

AL at Samsung[3] was introduced to the top leadership by the Samsung Human Resources Development (HRD) Department which, in turn, had been introduced to AL through benchmarking AL at sites such as General Electric (GE), attendance at AL forums, and consultations with World Institute for Action Learning staff. Conversations between Samsung HRD staff and the CEOs of Samsung led to AL being adopted as a strategic tool to develop business leaders as well as the key approach to cultivate the next-generation leaders who will create future business opportunities and lead global management at Samsung. The AL programs were designed to last 5 months in both offline and online training and would culminate in a final presentation in which all key executives, including CEOs, would participate. Samsung CEOs would be responsible for assigning strategic issues to the AL teams.

It was determined that the Samsung HRD Center would coordinate and supervise the AL programs for top management to accomplish the following purposes:

- develop future CEOs and senior managers,
- resolve mid- and long-term issues of strategic importance facing the Samsung group of companies,
- benchmark overseas subsidiaries and leading corporations,
- organize mixed AL teams to focus on creation of future value for Samsung, and
- facilitate communication within the organization and develop learning capabilities of team members to establish a learning organization.

Samsung's AL programs require the CEO's engagement from issue selection to final evaluation to make sure that proposed solutions are

---

[3]Information for this case was submitted by Sunhee Yoo, director, Samsung, HRD Center.

actually put to work. The CEO has official communication channels open in at least four steps of the AL process, including selection of trainee and issue, CEO proposal, interim strategy development reporting, and evaluation session.

Step 2—Putting Together a Program Management Team

After goal setting, an important next step is the development of a program management team. AL, more than almost any other work-based learning, requires organizational infrastructure in the form of leadership and organizational support (Marquardt, 2004). There are three roles or role categories that are most typically involved in an AL program management team: steering committee, program champion(s), and program manager. Each of these role categories plays an important part in successful AL.

STEERING COMMITTEE

An AL steering committee is a senior level executive group that has the final authority for approving the business goals, learning strategies, and budget. Just as important, the executive committee plays an important role in shaping the organizational learning environment. Active executive sponsorship may encourage greater risk tolerance and openness. All learning requires a certain amount of courage and a risk-tolerant environment that facilitates learning and performance by encouraging team members to engage in experiment and actively challenge assumptions. Because AL proposals may challenge currently accepted management orthodoxy, an open environment visibly supported by an executive steering committee sets the stage for true inquiry.

PROGRAM CHAMPIONS

Program champions include all organization members who are directly or indirectly involved in support of the AL process. Program champions include, but are not limited to, project sponsors and managers of participants.

PROGRAM MANAGER

The program manager's role is to plan, monitor, and measure the impact and effectiveness of the AL intervention. This includes the development of a program design linking program goals with business, talent, and learning strategies. An AL program plan, which addresses scope, quality and change issues, staffing requirements, communication plans, risk, evaluation strategies, and budget requirements, is also an important responsibility of the program manager.

MANAGERS OF PARTICIPANTS

An often overlooked member of the extended AL program team is the manager of the participant. Research supports the conclusion that the key to learning transfer is in the hands of the manager (Holton & Naquin, 2000; Swanson, 1996). Participation in AL requires time away from the core job. This time is an investment by both the participant and the manager and should be acknowledged as such from the very beginning. Some of the additional organizational support factors provided by managers include timely, relevant, and specific feedback as well as appropriate and meaningful consequences (Rummler & Brache, 1995).

PROGRAM MANAGEMENT TEAM AT CHRYSLER LLC

The program management team at Chrysler LLC[4] is central to the success of their AL program.

Executive Steering Committee

The Executive Steering Committee includes the heads of all major business units, including automotive, truck, and engine manufacturing as well as heads of sales and marketing. Openness, tolerance, and executive support are all important factors that can become constrained in the face of the unprecedented change and economic pressure faced by the organization. To mitigate against these constraints at Chrysler, its executive leadership is investing in AL as a countercyclical leadership development strategy and sees development as an important retention and morale factor. Each year, members of the executive steering committee help to identify strategic projects, speak at the opening conference, meet with individual AL teams, and participate in an executive panel at the end of the AL cycle. The following is a brief outline showing how project topics are identified:

- Discuss the following question: What would you like to see participants take away from their participation on an AL team? (15 minutes)

---

[4]Information for this case was provided by Katy Caschers, leadership development manager, Chrysler LLC.

- Dialogue activity: Four flip charts are positioned around the room; each flip chart identifies one of four strategic priorities. Participants are grouped into teams at each flip chart and then asked to list prospective projects linked to the strategic initiative on the flip chart. After 15 minutes the groups are asked to move to the next flip chart. Participants are asked to group the project ideas if necessary. (60 minutes)
- AL process review, including an introduction to the sponsor role, follows the brainstorming activity. (30 minutes)
- Sponsor identification: Participants are asked to review all projects on all four flip charts and assign them a priority (1 = *most critical* to 3 = *least critical*); finally, participants are also asked to sign up for project sponsorship. (30 minutes)

Continuing projects from the previous cycle of AL are also added to the overall list. Chrysler program champions include project sponsors, participant's managers, and individual coaches.

Project Sponsors

Once a project sponsor is associated with a business issue, he or she creates a "business issue briefing" document outlining the issue, important stakeholder information, key data, and past analysis. The project sponsor then attends a 2-day, AL launch in which the issue is presented to the team. Sponsors play an extremely important role in the Chrysler AL program. Sponsors are expected to challenge the team and, through their involvement, demonstrate the importance of the task to the organization. During AL, the sponsor attends meetings at the request of the AL team, sets the requirement for innovation from the team, encourages frank dialogue and questioning, and evaluates potential solutions. Finally, as the tasks of the AL team come to a conclusion, the sponsor keeps the focus on learning and performance by holding the team accountable for both.

Managers of Participants

The manager of each participant also plays an important part in the AL process. The manager nominates his or her participant for the process. The manager, individual coach, and participant meet prior to the start of the process to identify an individual development focus. The manager is invited to attend all group events including the final presentation.

Program Manager

The program manager is responsible for overall program quality; smooth functioning; and responding to steering committee, program champion, or team member requests. He or she is also responsible for evaluation and reporting. The program manager arranges for sponsor, team member, and steering committee education; manages budgeting, events, and communication; and is the human link between all of the stakeholders in the process.

Step 3—Program Design Planning

Once top leadership has determined that AL will be a tool used by the organization to solve important, urgent problems in the organization as well as to develop its leadership, teams, and culture, a number of decisions need to be made before beginning the actual AL programs, including the following:

1. *What resources and support will be necessary and provided for the AL projects?* AL programs require a commitment of time, money, and resources if they are to result in powerful, immediate strategies for the organization. Top leadership needs to determine who will be in the AL teams (see Step 4 later in this chapter for more information about group membership) and to work with the supervisors of the group members to make arrangements for their workload to be altered and handled in their absence. Financial resources, as necessary, need to be allocated for travel and lodging and other expenses.

2. *In addition to developing strategies for an urgent problem, what other benefits of AL should be emphasized?* AL, as noted elsewhere in the book, can be used to develop leadership competencies for all or specific managers in the organization, to build high performing teams, and to change the corporate culture. IBM, for example, implemented AL into the organization to "break down silos" and to create a culture of sharing and learning. Boeing uses AL to develop its high potentials leaders. Novartis brought in AL to create powerful teams and to develop team skills among its staff.

3. *How will the AL teams be coached?* As noted elsewhere in this book, a critical ingredient for successful AL projects is the presence of a skilled AL coach. The coach may be someone from within the organization or contracted from outside the organization. It is highly recommended that the coach be trained and certified in the skills and responsibilities of AL coaching. It should also be noted that the coach should not be the problem presenter, because it is difficult, if not impossible, for someone

to be responsible for both the action and the learnings. In addition, the power of the coach's questions to delve deep into the subconscious and to positively influence the workings of the group members will be lessened.

4. *Will the AL project be undertaken and completed in a tight time frame (a day, few days or a week) or occur over a period of time?* Depending on the urgency of the problem as well as the availability of the group members, AL projects can vary in length from a few hours to a few months. The circumstances and environment may be such that the organization will commit a group of people to work exclusively on an AL project for 2 or more consecutive days. The benefit of a massed design (a more detailed discussion of this issue can be found in chap. 7, this volume) is that the energy and commitment may remain high and results and action will occur quickly. Disadvantages of a short time frame are that the actions and the learnings may be less powerful because of the lack of reflection and lack of information that would be more likely in a spaced design. Potential disadvantages of a longer, less intensive time frame are (a) the difficulty of group members being able to attend all the meetings because of job changes, family or personal crises, or new urgencies or priorities and (b) the loss of enthusiasm or commitment to the AL project.

5. *How can AL be incorporated into other components of the organization?* What makes AL so valuable to an organization is the transfer of learning and skills from the AL group to the organization as a whole. In every AL session, there is knowledge, intelligence, and ideas that can be beneficial to other parts of the organization, if not the entire organization. Learning that one must first approach Mr. X in Organization Y before approaching Mr. Z to complete the sale will be critical for other salespeople to know as they work with Organization Y. A great strategy for overcoming an obstacle or achieving a success can likely be adapted and used in various other circumstances. Leadership skills developed in the AL group can be applied continuously by the individual during the remainder of his or her career with the company.

6. *Where and when will the group members meet? Will all meetings be onsite or virtual or a combination?* Determining when and where people will meet can have a significant impact on the quality and speed of work done by the AL groups. If the AL work is occurring only on evenings or weekends, the commitment and results will suffer. If facilities or technology is inadequate, people may show up late or not at all. Thus, careful planning and commitment relative to sites and timing are important for AL success.

NATIONAL AGRICULTURAL STATISTICAL SERVICE

A brief description of this program, including the results of an assessment of its effectiveness in developing a broad set of leadership skills, was presented in chapter 10.[5] The Leadership Development through Action Learning (LDAL) workshops were designed for National Agricultural Statistical Service (NASS) managers with direct supervisory responsibilities, including staff directors, state statisticians, branch chiefs, deputy state statisticians, and section heads. Any eligible NASS manager was encouraged to apply by completing an application form. Being chosen as a member of the LDAL program was considered a significant achievement. After applications were received, final selection of participants was made by the Human Resources Council, the United States Department of Agriculture executive group that gives approval for implementing training in NASS. The 14 participants selected for the LDAL were placed in two teams with consideration of the need for diversity on a number of important characteristics such as age, gender, ethnicity, job titles/levels/responsibility, region of the country, and organizational divisions and units.

Like most other federal government organizations, NASS has an aging management group and will need a number of well-trained managers and leaders to replace the group of baby-boomer managers who will soon be eligible for retirement. For this reason, the leadership development program was considered a high priority by senior leadership and was given sufficient money and resources to conduct this program. For example, each participant was allowed to devote the necessary time at work to complete preprogram assignments, to attend face-to-face team meetings, and to complete any required action steps resulting from the team's meeting.

Most federal agencies use a common 10-factor competency model for assessing and developing middle and senior management. Among these 10 competencies, 5 were considered by all 14 participants as critical for their future success at NASS: interpersonal skills, team building, decisiveness, conflict management, and continual learning. Three other competencies were listed by two or more of the participants as critical for future career success: oral communication, creativity and innovation, and integrity and honesty. On the basis of these personal needs assessments, the AL program focused on all eight of these leadership competencies.

NASS also made the decision to create a multiple-problem design. That is, participants were expected to attend and fully participate in each session by coming prepared to discuss a challenging human relations

---

[5]Information for this case was provided by Linda Raudenbush, PhD, NASS.

problem that they could impact in the area of four competencies: interpersonal skills, team building, conflict management, or communications. Participants realized that although the discussion focused on challenges in the four competencies just cited, they would also develop the remaining four competencies of decisiveness, continual learning, creativity and innovation, and integrity and honesty during the AL process.

Like many leadership development programs, the LDAL program was designed to be a 5-month, spaced design with each team meeting face to face regularly throughout this period. Each participant was expected to implement some specified actions aimed at resolving his or her leadership challenges between each face-to-face session. The program managers decided to use internal NASS managers rather than external consultants to provide coaching[6] for each team. The teams met again 6 months after the end of the AL program to discuss continued development and application of the respective leadership competencies as well as to support each other's progress and development.

BOEING

The Global Leadership Program (GLP) debuted in 1999 as one of several tools to enhance Boeing's[7] ability to operate as a global company and to develop leadership competencies within the executive population. To provide a structure for leadership development, the GLP management team divided Boeing leadership's 19 executive competencies into three categories:

- *Most critical:* adapting, thinking globally, building relationships, inspiring trust, leading courageously, aligning the organization, influencing and negotiating.
- *Very important:* shaping strategy, fostering open and effective communication, attracting and developing talent, driving for stakeholder success, demonstrating vision, using sound judgment.
- *Important:* driving execution, inspiring and empowering, working cross-functionally, focusing on quality and continuous improvement, applying financial acumen.

On the basis of the competency priorities detailed above, the GLP adopted AL as the methodology because it fit the objective of enhancing the most critical leadership competencies for success in the global marketplace. AL appeared to be able to produce a forum for senior level executives to learn while being challenged with real corporate issues related to the international environment in which they were placed.

---

[6]The NASS coaches were trained by one of the authors (Marquardt) to be AL coaches using the methods and principles described in this book.

[7]Information for this case was provided by Jim Eckels, Boeing.

The GLP had five key goals for its global executives:

- practice working together as one global company;
- value and seek understanding of the history, culture, politics, and customs of countries/regions;
- appraise the business practices, issues, and competitive dynamics within a country/region;
- assess business opportunities in a prospective country/region; and
- understand the opportunities for international joint ventures and partnerships.

All participants in the GLP are senior executives of the Boeing company, typically directors, division directors, and vice presidents. In addition, GLP participants were potentially identified on a company succession plan to be considered for the top company leadership assignments. The result was an extremely rigorous AL environment designed to strengthen executive global competencies at the highest level of corporate influence. Program participation was by nomination only through the candidate's business unit.

The program was divided into three sections: introduction, in-country, and report-out. The introduction section consisted of approximately 3 days in a location within the United States. These 3 days were filled with introductions, orientation, and guest speakers from within and outside of Boeing. The speakers addressing the group were subject experts who also had international credentials. In addition, experts within Boeing provided participants with insight from a U.S. perspective and a Boeing perspective.

The second section of the program was spent entirely within the country selected by the corporate executive board as a strategically important country. The 3 weeks were spent traveling to major portions of the country, interviewing business leaders, hearing from country experts, and becoming immersed in the culture and people. After approximately 10 days into this phase, the executives were introduced to a specific business issue that had been selected by the corporate executive board as an important and current issue for the company. The participants formed teams to develop solutions and recommendations to present to corporate decision makers. The participants returned to the United States for the final 2 days of the program. These days were spent reviewing, refining, and practicing their team's presentation before the executive committee at a regularly scheduled session. The executive committee considered recommendations presented by the participant teams for action.

This program had many design features in common with GE's well-known Work-Out Program (Davids, Aspler, & McIvor, 2002). The AL component of the program was embedded in a larger developmental program, which included traditional leadership development training delivered by senior management and guest speakers. Participants spent focused time "in-country" to gather background data to select and understand a problem. Finally, the AL component used an intensive 2-day massed schedule design concluding with a high-profile presentation to the senior-most-level corporate executives.

At various points in the GLP, AL coaches worked with the teams to help members reflect on how they could improve their capabilities as a team and how they could transfer their learnings to other aspects of Boeing operations. Both HRD staff as well as Boeing managers with no previous group facilitation background served as AL coaches. The AL coaches received an intensive 2-day training course based on the methods and principles presented in this book prior to serving as an AL team coach.

Step 4—Identifying and Defining the Problems to Be Addressed

Choosing the projects or problems that AL groups will work on is at the heart of the AL process and will have a significant impact on the image and impetus of AL within the organization. Giving AL groups urgent, complex problems and projects in need of innovative solutions will demonstrate the organization's commitment to AL and drive the quality of the action as well as the quality of the learning. Thus, whether chosen by the individual, by the business unit, or by the organization, the problem should be important, worth resolving, and have a definitive time frame for taking action.

A number of important decisions relative to the choice of the AL problem need to be made at this juncture:

1. *What types of problems should be chosen?* Any problem that is important to the organization and requires new breakthrough strategies to solve can be considered. Problems may be connected to operations, strategic planning, personnel, management, marketing, or customer relations. They may be significant and complex problems that require several months to complete or quick, urgent, and minor problems that need to be resolved before the end of the day. Whatever problem is chosen, it must be one in which the group has been given the power to develop and implement strategies.

2. *Who should choose the problem?* The problems can be chosen individually or collectively by the members of the AL group or, as is more common in organization-sponsored AL programs, by senior management or business unit leaders. There is also a hybrid

approach in which input from a number of sources—senior management, AL team members, or other sources such as organizational surveys—is used to identify and select appropriate AL problems.

The higher the level at which the problems are chosen, the more important the AL project will be perceived. For instance, in the GLPs at Boeing described in the previous step, the problems were initially chosen by HR staff. However, as the Boeing Executive Council recognized the high quality of strategic actions developed by the AL groups, it decided that it would choose future projects.

3. *Who will present the problem/project at the initial AL session?* The problem presenter is usually the person who is the true owner of the problem. If the problem being considered is an organizational one or one from a business unit, and two or more members of the group are familiar with the problem, then either or all of them can collaborate in presenting the problem and answering questions about it.

There may be instances, however, when the problem owner is a manager who is unable to commit to attend every meeting of the group or feels his or her presence would lessen the spontaneity and courage of the group in seeking fresh answers or examining root causes. In these circumstances, the problem owner may designate a representative to present the problem and assume responsibility to ensure that the group's proposed strategies will be implemented.

Of course, if the problem owner becomes a member of the AL group, this indicates his or her strong interest in solving the problem and a stronger commitment to implementing the solutions proposed. If the problem owner is not able to be a full-time member of the group, he or she should try to be available at the first session to answer questions from the group as well as between sessions to answer questions and to indicate support or uncertainty relative to strategies being considered (particularly because the problem owner may be the "who knows, who can, and/or who cares" person).

4. *What aspects of the problem should be presented?* It is a fine balancing act between providing too little information about the problem (thus leaving the members wondering aimlessly) or too much information (thus unintentionally or intentionally limiting the range of options that the group considers). It is therefore recommended that the problem presenter frame a presentation of the problem around the following:

- What is the background of the project?
- How will the organization measure the success of the project team?

- What is the critical information you can provide to the team relative to
  - business/strategic plans?
  - marketing plans?
  - competitive information?
  - financial results and plans?
  - benchmarking data?
- Who are the key people within the business/function that the team should meet with? Who will be responsible for scheduling people to meet with the project team (e.g., marketing, financial, manufacturing, legal, sourcing)?
- How can you help the project team access to key stakeholders? Who will schedule these meetings?
- What key people outside the company should the team engage—customers, suppliers, competitors, trade associations, government agencies?

5. *How quickly must the problem be resolved?* Problems usually have a deadline by which a decision needs to be made and tasks need to be completed. If the problem needs to be solved this afternoon, the AL group will be able to meet only one time. If the decision is due next week, the organization may arrange for the AL group to meet either on a part-time or full-time basis. If the final action date is a month or 6 months from now, then the AL group will probably meet on a part-time basis.

6. *What authority over the problem should the problem presenter retain?* Many managers are unable or unwilling to delegate their power and decision-making to a group that might come up with actions with which they are not fully comfortable. It is very difficult to sustain AL programs if the teams soon recognize that they are merely offering suggestions that may or may not be implemented by the organization. Possible ways of overcoming this resistance include the following:
   - relate case studies from organizations such as GE or Boeing that have successfully used AL over a number of years, and
   - select a problem that is important but has primarily internal impact and that can have sufficient time for interim testing and actions.

Three case examples are provided next to represent the three approaches to selecting problems (senior management, the AL teams themselves, and a hybrid process).

DEUTSCHE BANK

In the late 1990s, Deutsche Bank faced tremendous changes in its business and staff structure, with critical implications for corporate culture. Organizational change was critical and the following steps were considered:

- reconfiguration along divisional product lines,
- shift from regional to global operational structure,
- shift from multinational to global leadership structure,
- acquisition of several U.S. entities and their leadership model, and
- change in corporate language from German to English.

Developing leadership to handle these challenges was critical. Deutsche Bank recognized, however, that its existing leadership development courses were focused on individual not organizational development. As a result, little knowledge got transferred to the workplace or application of new skills to business challenges. In addition, the cost of off-the-job training and development was high and climbing. In searching for a tool that would develop leaders while simultaneously resolving these challenges, Deutsche chose AL because of its just-in-time learning and self-managed learning efficiency.

Key business challenges were identified and a 6-month AL program was begun. The CEO, program director, and program manager selected the problems best suited for Deutsche Bank and for the AL participants. Four criteria needed to be met:

- of strategic importance to bank;
- potential source of significant organizational change;
- strategic—not tactical—in nature; and
- to "stretch" participants, broad in scope, offering rich learning opportunities

Twenty participants were selected. Following a 2-day introduction to AL, the four groups met over a period of 6 to 8 weeks on a part-time basis to work on their problem. The final 2 days of the program included the presentation of actions taken as well as capturing the learning that could be applied throughout Deutsche Bank. The program was considered a great success, having attained innovative and cost-effective actions for each of the company's problems.

SIEMENS

In 1997 Siemens created a management learning architecture to develop leadership skills across all levels of management. A key objective of the programs within this architecture is to improve and sustain an entrepreneurial spirit at all levels of management across businesses and countries. Two thousand high-potential managers in cohorts of 35, at all levels of management, attend these programs each year.

After intense investigation into the best means to create and sustain entrepreneurial spirit within a corporate setting and in a learning environment, AL was chosen as the method of developing this critical competency. It was chosen mainly because it relies on learning in the real world of business with a focus on results and achievement, yet it could be supported by teaching from business school professors, such as those from Babson College, which is known for world-class teaching and research in corporate entrepreneurship.

Programs last for 8 to 12 months and provide a sufficient time frame for also implementing the AL projects. Suggestions for AL problems are solicited from the participants to leverage their energy, passion, and motivation for solving problems that had a direct impact on their work. This strategy was chosen because these projects would, in reality, create additional work for each of them. Every participant is asked to bring up at least one issue for AL in his or her program. The projects submitted have to be tangible, measurable, and achievable. Thus, a plan by itself would not be accepted if it was not quantifiable (e.g., in terms of money, cycle time, process time) and if a project could not be implemented within 3 to 4 months. Once a list of potential projects is complied, all members vote on what they consider would be the best projects for AL. Typical problems include cost cutting, sales growth, new market entry, new product development, process re-engineering, cross selling, and productivity improvement. Participant preferences are given significant priority in forming teams that have diverse membership (recognizing that not everyone can get their first choice).

Thus far, over 1,500 AL projects have been conducted by Siemens. Of this number, approximately 60% of the projects met their defined targets and about 20% were ultimately implemented. The main reason for teams not meeting their target was that they set goals that were too ambitious. Those projects that were strategic and scoped correctly, however, contributed substantially to the bottom line of the company. As a result, the program is strongly supported by line managers who willingly send their best performers to the program and contribute considerable time and energy to make these projects successful.

These AL programs provided Siemens managers a best-in-class and global approach to learning from working on "live" projects and also the critical experience of implementing the projects and experiencing tangible and measurable results for the organization. The individuals gained experience in virtual, multicultural, and multifunctional teamwork and learned a great deal from their colleagues while at the same time completing projects that benefited the corporation.

NATIONAL INSTITUTES OF HEALTH

Chapter 7 presents a more detailed account of a hybrid method for identifying problems that are of relevance to multiple stakeholders. Specifically, a creative problem-identification exercise was used to surface problems that had significant importance for participants. This process identified a number of latent or "root cause" issues that would not normally emerge in initial "top-of-mind" discussions of problems. Senior management considered these problems along with other strategic issues of concern to them. Finally, results from a survey of organizational functioning administered to all institute members were reviewed to identify additional problems. Ultimately, senior management decided that several problems, though important, were not appropriate for these AL teams to address.

Step 5—Forming Teams

Ideally, AL teams should be composed of four to eight members with diverse backgrounds, experience, and personal styles and preferences. There are a number of different approaches to forming AL teams.

NOMINATED/ASSIGNED BY ORGANIZATION

Many AL teams are composed of "high-potential" managers and employees nominated by the organization. The number of high-potential nominees may range from 15 to 100. In this situation, diverse teams are created by assigning nominees to teams so that they are balanced in terms of organization representation, gender, cultural background, age, personality style, and so forth.

NOMINATED/SELF-ASSIGNMENT

In this alternative method for team formation, the team problems are designated by the organization and nominees provide program managers with their preferences with respect to team problems. In forming teams, the program managers try to balance nominee preferences with diversity factors. This approach takes advantage of the natural interest of nominees but cannot guarantee that everyone will get their first choice.

An example of the nominated/self-assignment method was included in the description in chapter 7 of how the NIH institute created teams. Although most participants in this program were pleased with their assignment, there was a team (focused on a less popular problem) in which several members were unhappy with their team assignment. This created individual and team morale problems that were a continuous issue throughout the life of this team.

APPOINTED

This approach is popular when the organization charters a team to develop a solution for a strategic problem. Instead of setting up a traditional task force, the organization pulls together a diverse team and provides a coach trained in the principles and processes detailed in this book. In addition to selecting team members from a cross-section of the organization, the champions and managers of this process need to ensure diversity in other critical dimensions—end-users as well as techsperts, customers, members with different levels of experience and responsibility in the organization, members who represent the cultural diversity of the organization, and members with different personality styles (e.g., Meyers-Briggs types).

When a global engineering firm decided to use an AL approach to business planning, it chose to appoint teams according to business function. The overall objective of the AL process was to critically review the previous year's business and leadership performance, planning, and decision-making processes to identify and carry forward lessons learned to achieve higher performance in the future. To provide a market-focused look at the organization, senior managers appointed members from operations, business development, and shared services organizations to form three business function-diverse Action Learning teams representing major geographical regions.

To plan and to project the highest priorities for the next period, the AL teams were asked to analyze how the previous year's performance data compared with actual business results. After reviewing and analyzing the historical data, participants were asked to critique and suggest revisions to a simplified version of the forthcoming year's annual business plan. Each team presented its analysis and recommendations to the executive leadership team of the organization. The executive leadership team made it clear that it would hold the teams accountable for recommendations and challenged any recommendations that appeared incomplete or flawed. The executive leadership team also tested the participants' understanding of the underlying financial and leadership challenges.

Step 6—Building and Maintaining Team Morale and Motivation

Building and maintaining team morale and motivation is most important when conducting spaced programs. When an AL program is designed to last 3 or 4 months with a 1- to 3-week interval between meetings, it can be difficult to sustain the natural enthusiasm that results from the kick-off and chartering events that are a normal part of most AL programs, especially when they are part of a larger leadership development program.

It is also normal for teams to go through cyclical periods of enthusiasm and discouragement as they enter normal phases of team development and problem solving (see chap. 5, this volume). Many AL program managers anticipate these morale swings and build in events and structure to a help teams deal with and learn from these normal team phases.

SMITH INTERNATIONAL

Smith International's Senior Leadership Development Program (SLDP) is a good example of an AL-based leadership development program in which key events are spaced over time. Smith International is a global energy company whose headquarters are in Houston, Texas. The Smith SLDP is offered once a year to 24 first-level executives. The AL assignment spans 8 months during which three structured learnings are hosted at locations around the world. Senior executives are involved as sponsors, executive panel members, and speakers several times over the course of the program. The Smith organization comprises four business units and a corporate group. The program manager attempts to maximize diversity in backgrounds, experiences, geography, and expertise in each AL group. This team formation strategy enables networking and helps to develop a deeper understanding of all parts of the business.

Once enrollment is complete, three in-person sessions are spaced over time. Each of these sessions shares a dual purpose: to engage the participant in an intensive, structured learning experience and to provide the globally distributed teams with opportunities to meet in person. In each of the sessions, participants are expected to advance work on their projects and benchmark with the other teams in the program.

The SLDP officially begins in Session 1. Senior executives address the group, making a strong case for change and reinforcing the importance of leadership development. The first session also addresses key topics including strategy, change leadership, influence, team performance, and decision making. A large-scale business simulation challenges the team to apply the concepts presented and provides a preview of the coming AL experiences. These first 3 days are intense, purposefully designed to aid the team in forming bonds with fellow participants. The 4th and final day of Session 1 includes an official launch of the AL project. Participants meet with their sponsors, develop a team contract, and create an initial project plan.

Between Sessions 1 and 2, teams move from problem clarification through data gathering, analysis, and solution identification. The teams typically meet weekly during this time. During these initial 3 months, coaches report team development on a number of fronts. The bonding begun in Session 1 deepens, while informal roles associated with pre-ferred teaming behaviors become apparent. In some cases conflict arises when team members are seen to be dominating, controlling, or not con-tributing. The coach actively supports the team in addressing these issues. Authenticity levels and, to some extent, the potential of the team are established in this phase as the team either successfully confronts problem behavior or ignores it.

Session 2 follows 3 months after the launch. Prior to attending the session, participants are asked to provide a written project summary. The summary serves two purposes: first, it is one of the few reflective journaling tasks set before the team; second, it provides an opportunity for coaches from all four teams and the project manager to gauge progress across teams. Session 2 also spans 4 days and focuses on personal and organizational courage, skills for leading innovation, systems thinking, and collaboration. During the final day, time is available for the AL team working sessions.

The months following Session 2 are characterized by a growing awareness of the project deadline. Competing demands for time can be a key challenge at this stage. Coaches report that teams seem to dis-play greater energy, drive, and anxiety. They also tend to focus more exclusively on the task. If morale is going to be an issue, it generally surfaces during this period. Teams that have not adequately addressed conflict may continue to avoid confrontation. Emotions, whether pos-itive or negative, are an important factor. During this phase, the coach addresses morale issues by encouraging team members to confront engagement issues directly, to focus on the goal, and to celebrate inter-mediate wins.

In Session 3, teaching modules center on the interpersonal side of leadership. Coaching, managing with multiple generations, and presen-tation skills are the topics addressed. The presentation skills portion of the program is a working session designed to help the AL teams prepare their presentations that are conducted on the 4th day of Session 3.

Step 7—Maintaining Senior Management Involvement and Support

Sustained involvement and support by senior management is an impor-tant success factor for AL. There are many instances in which AL was readily adopted and initially supported by senior leadership, only to lose momentum and vital support as the process unfolded. Factors that erode support include competing demands, unexpected business challenges, and a lack of understanding of the process.

COMPETING DEMANDS

In the case of competing demands, it is not necessarily the demands that become the barrier but instead the response of the senior leaders themselves. AL works by encouraging participants to engage in reflective practices. These practices are central to the learning part of the AL equation, but they can be seen as distractions to a hard driving leader engaged in skillfully juggling demands.

UNEXPECTED BUSINESS CHALLENGES

Unexpected business challenges can also demand the time and the personal attention of senior leaders. When Chrysler was implementing its first year of AL, a planning error resulted in a temporary but very public and expensive overinvestment in inventory. As this crisis unfolded, senior leaders in sponsorship roles were in almost constant dialogue with their teams. These dialogues were sometimes uncomfortable because in many instances clear answers were not available.

LACK OF UNDERSTANDING OF THE PROCESS

The simplicity of AL is both its greatest strength and, in some ways, its greatest barrier. It takes less than an hour to become familiar with the most complex AL leadership development systems. It may take much longer to truly understand how this simple process has the power to transform through action. A lack of understanding of the process can lead to poor role clarity, missed coaching opportunities, and a gradual drop-off in executive support.

In organizations in which multiple AL teams are operating simultaneously, there are likely to be a large number of coaches, executive panel members, and sponsors involved in supporting the success of the process. An important lesson learned through a number of large-scale AL initiatives has been to take an AL approach to supporting AL. To be specific, this means planning opportunities for coaches, sponsors, and executive panel members to come together to share their experiences with each team and to develop a better sense of confidence as a coach, sponsor, or panel member.

CHRYSLER LLC

In a 2008 interview, Katy Caschers, Chrysler's leadership development manager, was asked, "How did you engage the organization and generate support for an AL leadership development system?" Katy began by saying that she viewed that challenge as she would any organizational change initiative. As a starting place, she performed an inventory of what was already available and working in terms of leadership development. Next, Katy conducted individual interviews with organizational leaders at multiple levels.

Once a core group of supportive leaders was identified, she arranged for focus group meetings to gain input and perspective about what leadership means to them. What kinds of experiences or learning experiences were most memorable? Which were most meaningful? What does not work? With this information in hand, Katy engaged with internal and external thought leaders and subject-matter experts to discuss best practices in leadership development and also benchmarked with other companies. On the basis of all of this input, Katy developed a vision and framework that addressed the needs/issues of the stakeholders.

With this initial plan in place, Katy went back to all stakeholders individually as well as in focus groups to "teardown and build" the initial framework so it worked for them and they felt that they were definitely part of the design process. The initial learning system was reworked a number of times during this process.

Once an acceptable solution was created, a more detailed framework and business case was presented to senior management. Following this initial presentation, a senior executive advisory board was created for the new leadership development process. This advisory board participated in and supported the creation of a final design, as well as the subsequent development, launch, implementation, and evaluation of the process.

SMITH INTERNATIONAL

At Smith International, for example, a brief orientation to AL is provided during the issue identification session prior to the launch phase. During the AL process, the sponsor and coach for each team meet frequently to share observations and perspectives on the team performance. Prior to Session 2, about 3 months into the AL process, sponsors and executive panel members are brought together for their own AL experience. In preparation for this meeting, sponsors and coaches are asked to complete a brief reflection document (see Exhibit 11.1), and each team is also asked to provide a report on progress (see Exhibit 11.2). A sample agenda for a half-day Leadership Learning Session includes an overall progress report, an update on the team's progress, a discussion focusing on the value of storytelling, a preview for the next stage, and an orientation for the final presentations.

One way to create greater motivation among members of the senior leadership team is to make their lessons of experience more accessible

EXHIBIT 11.1

Team Progress Surveys for Coaches and Sponsors

Coach/Sponsor Team Progress Survey

How would you rate your team on each of the following issues as they are defined?

1. Team Direction: The team I sponsor has a clear purpose. (1) Ineffective, (2) Neutral, and (3) Very Effective. For ratings of Ineffective or Neutral, what should your team do to improve its direction? For Very Effective ratings, how did the team gain its clarity of purpose?

2. Team Decision Making and Interaction: The team maintains a clear focus on getting the job done, all team members contribute equally and are able to make effective decisions. (1) Ineffective, (2) Neutral, and (3) Very Effective. For ratings of Ineffective or Neutral, what should your team do to improve? For teams that achieve Very Effective ratings, what makes this team successful?

3. Creativity and Innovation: The first phases of the project should be characterized by open-ended questioning, multiple potential solutions, and creative idea generation. Rate your team's creativity and innovation: (1) Ineffective, (2) Neutral, and (3) Very Effective. For ratings of Ineffective or Neutral, what should your team do to become more innovative? For teams that achieve Very Effective ratings, what makes them innovative?

through storytelling. Sponsors and executives pair up with coaches in the Leadership Learning Session to discuss the following questions:

- Where do you see the organization heading? Where do you want it to head? How are we going to get there? What are the most critical activities for leaders in making it happen?

- What mistakes have you made that you thought would have a negative impact on our career? How did you learn from these mistakes? What would you have done differently? How did you become aware of a personal shortcoming? What did you do about it?

- In regard to work–life balance, what compromises have you made? How do you feel about them? What have you learned that you could share with others? Discuss strategies to balance work and personal life.

EXHIBIT 11.2

Team Progress Report Form

Team Progress Report

Team Name:
Team Members:
Problem Statement:
Initial Actions:
Potential Solutions:
Barriers and obstacles you have faced so far:

AL often comes as a surprise for the organization in many ways. It is surprisingly powerful, and it is surprising in the depth of commitment it takes from multiple levels of leadership to make it work effectively. During its execution, AL teams often challenge the organization's established ways of doing business. At times a great deal of personal courage is required of some members of the learning community. Our experience shows that communication and engagement are effective ways to maintain motivation throughout an AL life cycle.

Step 8—Solution Presentations

As AL teams enter into the final phases of the AL process, the looming deadline tends to increase the sense of urgency and move all toward completing their work on the project. Teams are challenged to complete their collection of data, analyze test results, prepare recommendations, preview with stakeholders, and develop an executive report and presentation. Logistics for the presentation can be very complex. In some organizations AL teams present their recommendations to executive sponsors individually at an agreed on day and time. At other organizations, such as Chrysler, Smith, and Goodyear, all teams present to a panel of executives, and the presentations are spaced out over the course of a day. With four or more teams presenting in a given day, orchestrating the process and ensuring that each team's recommendations have a proper hearing can be challenging.

PREPARATION OF TEAMS

Participants are provided with an outline that they are encouraged to use in structuring their presentations.

- *Tell them what you will tell them.* Identify three to five key messages and state them in simple, declarative sentences. Each message should have a variety of supporting information such as examples, financial and other statistics, explanations, comparisons/analogies, and/or expert or customer quotations. (Use a good mix and variety of support.)
- *Tell them who you are.* Introduce your team and its members (including sponsor and coach). Acknowledge people who have provided important assistance to your team.
- *Make a case for change.* State your case in a way that will address potential reluctance and demonstrate the importance of this project vis-à-vis your organization's strategy, vision, or values. Answer

the question, "Why should we be unhappy with the way that things are right now?"

- *Provide a brief summary of the proposed solution.* It may include a statement of the solution purpose, the project goal(s), the scope of the project, a general time frame for completing the project, key project members, overall budget/cost estimate, and so forth.
- *Present your business case for change.* Present return-on-investment (ROI), cash flow, or other business impact calculations. Set specific measures of success for evaluating the proposal. Include a deadline for attaining the goal.
- *Provide a realistic estimate of the cost and/or resources required.* The estimates should include human resource requirements in terms of roles, skills required, and time commitment and costs necessary to implement your solution.
- *Identify important milestone events.* Include timeframe, staging, and accountability.
- *Close with a concise conclusion.* Give a brief summary of the key messages.

Smith International provides presentation skills training (on the basis of Lee & Nelson-Neuhaus, 2003) 2 days before the presentation. After the training, each team is videotaped while practicing its presentation. Coaches review the tapes with each team and assist the team in identifying areas for improvement. At Chrysler all teams are provided an opportunity to conduct a trial presentation with a group of coaches prior to the final presentation. The coaches focus on a very specific set of criteria: Are the teams believable? Do they support one another? Is the argument compelling? Is the case for change clear? Are risks and benefits identified? What are the immediate action requirements? Each team receives feedback from at least one other team and a panel of three coaches.

PREPARATION OF EXECUTIVE PANEL

Typically, executive panel members, sponsors, and coaches all receive preparation for their role as evaluators or feedback providers either during the face-to-face mid-course meeting or in a virtual meeting. On average, most teams receive 30 minutes to make their presentation, and then 30 minutes are allowed for question and answers posed by the executive panel. The executive panel uses a feedback template like the one provided in Exhibit 11.3.

Following the presentation, the executive panel gathers to share impressions and reactions to the various presentations. The coaches accompany the team back to the preparation/debrief staging room. There a team photo is taken and a rapid debrief takes place. The coach explains that this moment is just like the moments after reaching the

EXHIBIT 11.3

Sample Presentation Evaluation Form

Team:
General Presentation Observations

Presentation Characteristics	**Yes**	**No**
1. Key messages stated in simple declarative sentences		
2. A variety of supporting materials including examples, statistics, comparisons, and quotations were employed		
3. Clear organizing concept for the presentation		
4. Strong opening		
5. Concise conclusion		
6. Adapted to audience		

peak of a mountain or crossing the finish line of a marathon. It can be a moment of great clarity and perspective. The coach asks participants to reflect on two key questions: What did they learn about themselves (triple-loop learning) as they went through the entire process? What did they learn about the organization (double-loop learning)? The coach asks each person to take a few minutes to respond. Last, the coach hands out reflection guidelines for the peer coaching wrap-up session to be conducted 1 month following the presentation.

While the team is debriefing, the executive panel members complete their feedback session. One executive panel member volunteers to be the executive sponsor responsible for action on the project. This volunteer takes notes regarding evaluation discussions among the executives and later delivers initial feedback to the AL team.

PRESENTATION FEEDBACK AND FOLLOW-UP

At Chrysler, 1 month after the presentation session, members from the AL management team interview each sponsor and key stakeholder. Interviewers also develop metrics to measure tangible action on the basis of project recommendations. Two months later, the executive panel member will call a second feedback meeting with the team to identify action items going forward.

Step 9—Program Evaluation

Because most organizations are interested in assessing the value of their investments, they are most receptive to, and more likely to financially support, program evaluations that are based on (a) the Kirkpatrick training evaluation model (1998) or (b) an ROI analysis (see chap. 10, this volume, for a fuller description of these evaluation methodologies). Owing to the difficulty in estimating the financial value of some AL solutions, few ROI analyses have been conducted for AL programs (we were unable to find any in the literature).

To ensure that an organization is fully capturing the power and benefits of AL, AL programs should be regularly and systematically evaluated. Most program evaluations based on the Kirkpatrick evaluation model focus on Levels 1 (participant reactions) and 2 (participant learning). Several cases, however, are available to illustrate how to assess at Kirkpatrick's Level 3 (participant application of what they learned to the workplace) and Level 4 (organizational results).

BOEING

Approximately 3 months after completion of the GLP at Boeing[8] described earlier and then again 1 year following the completion of an AL program component of the program, a sampling of graduates are interviewed in an effort to determine whether the skills developed in the GLP have also been demonstrated by graduates in their jobs. Graduates are asked whether they have used what they learned, and how. On the basis of Kirkpatrick's four levels of learning to structure the analysis (Kirkpatrick, 1998), the responses are coded as demonstrating awareness, learning, behavior changes, or performance stories.

Here are some of the findings following a recent AL program: All respondents showed an increased awareness of the global environment; 90% of the respondents demonstrated at least one new learning about themselves or their job; 40% of the respondents could identify a behavior change since they had been back on the job; and 8% of the respondents identified specific and quantifiable performance stories that resulted from the program. One participant credited the GLP for being instrumental in his successful negotiation of a new international business venture that was worth multimillions of dollars in new business. He cited the fact that being in a new country, being part of a working team, learning reflection techniques, and developing cultural awareness all directly contributed to the global competencies he needed to be successful. Although these success stories cannot be credited solely to the AL component of the GLP, one can see how the structure and process of AL clearly contributes to these positive outcomes.

---

[8]See Footnote 7.

NATIONAL INSTITUTES OF HEALTH

Most assessments of behavior change in individuals or organizations use a pre–post assessment approach, measuring dependent variables before and after a program and assuming that any differences are attributable to the program. There are a number of statistical and methodological difficulties with pre–post designs, however, that often make it difficult to detect changes even when real changes occur.[9]

The assessment strategy used to measure changes in the NIH program described earlier avoids these difficulties.[10] In this design, bosses, colleagues, and subordinates of participants were asked to rate (via a 360-degree feedback type survey[11]) perceived changes in leadership behavior that the participants were targeting for improvement in the LDP. Using this methodology, raters noted some change for all participants; 44% of participants demonstrated "slight positive change," 50% demonstrated "noticeable positive change," and 6% displayed "dramatic positive change."

The NIH program also illustrates a methodology for assessing a program at Kirkpatrick's Level 4. NIH was particularly interested in assessing the impact of the LDP on the functioning of the organization as a whole. An organizational culture survey was administered to all institute employees (not just LDP participants) to assess their perceptions of organizational life along 21 dimensions.[12] Despite the difficulties inherent in using a pre–post assessment approach, clear and consistent improvements in ratings of organizational functioning were observed for all 21 organizational dimensions. Mean pre–post differences were significant at the .01 level, $F(5, 531) = 3.96$ (Leonard & Goff, 2003).

Only through ongoing assessments is it possible to determine the true impact of AL and identify how a program or process can be modified and adapted to yield even greater results for the organization.

---

[9]For a fuller technical discussion of these difficulties, the reader is referred to Linn and Slinde (1977) and Goff (1998).

[10]Because the methodology described here was used to assess the impact of the entire LDP program, the impact of the AL program alone could not be determined. However, this evaluation strategy can easily be used in future programs to assess the impact of the AL component of any program.

[11]The Time2Change survey (Personnel Decisions International, Minneapolis, MN) was used.

[12]The organizational survey, The Organizational Success Profile (Personnel Decisions International, Minneapolis, MN), contains the following 22 dimensions assessing organizational functioning: strategy, planning and goal setting, leadership, innovation, risk taking, anticipating and adapting to change, absence of obstacles, commitment to the whole team, handling conflict, consistency and fairness, respecting and supporting others, sharing learnings and ideas, working with other groups, accountability, facilitating structure, informing, making decisions, managing results, recruiting and staffing, training and developing, financial resources, physical resources.

Therefore, strategies and resources for assessing should be determined before the AL project begins. Quick evaluations should also occur during and after each AL session. Comprehensive, deep evaluations should be undertaken at critical junctures and at the conclusion of the program. Elements to be assessed during and after the AL sessions include the quality of the questions, the listening and reflection, the problem framing and problem solving, the actions and strategies being considered, and the quality of the learning. Components to be evaluated at the critical junctures and at the conclusion of the AL program include the impact of the actions taken, the development of leadership skills, and the change in the corporate culture.

Step 10—Making Action Learning Part of the Corporate Culture

As the organization continues to have success with its AL projects, top management will naturally seek to institutionalize the process and make it an ongoing, integrated part of the corporate culture. Whenever urgent problems or projects arise that require innovative, powerful, and rapid actions, AL teams are quickly established. All high-potential managers are assigned to AL projects to develop the critical leadership competencies needed by the organization. Internal or external coaches are available as needed to coach the AL groups.

The principles and practices of AL are incorporated in day-to-day actions. Questions are more a part of corporate communications. Following events such as a performance appraisal, the manager and staff person reflect on what went well and how the next performance appraisal could go better. On completing a phone call with a customer, the salesperson asks himself: How did that call go? What could I do better next time? How can I improve my telephone sales techniques?

SAMSUNG

In Samsung,[13] AL is seen as an integral part of the corporate culture and a tool and strategy that drives the future of the company. Because AL team members are future corporate leaders, graduates of AL programs will model the methods and principles they learned through AL as they

---

[13]See Footnote 3.

progress through their career. Their subordinates will learn through the inquiring and reflective management style of their mentors how to be more effective leaders and managers and will come to regard the challenging AL processes as essential preparatory steps in their path toward future senior leadership positions. AL has also provided them invaluable opportunities to develop both a global and a multidimensional mind-set.

Samsung's AL programs have also provided momentum for change and innovation throughout the company and have brought together people from all sectors of the organization. The significance of Samsung's AL program lies in the fact that the program has trained 800 management leaders strategically and produced more than 150 solutions and strategies that are being applied worldwide.

Samsung's AL program has fostered an ingenious management style built on reflection and questions and on seeking ongoing feedback following field execution. Notably, the creative methodologies developed in the AL teams that have resulted in new businesses or pioneered technological standards are being applied to similar cases across the many industries and business units to secure market leadership for Samsung. AL at Samsung has become the strategic tool and methodology to transform Samsung into a first-class global organization by 2010.

CONSTELLATION ENERGY

Constellation's culture has always been results driven and has not given strong thought to the learning aspects of performance.[14] The goals of the organization, set both internally and by Wall Street, are performance driven. It is only recently that the concept of learning as a necessity has been introduced to the organization.

AL is credited with helping Constellation Energy become truly a learning organization. The entire company understands that learning is the necessary precursor to higher performance. Every new manager is required to participate in a leadership training program that involves AL. In this training, participants are encouraged to question everything. AL has been added to the arsenal of tools the employees have at their disposal as the company continually strives for better ways of doing business.

Constellation has trained a cadre of 50 skilled AL coaches. Every plant has a trained coach who can be called in to work with groups to solve problems that arise. The language of AL has become apart of the everyday language of the employees. It is not unusual to overhear someone looking for a "pizza person" for his or her AL session.

---

[14]Information for this case was provided by Bernadette Carson, vice president, World Institute for Action Learning, and Frank Andracchi, vice president, Constellation Energy.

Reflection Questions

1. How could you make AL in your organization a best practice?
2. How would an external consultant introduce AL differently from an internal agent?
3. What are the challenges in sustaining AL versus introducing AL in an organization?
4. Several examples of best practices of AL were presented in this chapter. Which one did you find most impressive and why?
5. Would you appoint group members or allow individuals to self-select? What are the advantages of each approach?
6. What are the challenges in getting senior management to accept the strategies suggested by an AL group? How would you overcome these?

Action Learning From the Future 12

A ction learning (AL) has accomplished many amazing results over the past 50 years—developing teams to work with refugees in Sudan, community development in the Solomon Islands, serving as the foundation for corporate change at a business school in Mauritius, solving complex problems for Samsung, building leaders at Microsoft, and changing corporate culture at IBM. However, we believe the best is yet to come. As the processes and dynamics of AL continue to improve, AL can reach places and transform people in ever more powerful ways.

In this chapter, we present what could be a very likely scenario for a global AL conference in which the new and wider successes of AL are explored. Those who have experienced these successes will share how AL has worked in a variety of new venues, new countries, and new applications.

We thus ask the reader to jump to the future—to the year 2012—to listen in on a global AL forum in which leaders from a variety of cultures and organizations share how AL has developed their leaders and teams as well as changed their organizations and communities.

Action Learning Forum—
Geneva, 12 April 2012

WELCOME BY MODERATOR
(CEO OF A MAJOR CORPORATION)

I am pleased to open the fifth Global Action Learning Forum sponsored by the World Institute for Action Learning. We have certainly seen an amazing increase in the use of AL for leadership development and organizational change over the past 5 years, and every day we see more and more stories appearing in the press about the power of AL.

It reminds me of the words of Margaret Mead (1964) in which she discusses how a small group of thoughtful people can change the world. Indeed, it's the only thing that ever has. AL groups have indeed begun to change the world in which they work and the environment in which they live. AL groups have inexorably, through the use of fresh questions, discovered new insights into everyday problems.

We are fortunate today to have seven AL practitioners from all over the world who will share their successes and their challenges relative to AL. Allow me to briefly introduce the panelists:

- Franklin Sanchez, who has had over 20 years of experience in local and national government service;
- Ingrid Johnson, who works for a nonprofit community-based organization;
- Choon Hee, a senior corporate leader, in a global manufacturing firm;
- Shamuko Gorbuku, director of a rapid-growing personnel association;
- Ali Nassan, senior director for the United Nations Development Programme;
- Jennifer Sumatra, owner of a global high-tech company; and
- Norat Sumingasan, professor and researcher for a large university.

During today's forum, I will be asking panelists to respond to the following questions:

1. What have been your greatest successes in the use of AL for leadership and organization development as well as delivering a service/product? Can you share any examples of skills developed and unique results?
2. For those who might be interested in establishing AL in their organizations, what advice would you offer to them?
3. What do you see as some future trends in practice and application of AL?

QUESTION 1

Moderator: Okay, let's now move to our first question for the day. What have been your greatest successes over the past 2 years in the use of AL for leadership and organization development? Can you share any examples of skills developed and unique results?

Franklin Sanchez (Government)

First, let me say how AL has helped create a new leadership capability in our federal agency. We have developed the leadership skills that are needed by public officials in today's environment—being more decisive, thinking in a more systemic and strategic way, being able to lead teams, and encouraging leadership to flow among all team members as appropriate. AL has changed our mind-set to be more entrepreneurial and more responsive to our citizens. Over the past 3 years, whenever we had a major crisis or issue facing our government, our agency put together an AL team of government officials and citizens. Inevitably the group identified valuable and effective strategies and actions. As a result, government resistance has changed to one of embracing AL.

Perhaps one of our greatest successes was the work we did with our neighbors in developing a regional commitment to reduce the pollution in our countries and to have a significant impact on global warming. It was a difficult challenge with each government seeking to protect its industries and yet protect its present and future citizens.

Ingrid Johnson (Nonprofit Community Hospital)

Although AL groups in our hospital have not discovered the cure to diseases (that is the province of experts working on puzzles), they have been able to expand the quality and speed of health services to our patients. Over the past several years, we have used AL in converting our hospital from an inefficient, money-wasting, poor-service health institution to one of the top success stories in our region. AL teams composed of the board of directors, staff, and the community at large have used AL to determine our long-term goals, improve our patient care, develop quality care reviews, and establish business and health system collaborations that provide high-quality, low-cost health insurance to small businesses. We have also used AL to design a health care delivery system for a community health care center.

Choon Hee (Corporate)

AL has been a valuable tool for us over the past 5 years because it has enabled us to quickly move a number of our ideas to the marketplace with successful launches. We have also used AL in our Six Sigma projects with over $1 billion in savings over the past 2 years.

Probably our biggest and most successful AL project was the one that enabled us to have a successful merger. As you know, most mergers are unsuccessful, and rarely do the merged companies exceed the combined value of the two individual companies. However, our merger proved to be different. As soon as the merger was approved, an AL team of three folks from our company and three folks from the acquired company met 1 day a week for 2 months to develop strategies and actions on issues such as product priorities, marketing foci, personnel integration, and so forth.

Shamuko Gorbuku (Association)

Several years ago, our association decided to make the move from being a small national association that was losing members to a global association. AL was the key in helping us move in that direction. Included in our AL teams was a globally famous musician as well as representatives from all the continents. Much was done virtually. Our membership doubled within 2 years as we improved our membership services, greatly enhanced the quality of our newsletter, and quickened our response rate.

Ali Nassan (United Nations)

AL has become an integral part of many agencies in the UN family as we search for global solutions to war, poverty, housing, food, and so on. Our greatest success was the recently completed AL project that brought together people from within and outside of the refugee camps in Africa. A strategy emerged that enabled us to reintegrate over 1 million refugees back into their home communities. What was most amazing about AL was its ability to bring together people of various cultures, values, experiences and allow them to truly work as a high-performing team. Differences served as a source of synergy and creative energy rather than as a cause of strife and divisiveness.

Jennifer Sumatra (Owner of a Global High-Tech Company)

In our global high-tech firm, we operate almost exclusively on a virtual and asynchronous basis. Although we were initially doubtful whether a tool like AL could work under these conditions, we have found AL to be remarkably effective for groups that operate in this manner. Now, most of our global teams use the AL process on a regular basis. It has indeed allowed us to accelerate the transfer and application of our new products.

Perhaps one of our greatest successes as a company occurred with our utilization of AL in helping us to enter the global learning field via the mobile devices market. Mobile learning, as you know, is the provision of education and training on PDAs (personal digital assistants), smartphones, and mobile phones. In 2010 the number of mobile devices reached over 3 billion, this for a world population of just over 6 billion. We regarded the mobile phone as a necessity, not a luxury, and recognized that this is precisely the age grouping of the higher and further education market.

The objective of this project is to bring this unprecedented ownership of mobile devices into European education and training. For this reason the first target group was decision makers and decision makers in the 25 European Union states to whom the products of the project were sent. Further target groups were the students and institutions in the partner countries, and eventually in the whole 25 countries.

The problem is that students use their mobile phones constantly but not yet in their education. The main results of this AL project were development of a policy and strategy on the role of mobile learning; development of potential achievements of mobile learning; pedagogical aspects of mobile learning; adapting information and learning technologies and e-learning materials to mobile learning; and the development, adaptation, teaching, and evaluation of mobile learning courseware for real students.

Norat Sumingasan (Professor and Researcher)

Through AL, our university has quickly moved to the forefront of academic excellence and relevance in our country. We have decided to have all of our incoming students take an AL workshop prior to beginning their courses, because we want all of our students to (a) be able to work effectively in teams and (b) be more comfortable and confident asking questions of our teachers. All of our professors were introduced to AL so that they could incorporate the new expectations and abilities of the students. AL has thus dramatically changed the role of professors in how we teach in the classroom and how we conduct research. It has also changed the role and capabilities of our students. We have received numerous raves from employers who now see graduates quickly becoming valuable in the workplace; who understand the importance of having clear performance targets and results; and who are not afraid to challenge, to be creative, to ask questions.

We have also used AL on our online courses. Online instructors now play the role of an AL coach as well as a teacher. Prior to converting our e-learning courses to e-action learning courses, nearly 70% of these students dropped out. Now less than 25% of our online students do not complete courses.

Moderator: Thank you all. It's amazing to see the breath and depth of the power of AL—from saving a company $1 billion to saving 1 million refugees, from expanding the power of learning to expanding the power of people.

QUESTION 2

Moderator: Let's now move to our second question. What advice would you offer for those interested in introducing AL into your type of organization?

Franklin Sanchez (Government)

Government agencies, properly so, need to be fairly safe and reasonably confident that their strategies will not only work but also be perceived by the public as not too risky. Thus an important element of all of our AL programs was (a) to pilot test the strategies and (b) to reflect on how the actions might read in the front pages of the national newspapers. Our AL groups, recognizing these necessary elements, have indeed come up with such kinds of strategies.

Ingrid Johnson (Nonprofit Community Hospital)

For our type of organization, it is important that we have top management support and that our projects attack really urgent issues in the community. My experience has been that the best way to introduce AL into our type of organization is to encourage top management to take their toughest, most persistent problem and put an AL group on it. Of course, this makes it necessary that for us to have well-trained, competent AL coaches.

Choon Hee (Corporate)

Corporate leaders are very concerned that any expenditure, be it for services or for people or for training, lead to significant, measurable results. Thus it is important that we do solid research, particularly a well-done ROI analysis, on all of our AL projects. Thus far, I can proudly say that all of our AL projects have an ROI of more than 10 to 1, with some as high as 50 to 1.

Shamuko Gorbuku (Association)

For us, the projects and issues must be tackled by a wide array of our members. AL has helped us create a new problem-solving mind-shift by making sure that we focus first on gaining problem clarity. This may be difficult with many folks from different orientations and goals. Yet the group formation process must be fast; fortunately, "storming" among people in AL is virtually nonexistent. Our members want to be empowered, and the fact that anyone can ask great questions is critical for our success. We put a premium on the presence of nonexperts, integrate continuous improvement into problem solving, and really follow the AL axiom of no learning without action, and no action without learning.

Ali Nassan (United Nations)

When working with a UN agency, one must always be sensitive to the bureaucracy, politics, and cultural dynamics of having people from so many nations involved in any activity or project. Determining membership of an AL group is a very important consideration. Fortunately, we have found that only AL groups truly overcome these challenges.

Jennifer Sumatra (Owner of a Global High-Tech Company)

Will it work globally and virtually?—that was the key question/concern that AL had to address for our high-tech firm. What we have discovered is that successful AL teams blend limited structure around responsibilities and priorities with extensive communication (careful listening, questions, all perspectives, etc.) and design freedom.

The limited structure of AL helps group members make sense of complex problems and to operate within a complicated environment. Clear autonomy, communications, and responsibilities enable the group to move forward and apply appropriate solutions. To stay at the edge of chaos, the team needs to have a few simple rules and a minimum set of guidance or norms. For our virtual teams to work, the rules should be simple but able to be adapted—and that is what AL is able to do.

AL needs to avoid being too structured, which would lead to rigidity, constraint, and suppression of needed information as well as constrict innovation and make it hard for the team to adapt. On the other hand, providing too little structure which would lead to disorder, lack of focus, fragmentation, and become too permeable to disruptive inputs, making AL groups and projects too difficult to coordinate.

At the first meeting of the AL group, norms and group ground rules, in which there are clear responsibilities and priorities, must be established. The structure and stability in AL come about as a result of the six components of all AL programs and the group ground rules (norms established for all AL groups). This structure is counterbalanced by the freedom and flexibility, the encouragement of fresh questions, and the use of diverse people with and without familiarity with the problem or context. A few firm, clear rules and structure agreed to up front allows for great flexibility later on.

Norat Sumingasan (Professor and Researcher)

An ongoing challenge for our instructors as well as our students is the difficulty of moving from theory into action. Our students want plenty of application, and our professors want to be sure that there are theoretical foundations to proposed actions. I am reminded of two well-known axioms: Lewin's axiom that there is nothing as practical as a good theory, and Revans's belief that there can be no learning without action and no action without learning.

QUESTION 3

Moderator: Thank you, panel members, for those valuable bits of advice. Now to our final question. What do you see as some future trends in the way AL might be implemented? Do you see any new applications for AL?

Franklin Sanchez (Government)

I believe that AL can play a major role in changing the relationship between government and its citizens. As you know, democratic governance cannot be successful unless there is a vibrant civil society that is in some way involved in influencing public policy making. Civil society interest groups promote a variety of missions—ranging from those rather narrow in scope to issues that impact on the regional and even national/international polity.

Without the collective interplay and interdependency between government and such interest groups (as long as they are independent and not simply a government-controlled mouthpiece), government at all levels will remain closed and unresponsive to legitimate outside pressures. In any governmental system, there must be a balance between the right of citizens to expect open and accountable and transparent governance and government's concert with efficiency, autonomy, and national security.

A good AL program, therefore, includes a cross-section of interest groups in a given country. This helps the teams, through the unique AL format, to transcend their particular agendas and concentrate on the larger agenda of identifying those common issues that will lead to more responsive public policy formulation.

Initially, in some countries, it may be necessary to hold separate AL sessions with government representatives. Once they, too, have developed more inclusive programs, the two groups (civil and government) would be merged and could possibly agree on a united program of action. It probably would be best to first do a pilot project, perhaps at the local level, and if this venue is successful, move to the regional or national government level.

Finally, I would like to see more collaboration between local, provincial, and national levels of government in the future. Certainly, we can learn from each other as well as work with each other.

Ingrid Johnson (Nonprofit Community Hospital)

There are a couple areas in which AL has not been utilized to its full potential—namely, neighborhoods and prisons.

Here's a community application: it could be a neighborhood event in which any family in the neighborhood can form a team to solve conflict between neighbors, or a family having some problems and needs that the neighbors can help to solve. This would help build neighborliness as well as build the community.

I'll also offer a rehabilitation application. We could use AL to help prison inmates to solve problems they face within the prison or when they are about to be released. I am trying to see if I can try it out with young offenders in one of our prisons. Fellow inmates can be the AL team members with an external coach. And inquiry will help these inmates with greater reflection.

Choon Hee (Corporate)

I think that it would also be important to highlight the need for consistent standards and practice worldwide so that AL will be attractive to global corporations not only for tackling tough problems but also for establishing an organizational learning culture. I am strongly in favor of well-trained AL coaches. We, as a matter of fact, make sure that all of our internal AL coaches have been certified by a training and certifying body such as the World Institute for Action Learning.

Shamuko Gorbuku (Association)

Another issue that might be addressed is whether to offer AL training to everyone in the organization in an effort to build a learning organization. This is being done in the United States as well as in some Asia/Pacific countries such as Singapore and Korea. Europe has an association called the European Council on Learning Organizations; perhaps the use of AL at the regional and national levels could enable this association to more quickly and effectively to build learning organizations across Europe.

Ali Nassan (United Nations)

One of the major goals of the UN is to stop armed conflicts and build a world of peaceful coexistence among nations. I believe that AL could be extremely helpful and powerful in helping us achieve these objectives. At the UN Staff College in Turin, Italy, we could bring together people from within and from outside the conflict to find ways that benefit all sides in the long term—AL can do that! AL might help us move from a debating organization to one that uses dialogue, from an organization that often makes accusatory statements to one that asks open-ended questions.

Becoming a world of peace rather than one of war requires changing what we do, changing how we work together, and changing ourselves. Reg Revans recognized this when he indicated that change is possible only if the entire system is changed—the people seeking the change as well as those who are to be changed.

Jennifer Sumatra (Owner of a Global High-Tech Company)

I would like to see AL used more frequently in the day-to-day crises that small entrepreneurial companies face on an almost daily basis. Organizational theorists have recently discovered the importance of what is called the "edge of chaos," or "a natural state between order and chaos, a compromise between structure and surprise." It is the place in which maximum creativity and possibility exist and learning best occurs, in which a team or organization is optimally responsive to the complexity of the environment but still structured sufficiently to succeed. For any team to succeed, it needs to walk the fine line between stability and change (i.e., to stay poised on the edge of chaos). I have found that AL allows us to use elements such as chaos, diversity, and change and convert these elements into powerful actions.

Norat Sumingasan (Professor and Researcher)

We in academia must continue to expand the use of AL in helping our students and ourselves to better translate great business theories into valuable business practices. We therefore have to more fully optimize the power of AL, to capture both (a) the flexibility and chaos of AL (elements such as diversity of membership, complex challenges, creative questions, lack of familiarity with problem and/or context) and (b) the practical, time-urgent structure and order of AL (elements such as real problems, accountability and responsibility, careful listening, pilot testing, and action).

If we do, we will be able to help our students and future leaders to operate in an environment that encourages innovation while maintaining minimal, but crucial, guidelines, norms, and group ground rules that produce sound, practical, and workable results.

CONCLUDING REMARKS FROM THE MODERATOR

Thank you all. This has been a wonderful opportunity for us to learn how AL has proven to be a tremendous tool for developing leaders and transforming organizations. Any questions from the audience (readers)?

Reflection Questions

1. What are some changes and challenges you foresee your organization facing within the next 5 years? How could AL respond to those?
2. What could you do to introduce AL programs to community groups and sustain them with limited resources and funds?
3. What would be some of the cultural challenges of bringing AL to a multicultural organization?

References

Acker-Hocevar, M., Pisapia, J., & Coukos-Semmel, E. (2002, April). *Bridging the abyss: Assign value and validity to leadership development through action learning—case-in-point.* Paper presented at the American Educational Association annual conference, New Orleans, LA.

Adams, J. S. (1963). Toward an understanding of inequity. *Journal of Abnormal Social Psychology, 67,* 422–436.

Alinsky, S. (1989). *Reveille for radicals.* New York: Vintage Books.

Argyris, C. (1993). *Knowledge for action: A guide to overcoming barriers to organizational change.* San Francisco: Jossey-Bass.

Argyris, C. (1999). *On organizational learning.* Oxford, England: Blackwell.

Argyris, C., Putnam, R., & Smith, D. M. (1985). *Action science: Concepts, methods, and skills for research and intervention.* San Francisco: Jossey-Bass.

Argyris, C., & Schön, D. (1978). *Organizational learning: A theory of action perspective.* Reading, MA: Addison-Wesley.

Argyris, C., & Schön, D. (1996). *Organizational learning II.* Reading, MA: Addison-Wesley.

Bandura, A. (1977). *Social learning theory.* Englewood Cliffs, NJ: Prentice Hall.

Bandura, A. (1986). *Social foundations of thought and action: A social cognitive theory.* Englewood Cliffs, NJ: Prentice Hall.

Bandura, A. (1997). *Self-efficacy: The exercise of control.* New York: W. H. Freeman.

Bass, B. M. (1990). *Bass & Stogdill's handbook of leadership: Theory, research, and managerial applications* (3rd ed.). New York: The Free Press.

Bass, B. M., & Avolio, B. J. (1990). The implications of transactional and transformational leadership for individual, team, and organizational development. *Research in organizational change and development, 4,* 231–272.

Bazerman, M. H., & Watkins, M. D. (2008). *Predictable surprises: The disasters you should have seen coming and how to prevent them.* Boston: Harvard Business Press.

Beal, D., Cohen, R., Burke, M., & McLendon, C. (2003). Cohesion and performance in groups: A meta-analytic clarification of construct relations. *Journal of Applied Psychology, 88,* 989–1004.

Beaty, L., Bourner, T., & Frost, P. (1993). Action learning: Reflections on becoming a set member. *Management Education and Development, 24,* 350–367.

Beckhard, R., & Harris, R. (1987). *Organizational transitions: Managing complex system change.* Reading, MA: Addison-Wesley.

Bell, M. P., & Berry, D. P. (2007, November). Viewing diversity through different lenses: Avoiding a few blind spots. *Academy of Management Perspectives, 21*(4), 21–25.

Bennis, W. (2000). *Managing the dream: Reflections on leadership and change.* Cambridge, MA: Perseus.

Bennis, W. G., Beane, K. D., & Chin, R. (1969). *The planning of change* (2nd ed.). New York: Holt, Rinehart & Winston.

Bennis, W., & Nanus, B. (1985). *Leaders: Strategies for taking charge.* New York: HarperCollins.

Berger, P. L., & Luckmann, T. (1966). *The social construction of reality: A treatice in the sociology of knowledge.* Garden City, NY: Doubleday.

Bion, W. (1961). *Experiences in groups.* New York: Basic Books.

Blake, R. R., & Mouton, J. S. (1964). *The managerial grid.* Houston, TX: Gulf.

Blanchard, K. H. (1992, October). The seven dynamics of change. *The Inside Guide.*

Block, P. (2000). *Flawless consulting.* San Francisco: Jossey-Bass.

Bohm, D. (1996). *On dialogue.* London: Routledge.

Boshyk, Y. (2002). *Action learning worldwide: Experiences of leadership and organizational development.* New York: Palgrave Macmillan.

Bossidy, L., & Charan, R. (2002). *Execution: The discipline of getting things done.* New York: Crown Business.

Botham, D., & Vick, D. (1998). Action learning and the program at the Revans Center. *Performance Improvement Quarterly, 11*(2), 5–16.

Boud, D. L., Keough, R., & Walker, D. (1985). *Reflection: Turning experience into learning.* Oxford, England: Routledge.

Bradford, D. L., & Burke, W. W. (2005). *Reinventing organization development: Addressing the crisis, achieving the potential.* San Francisco: Pfeiffer.

Breyfogle, F. W. (1999). *Implementing Six Sigma: Smarter solutions using statistical methods.* New York: Wiley-InterScience.

Broad, M. L., & Newstrom, J. W. (1992). *Transfer of training: Action-packed strategies to ensure high payoff from training investments.* Reading, MA: Perseus.

Brookfield, S. D. (1987). *Developing critical thinkers: Challenging adults to explore alternative ways of thinking and acting.* San Francisco: Jossey-Bass.

Brown, T. (2007, November 12). Bringing design to blue chips. *Fortune, 32.*

Brown, T. A. (2006). *Confirmatory factor analysis for applied research.* New York: Guilford.

Bruch, H., & Ghoshal, S. (2003). Unleashing organizational energy. *Sloan Management Review, 45*(1), 45–51.

Buckingham, M., & Clifton, D. O. (2001). *Now, discover your strengths.* New York: Free Press.

Burke, W. W. (2002). *Organization change: Theory and practice.* Thousand Oaks, CA: Sage.

Burley-Allen, M. (1982). *Listening: The forgotten skill.* New York: Wiley.

Burns, J. M. (1978). *Leadership.* New York: Harper & Row.

Butterfield, S. D. (1999). *Action learning: Case study of learning and transfer for personal and professional development.* Unpublished doctoral dissertation, Georgia State University.

Butterfield, S. D., Gold, K., & Willis, V. (1998). Creating a systematic framework for the transfer of learning from an action learning experience. *Academy of HRD Proceedings,* 490–496.

Byrnes, N. (2005, October 10). Star search: How to recruit, train, and hold on to great people: What works, what doesn't. *Business Week, 71.*

Campbell, D. T., & Stanley, J. C. (1966). *Experimental and quasi-experimental designs for research.* Chicago: Rand McNally.

Carlyle, T. (1841/2003). *Heroes, hero worship and the heroic in history.* Whitefish, MT: Kessinger.

Carr, A., & McNulty, M. (Eds.). (2006). *The handbook of adult clinical psychology: An evidence-based practice approach.* New York: Routledge.

Carson, B. (2006). *Balancing your scorecard via action learning.* Retrieved December 29, 2006, from http://carson-consultants.com/BSC.PDF

Cartwright, D. (1968). The nature of group cohesiveness. In C. Cartwright & A. Zander (Eds.), *Group dynamics: Research and theory* (3rd ed.; pp. 91–107). New York: Harper & Row.

Castore, C. H. and Murnighan, J. K. (1978). Determinants of individual support of group decisions. *Organizational Behavior and Human Performance, 22,* 75–92.

Chapman, A. (n.d.) *Conscious competence learning model.* Retrieved February 25, 2007, from http://www.businessballs.com/conscious competencelearningmodel.htm

Charan, R., Drotter, S., & Noel, J. (2001). *The leadership pipeline: How to build the leadership-powered company.* San Francisco: Jossey-Bass.

Chemers, M. M. (1997). *An integrated theory of leadership.* Mahway, NJ: Erlbaum.

Choi, J. S. (2005). *A case study of an action learning program: Can action learning be an approach to enhance a manager's coaching skills?* Unpublished dissertation, George Washington University.

Ciampa, D. (2005, January). How leaders move up. *Harvard Business Review, 83*(1), 46–53.

Cohen, A. R., & Bradford, D. L. (1991). *Influence without authority.* New York: Wiley.

Cohen, A. R., & Bradford, D. L. (2005). *Influence without authority* (2nd ed.). Hoboken, NJ: Wiley.

Cohen, J. (1988). *Statistical power analysis for the behavioral sciences* (2nd ed.). Hillsdale, NJ: Erlbaum.

Cohen, J., Cohen, P., West, S. G., & Aiken, L. S. (1983). *Applied multiple regression/correlation analysis for the behavioral sciences.* Mahway, NJ: Erlbaum.

Conner, J. (2000). Developing the global leaders of tomorrow. *Human Resource Management, 39,* 147–157.

Corporate Leadership Council. (2000). *Corporate Leadership Council 2000/ Leadership Survey.* Washington, DC: Author.

Covey, S. (1989). *The seven habits of highly effective people.* New York: Simon & Schuster.

Cronbach, L. J., & Suppes, P. (1969). *Research for tomorrow's schools: Disciplined inquiry for education.* New York: McMillan & Co.

Cummings, T. G., & Worley, C. G. (2005). *Organization development and change* (8th ed.). Mason, OH: South-Western.

Davenport, T. H. (1995). The fad that forgot people. *Fast Company, 1*(1), 70–73.

Davids, B., Aspler, C., & McIvor, B. (2002). General Electric's action learning change initiatives: Work-Out™ and the change acceleration process. In Y. Boshyk (Ed.), *Action learning worldwide: Experiences of leadership and organizational development* (pp. 76–89). New York: Palgrave Macmillan.

Day, D. V. (2005, April). Identifying, evaluating, and using indigenous leadership theories: Building a leadership brand. In R. Kaiser (Chair), *Making leadership research more relevant.* Symposium conducted at the annual convention of the Society for Industrial and Organizational Psychology, Los Angeles.

de Haan, E., & de Ridder, I. (2006). Action learning: How do participants learn? *Consulting Psychology Journal, 58,* 216–231.

Delbecq, A., Van de Ven, A., & Gustafson, D. (1975). *Group techniques for program planning: A guide to nominal group and Delphi processes.* Glenview, IL: Scott Foresman.

Dewey, J. (1916/1997). *Democracy and education: An introduction to the philosophy of education.* New York: Simon & Schuster.

Dewey, J. (1933/1997). *How we think.* Toronto, Canada: Dover.

Dilworth, R. L. (1995). The DNA of the learning organization. In S. Chawla and J. Renesch (Eds.), *Learning organizations* (pp. 243–256). Portland, OR: Productivity Press.

Dilworth, R. L. (1998). Action learning in a nutshell. *Performance Improvement Quarterly, 11*(1), 28–43.

Dilworth, R. L., & Willis, V. (2003). *Action learning: Images and pathways.* Malabar, FL: Krieger.

Dixon, N. (1996). *Perspectives on dialogue.* Greensboro, NC: Center for Creative Leadership.

Drucker, P. F. (1954/2006). *The practice of management.* New York: HarperCollins.

Druckman, D., & Bjork, R. A. (1991). *In the mind's eye: Enhancing human performance.* Washington, DC: National Academy Press.

Dykhuizen, G. (1973). *The life and mind of John Dewey.* Carbondale: Southern Illinois University Press.

Ecclestone, K. (1996). The reflective practitioner: Mantra or model for emancipation. *Studies in the Education of Adults, 28,* 146–161.

Elinor, L., & Gerard, G. (1998). *Dialogue: Creating and sustaining collaborative partnerships at work.* New York: Wiley.

Evidence-Based Working Group. (1992). Evidence-based medicine: A new approach to teaching the practice of medicine. *JAMA, 268,* 2420–2425.

Festinger, L. (1954). A theory of social comparison process. *Human Relations, 7,* 117–140.

Fiedler, F. E. (1964). A contingency model of leadership effectiveness. *Advances in experimental social psychology, 51,* 227–235.

Fisher, K. (1999). *Leading self-directed work teams.* New York: McGraw-Hill.

Flavell, J. H. (1987). *Speculations about the nature and development of metacognition: Metacognition, motivation and understanding.* Hillside, NJ: Erlbaum.

Fox, M. (1998). Closing the global leadership competency gap: The Motorola GOLD process. *Organization Development Journal, 16*(4), 5–12.

Freedman, A. M. (1987). *One of Kurt Lewin's practical theories: Force field analysis.* Chicago: Quantum Associates/Washington, DC: Freedman, Leonard & Marquardt Consultancy.

Freedman, A. M. (1997). The undiscussable sides of implementing transformational change. *Consulting Psychology Journal, 49,* 51–76.

Freedman, A. M. (1998). Pathways and crossroads to institutional leadership. *Consulting Psychology Journal, 50,* 131–151.

Freedman, A. M. (2005). Swimming upstream: The challenge of managerial promotions. In R. Kaiser (Ed.), *Filling the leadership pipeline* (pp. 25–44). Greensboro, NC: CCL Press.

Freedman, A. M. (2006). Action research: Origins and applications for OD&C practitioners. In B. B. Jones, & M. Brazzel (Eds.), *The NTL handbook of organization development and change* (pp. 83–103). San Francisco: Jossey-Bass/Pfeiffer/NTL Institute.

Freedman, A. M., & Leonard, H. S. (2002). Organizational consulting to groups and teams. In R. L. Lowman (Ed.), *The handbook of organizational consulting psychology: A comprehensive guide to theory, skills, and techniques* (pp. 27–53). San Francisco: Jossey-Bass.

Freedman, A. M., & Zackrison, R. E. (2001). *Finding your way in the consulting jungle.* San Francisco: Jossey-Bass/Pfeiffer.

Freeman, C., & Power, M. (Eds.). (2007). *Handbook of evidence-based psychotherapies: A guide to research and practice.* Chichester, England: Wiley.

French, W. L., Bell, C. H., Jr., & Zawacki, R. A. (2000). *Organization development and transformation: Managing effective change* (5th ed.). Boston: Irwin McGraw-Hill.

Gambrill, E. (2003). Evidence-based practice: Implications for knowledge development and use in social work. In A. Rosen & E. Proctor (Eds.), *Developing practice guidelines for social work intervention* (pp. 37–58). New York: Columbia University Press.

Gharajedaghi, J. (1999). *Systems thinking: Managing chaos and complexity.* Boston: Butterworth-Heinemann.

Glass, G. V., McGaw, B., & Smith, M. L. (1981). *Meta-analysis in social research.* Beverly Hills, CA: Sage.

Goff, M. (1998). *The perils of change scores, or, how to be misled by numbers without really trying.* Minneapolis, MN: Personnel Decisions International.

Gordon, J. J. (1961). *Synectics: The development of creative capacity.* New York: HarperCollins College Division.

Gorsuch, R. (1983). *Factor analysis* (2nd ed.). Hillsdale, NJ: Erlbaum.

Greenleaf, R. K., Vaill, P. B., & Spears, L. C. (1998). *The power of servant leadership.* San Francisco: Berrett-Koehler.

Gustafson, K., & Bennett, W. (1999). *Issues and difficulties in promoting learner reflection: Results from a three-year study.* Retrieved November 24, 2007, from http://www.nwlink.com/~donclark/learning/reflecting.html

Gyllenhamer, E. (1977). *People at work.* Reading, MA: Addison-Wesley.

Hare, R. P. (1980). Consensus versus majority vote: A laboratory experiment. *Small Group Behavior, 11,* 405–408.

Harris, R. P., Helfand, M., Woolf, S. H., Lohr, K. N., Mulrow, C. D., Teutsch, S. M., & Atkins, D. (2001). Current methods of the U.S. Preventative Services Task Force: A review of the process. *American Journal of Preventative Medicine, 20*(Suppl. 3), 21–35.

Helsing, J., Geragherty, B., & Napolitano, L. (2003). *Impact without authority: How to leverage internal resources to create customer value.* Chicago: SAMA.

Hersey, P., & Blanchard, K. H. (1977). *Management of organizational behavior*. Englewood Cliffs, NJ: Prentice Hall.

Herzberg, F. (1968/2003). One more time: How do you motivate employees? *Harvard Business Review 1*, 87–96. (Original work published 1968)

Hicks, M. D., & Peterson, D. E. (1999). The developmental pipeline: How people really learn. *Knowledge Management Review, 9*, 30–33.

Hii, A. (2000). *The impact of action learning on the conflict-handling styles of managers in a Malaysian firm*. Unpublished doctoral dissertation, George Washington University.

Hill, C., Leonard, H. S., & Sokol, M. B. (2006). *Action learning guide: Real learning, real results*. Minneapolis, MN: Personnel Decisions International Publications.

Hodgkinson, G. P., & Clarke, I. (2007). Conceptual note: Exploring the cognitive significance of organizational strategizing: A dual-process framework and research agenda. *Human Relations, 60*, 243–255.

Holder, R. J., & McKinney, R. N. (1993, Fall). Scouting: A process for dealing with the frontiers of an uncertain world. *OD Practitioner*, 20–25.

Holton, E. F. (1996). The flawed four-level evaluation model. *Human Resource Development Quarterly, 7*(1), 5–21.

Holton, E. F., & Naquin, S. S. (2000). Implementing performance-based leadership development. *Advances in Developing Human Resources, 6*, 104–113.

Homans, G. C. (1961). Social behavior: Its elementary forms. New York: Harcourt, Brace & World.

House, R. J. (1971). A path goal theory of leader effectiveness. *Administrative Science Quarterly, 16*, 321–338.

Isaacs, W. (1999). *Dialogue and the art of thinking together*. New York: Currency Doubleday.

Jennings, D. (2002). Strategic management: An evaluation of the use of three learning methods. *Journal of Management Development, 21*, 655–665.

Johnson, B. (1997). *Polarity management*. Amherst, MA: Human Resource Development Press.

Johnson, D., & Johnson, P. (1997). *Joining together: Group theory and group skills* (6th ed.). Boston: Allyn & Bacon.

Johnson-Laird, P. (1994). Mental models and probabilistic thinking. *Cognition, 50*, 189–209.

Jones, B. B., & Brazzel, M. (Eds.). (2006). *The NTL handbook of organization development and change*. San Francisco: Pfeiffer.

Kaiser, R. B., & Craig, S. B. (2007). *Testing the leadership pipeline: Do the behaviors related to managerial effectiveness change with organizational level?* Manuscript under review.

Kaplan, R. S., & Norton, D. P. (1996). *The balanced scorecard: Translating strategy into action*. Cambridge, MA: Harvard Business School Press.

Katz, D., & Kahn, R. I. (1951). Human organization and worker motivation. In L. R. Tripp (Ed.), *Industrial productivity* (pp. 146–171). Madison, WI: Industrial Relations Research Association.

Keirsey, D., & Bates, M. (1984). *Please understand me: Character and temperament types.* Del Mar, CA: Prometheus Nemesis.

Kim, J. (2007). *Action learning factors perceived by action learning participants in companies in South Korea.* Unpublished doctoral dissertation, University of Minnesota.

Kim, M. (2002). Leadership development using action learning: CJ case. *Fall proceedings of the Korean Association of Personnel Administration,* 205–227.

Kim, S. H. (2003). *An examination of action learning as a method for developing transformational leadership behaviors and characteristics.* Unpublished doctoral dissertation, George Washington University.

Kim, Y. (2003). *An examination and key success factors of practical learning methods in businesses: Focusing on the case of company T.* Unpublished master's thesis, Yonsei University, Republic of Korea.

Kirkpatrick, D. L. (1998). *Evaluating training programs: The four levels.* San Francisco: Berrett-Koehler.

Klein, K. J., & Harrison, D. A. (2007, November). On the diversity of diversity: Tidy logic, messier realities. *Academy of Management Perspectives, 21*(4), 26–33.

Knowles, M. S. (1970). *The modern practice of adult education: Andragogy vs. pedagogy.* New York: The Association Press.

Knowles, M. S. (1978). *The adult learner: A neglected species* (2nd ed.). Houston, TX: Gulf.

Knowles, M. S. (1980). *The modern practice of adult education: From pedagogy to andragogy* (Rev. ed.). New York: Cambridge Book Company.

Knowles, M. S. (1984a). *The adult learner: A neglected species* (3rd ed.). Houston, TX: Gulf.

Knowles, M. S. (1984b). *Andragogy in action: Applying modern principles of adult learning.* San Francisco: Jossey-Bass.

Knox, J. A. (2000). *Action dialogue: Developing leadership effectiveness at the individual and organizational levels through action learning.* Unpublished doctoral dissertation, California School of Professional Psychology, Los Angeles.

Koberg, D., & Bagnall, J. (1974). *The universal traveler: A soft-system guide to creativity, problem-solving and the process of reaching goals.* Los Altos, CA: William Kaufmann.

Kofman, F., & Senge, P. M. (1995). Communities of commitment: The heart of learning organizations. In S. Chawla & J. Renesch (Eds.), *Learning organizations: Developing cultures for tomorrow's workplace* (pp. 14–43). Portland, OR: Productivity Press.

Kolb, D. (1984). *Experiential learning: Experience as the source of learning and development.* Englewood Cliffs, NJ: Prentice Hall.

Kouzes, J. M., & Posner, B. Z. (1995). *The leadership challenge*. San Francisco: Jossey-Bass.

Kroeger, O. (with Thuesen, J. M.). (1992). *Type talk at work*. New York: Delacorte Press.

Lee, D. G., & Nelson-Neuhaus, K. (2003). *Presentations: How to calm down, think clearly, and captivate your audience*. Minneapolis, MN: Personnel Decisions International.

Lee, T. B. (2005). *A case study of an action learning program with regard to leadership behaviors and characteristics*. Unpublished doctoral dissertation, George Washington University.

Leonard, H. S. (2003). Leadership development in the post-industrial, postmodern, information age. *Consulting Psychology Journal, 55,* 3–14.

Leonard, H. S. (2005). When leadership development fails managers: Addressing the right gaps when developing leadership. In R. Kaiser (Ed.), *Filling the leadership pipeline* (pp. 69–84). Greensboro, NC: CCL Press.

Leonard, H. S., & Goff, M. (2003). Leadership development as an intervention for organizational transformation. *Consulting Psychology Journal, 55,* 58–67.

Levi, D. (2007). *Group dynamics for teams* (2nd ed.). Los Angeles: Sage.

Levinson, H. (1993). The practitioner as diagnostic instrument. In A. Howard (Ed.), *Diagnosis for organizational change* (pp. 27–52). New York: Guilford.

Lewin, K. (1931). The conflict between Aristotelian and Galilean modes of thought in contemporary psychology. *Journal of General Psychology, 5,* 141–177.

Lewin, K. (1943). Psychological ecology. In K. Lewin (Ed.), *Field theory in social science: Selected theoretical papers* (pp. 170–187). New York: Harper & Row.

Lewin, K. (1946). Action research and minority problems. *Journal of Social Issues, 2*(4), 34–46.

Lewin, K. (1948). Group decision and social change. In M. Gold (Ed.), *The complete social scientist: A Kurt Lewin reader* (pp. 265–284). Washington DC: American Psychological Association.

Lewin, K. (1961). Quasi-stationary social equilibria and the problem of permanent change. In W. G. Bennis, K. D. Benne, & R. Chin (Eds.), *The planning of change* (pp. 235–238). New York: Holt, Rinehart and Winston.

Likert, R. (1961). An emerging theory of organization, leadership and management. In L. Petrullo & B. M. Bass (Eds.), *Leadership and interpersonal behavior*. New York: Holt, Rinehart and Winston.

Limerick, D., Passfield, R., & Cunnington, B. (1994). Transformational change: Towards an action learning organization. *The Learning Organization, 1*(2), 29–40.

Linn, R. L., & Slinde, J. A. (1977). The determination of the significance of change between pre and posttesting periods. *Review of Educational Research, 47,* 121–150.

Lipnack, J., & Stamps, J. (1997). *Virtual teams: Reaching across space, time, and organizational technology.* New York: Wiley.

Lippitt, G., & Lippitt, R. (1986). *The consulting process in action* (2nd ed.). San Francisco: Pfeiffer.

Lowe, K. B., Kroeck, K. G., & Sivasubraniam, N. (1996). Effectiveness correlates of transformational and transactional leadership: A meta-analytic review of the MLQ literature. *The Leadership Quarterly, 7,* 385–425.

Luft, J. (1961). The Johari window. *Human Relations Training News, 5,* 6–7.

Lynham, S. A. (2000). Leadership development: A review of the theory and literature. In P. Kuchinke (Ed.), *Proceedings of Academy of Human Resource Development* (pp. 285–292). Baton Rouge, LA: AHRD.

Lyotard, J. (1992). *The postmodern explained.* Minneapolis: University of Minnesota Press.

Mahler, W. F., & Wrightnour, W. F. (1973). *Executive continuity: How to build and retain an effective management team.* Homewood, IL: Dow Jones-Irwin.

Maier, N. (1970). *Problem solving and creativity in individuals and groups.* Belmont, CA: Brooks/Cole.

Manz, C. C., & Sims, H. P. (2001). *The new superleadership.* San Francisco: Berrett-Koehler.

Marquardt, M. J. (1999). *Action learning in action: Transforming problems and people for world-class organizational learning.* Palo Alto, CA: Davies-Black.

Marquardt, M. J. (2000). Action learning and leadership. *The Learning Organization, 7*(5), 233–240.

Marquardt, M. J. (2002). *Building the learning organization: Mastering the 5 elements of corporate learning* (2nd ed.). Palo Alto, CA: Davies-Black.

Marquardt, M. J. (2004). *Optimizing the power of action learning: Solving problems and building leaders in real time.* Palo Alto, CA: Davies-Black.

Marquardt, M. J. (2005). *Leading with questions.* San Francisco: Wiley.

Marquardt, M. J., & Carter, T. (1998). Action learning and research at George Washington University. *Performance Improvement Quarterly, 11*(2), 59–71.

Marrow, A. J. (1969). *The practical theorist: The life and work of Kurt Lewin.* New York: Basic Books.

Marrow, A. J. (1972). The effects of participation on performance. In A. J. Marrow (Ed.), *The failure of success* (pp. 90–102). New York: Amacom.

Marshak, R. (2006). *Covert processes at work.* San Francisco: Berrett-Koehler.

McGill, I., & Beatty, L. (1995). *Action learning: A practitioner's guide* (2nd ed.). London: Kogan Page.

McGregor, D. (1960). *The human side of enterprise.* New York: McGraw-Hill.

McNulty, N., & Canty, G. R. (1995). Proof of the pudding. *Journal of Management Development 14*, 53–66.

Mead, M. (1964). *Continuities in cultural evolution.* New Haven, CT: Yale University Press.

Mezirow, J. (1991). *Transformative dimensions of adult learning.* San Francisco: Jossey-Bass.

Moreno, J. L. (1951). *Sociometry, experimental method and the science of society: An approach to a new political orientation.* Beacon, NY: Beacon House.

Murphy, K., & Cifuentes, L. (2001). Using web tools, collaborating and learning online. *Distance Education, 22,* 285–305.

Neary, D., & O'Grady, A. (2000). The role of training in developing global leaders: A case study at TRW Inc. *Human Resource Management, 39*(2), 185–193.

Nelson-Neuhaus, K. J., Skube, C. J., Lee, D. G., Stevens, L. A., Hellervik, L. W., Davis, B. L., & Gebelein, S. H. (Eds.). (2004). *Successful manager's handbook.* Minneapolis, MN: ePredix.

Nonaka, I. (1994). A dynamic theory of organizational knowledge creation. *Organization Science, 5*(1), 14–37.

Norcross, J. C., Beutler, L. E., & Levant, R. F. (2006). *Evidence-based practices in mental health: Debate and dialogue on the fundamental questions.* Washington, DC: American Psychological Association.

Odiorne, G. S. (1965). *Management by objectives: A system of managerial leadership.* New York: Pitman.

O'Neil, J. A. (1999). *The role of the learning advisor in action learning.* Unpublished doctoral dissertation, Teachers College, Columbia University.

The Organizational Development Institute. (2008). *The international registry of organization development professionals and organization development handbook.* Chesterfield, OH: Author.

Osborn, A. F. (1979). *Applied imagination.* New York: Scribner.

Page, S. E. (2007, November). Making the difference: Applying a logic of diversity. *Academy of Management Perspectives, 21*(4), 6–20.

Paris, S. G., & Winograd, P. (1990). How metacognition can promote learning and instruction. In B. F. Jones & L. Idol (Eds.), *Dimensions of thinking and cognitive instruction* (pp. 15–52). Hillsdale, NJ: Erlbaum.

Park, S. H. (2004). *A study on drawing critical success factors for planning and management of leadership development programs by applying action learning methods: Delphi method approach.* Unpublished master's thesis, Chon-Buk National University, Republic of Korea.

Patton, M. Q. (1990). *Qualitative evaluation and research methods.* Newbury Park, CA: Sage.

Patton, M. Q. (2002). *Qualitative research and evaluation methods* (3rd ed.). Thousand Oaks, CA: Sage.

Pavlov, I. P. (1927). *Conditioned reflexes.* (G. V. Anrep, Trans.). London: Oxford University Press. (Original work published 1927)

Pearce, C. L., & Conger, J. A. (Eds.). (2003). *Shared leadership: Reframing the hows and whys of leadership.* Thousand Oaks, CA: Sage.

Pearce, C. L., & Sims, H. P. (2002). Vertical versus shared leadership as predictors of the effectiveness of change management teams: An examination of aversive, directive, transactional, transformational, and empowering leader behavior. *Group Dynamics, 6,* 172–197.

Pearce, C. L., Sims, H. P., Cox, J. F., Ball, G., Schnell, E., Smith, K, & Trevino, L. (2003). Transactors, transformers, and beyond: A multi-method development of a theoretical typology of leadership. *Journal of Management Development, 2,* 273–301.

Pedlar, M. (1996). *Action learning for managers.* London: Lemos & Crane.

Pedler, M. (Ed.). (1983/1991/1997). *Action learning in practice* (1st, 2nd, and 3rd eds.). Aldershot, England: Gower.

Peterson, D. B., & Hicks, M. D. (1996). *Leader as coach: Strategies for coaching and developing others.* Minneapolis, MN: PDI.

Pfeffer, J., & Fong, C. (2002). The end of business schools? Less success than meets the eye. *Academy of Management Learning and Education, 1*(1), 78–95.

Phillips, J. J. (1997). *Handbook of training evaluation and measurement* (3rd ed.). Houston, TX: Gulf.

Piaget, J. (2000). *The psychology of the child* (H. Weaver, Trans.). New York: Basic Books. (Original work published in 1966)

Prochaska, J. O., DiClemente, C. C., & Norcross, J. C. (1992). In search of how people change: Applications to addictive behaviors. *The American Psychologist, 47,* 1102–1114.

Putnam, R. (2000). *Bowling alone.* New York: Simon & Schuster.

Raudenbush, L., Marquardt, M. J., & Walls, T. (2003). Growing leaders at the U.S. Department of Agriculture: A case study of leadership development using action learning. *Proceedings of the 2003 Annual AHRD Conference.* Minneapolis, MN: AHRD Publications.

Ray, M., & Myers, R. (1986). *Creativity in business.* New York: Doubleday.

Revans, R. (1980). *Action learning: New techniques for management.* London: Blond & Briggs.

Revans, R. (1982a). *The origins and growth of action learning.* Bromley, England: Chartwell-Bratt.

Revans, R. (1982b). What is action learning? *Journal of Management Development, 1*(3), 64–75.

Revans, R. (1998). *ABC of action learning: Empowering managers to act and learn from action.* London: Lemos & Crane.

Rice, A. K. (1958). *Productivity and social organization: The Ahmedabad experiment.* London: Tavistock.

Rimanoczy, I. (1999). *Action reflection learning: Application for individual learning.* Retrieved November 7, 2008, from http://www.limglobal.net/Readings/Articles/ARL%20-%20Application%20for%20Individual%20Learning%20-%20I%20Rimanoczy.doc

Robinson, R. (1953). *Plato's earlier dialectic* (2nd ed.). Oxford, England: Clarendon Press.

Rodgers, C. R. (1961). *On becoming a person: A therapist's view of psychotherapy.* New York: Houghton-Mifflin.

Roh, H. R. (2003). *The field research for identification of factors to facilitate transfer in the context of action learning.* Unpublished doctoral dissertation, Hanyang University, Republic of Korea.

Rothwell, W. J., Sullivan, R., & McLean, G. N. (1995). *Practicing organization development: A guide for consultants.* San Diego, CA: Pfeiffer.

Rummler, G. A., & Brache, G. P. (1995). *Improving performance: How to manage the white spaces on your organization chart.* San Francisco: Jossey-Bass.

Sackett, D. L., Rosenberg, W. M. C., Gray, J. A. M., Haynes, R. B., & Richardson, W. S.(1996), Evidence based medicine: What it is and what it isn't. *British Medical Journal, 312*(7023), 71–72.

Sandelands, E. (1998). Creating an online library to support a virtual learning community. *Internet Research, 8*(1), 75–84.

Sashkin, M. (1998). *Development and validity of the leadership profile* (Working paper 311-98). Washington, DC: George Washington University, Program in Human Resource Development.

Sashkin, M., Rosenbach, W. E., & Sashkin, M. G. (1998, August). *The leadership profile: Psychometric development of a leadership assessment tool and its use in leadership development.* Paper presented at the annual meeting of the Academy of Management, Boston.

Sashkin, M., & Sashkin, M. G. (2003). *Leadership that matters: The critical factors for making a difference in people's lives and organizations' success.* San Francisco: Berrett-Koehler.

Schaffer, R. H., & Thomson, H. A. (1992). Successful change programs begin with results. *Harvard Business Review, 70*(1), 80–89.

Schmidt, F. L., & Hunter, J. E. (1977). Development of a general solution to the problem of validity generalization. *Journal of Applied Psychology, 62,* 529–540.

Schön, D. A. (1987). *Educating the reflective practitioner.* San Francisco: Jossey-Bass.

Schwarz, R. (2002). *The skilled facilitator: A comprehensive resource for consultants, facilitators, managers, trainers, and coaches.* San Francisco: Jossey-Bass.

Senge, P. (1990). *The fifth discipline.* New York: Doubleday.

Sessa, V. I., & Taylor, J. J. (2000). *Executive selection: Strategies for success.* San Francisco: Jossey-Bass.

Shartle, C. L. (1950). Studies of leadership by interdisciplinary methods. In A. G. Grace (Ed.), *Leadership in American education.* Chicago: University of Chicago Press.

Skinner, B. F., & Ferster, C. B. (1957). *Schedules of reinforcement.* Boston: Appleton-Century-Croft.

Spector, B., & Beer, M. (1994). Beyond TQM programmes. *Journal of Organizational Change Management, 7*(2), 63–70.

Stacey, R. D. (1992). *Managing the unknowable: Strategic boundaries between order and chaos.* San Francisco: Jossey-Bass.

Stein, D. (2000). *Teaching critical reflection: Myths and realities, No. 7.* Columbus, OH: ERIC Clearing House on Adult, Career, and Vocational Education. (ERIC Document Reproduction Service No. ED445256)

Stogdill, R. M. (1950). Leadership, membership and organization. *Psychological Bulletin, 47,* 1–14.

Swanson, R. (1996). *Analysis for improving performance.* San Francisco: Berrett-Koehler.

Tamkin, P., Yarnall, J., & Kerrin, M. (2002). *Kirkpatrick and beyond: A review of models of training and evaluation* (IES Report). Grantham, England: Grantham Book Services.

Thomas, R. R. (2008). Consulting in the midst of differences: Related tensions and complexities. *Consulting Psychology Journal: Practice and Research, 60,* 203–214.

Thompson, B. (2004). *Exploratory and confirmatory factor analysis: Understanding concepts and applications.* Washington, DC: American Psychological Association.

Thorsrud, E., Sorensen, B., & Gustavsen, B. (1976). Sociotechnical approach to industrial democracy in Norway. In R. Dubin (Ed.), *Handbook of work organization and society* (pp. 648–687). Chicago: Rand McNally.

Tourloukis, P. (2002). Using action learning to develop human resource executives at General Electric. In Y. Boshyk (Ed.), *Action learning worldwide: Experiences of leadership and organizational development* (pp. 90–109). New York: Palgrave Macmillan.

Trist, E., & Bamforth, K. (1951, January). Some social and psychological consequences of the longwall method of coal-getting. *Human Relations, 4,* 1–38.

Tuckman, R., & Jensen, M. (1977). Stages of small group development revisited. *Group and Organizational Studies, 2,* 419–427.

Tyre, M. J., & von Hippel, E. (1997). The situated nature of adaptive learning in organizations. *Organization Science, 8*(1), 71–83.

Usher, R., & Edwards, R. (1994). *Postmodernism and education.* New York: Routledge.

Vaill, P. B. (1996). *Learning as a way of being: Strategies for survival in a world of permanent whitewater.* San Francisco: Jossey-Bass.

Van Schuyver, M. E. (2004). *Action learning: Set member learning experiences.* Unpublished doctoral dissertation, Fielding Graduate Institute.

Van Woerkom, M. (2003). *Critical reflection at work: Bridging individual and organizational learning.* Enschende, The Netherlands: Twente University.

von Bertalanffy, L. (1963). *General systems theory.* New York: Braziller.

Vroom, V., & Yetton, P. (1973). *Leadership and decision making*. Pittsburgh, PA: University of Pittsburgh Press.

Waddill, D. D. (2001). Action e-learning: An exploratory case study of action learning applied online. *Human Resource Development International, 9*, 157–171.

Waddill, D., & Marquardt, M. (2004). Action learning and the schools of adult learning. *Human Resource Development Review, 2*, 406–429.

Wagner, K. V. (2006). *Kurt Lewin quotes*. Retrieved December 29, 2006, from http://psychology.about.com/od/psychologyquotes/a/lewinquotes.htm

Weick, C. E. (1979). *The social psychology of organizing*. New York: McGraw-Hill.

Weick, C. E. (1995). *Sensemaking in organizations: Foundations for organizational science*. Thousand Oaks, CA: Sage.

Weinstein, K. (1995). *Action learning: A journey in discovery and development*. London: HarperCollins.

Weinstein, K. (1997). A dialogue with participants. In A. Mumford (Ed.), *Action learning at work* (pp. 340–366). Aldershot, England: Gower.

Whitney, D., & Giovagnoli, M. (1997). *75 cage-rattling questions to change the way you work*. New York: McGraw-Hill.

Yang, B. (2005). Factor analytic methods. In R. A. Swanson & E. F. Holton III (Eds.), *Research in organizations: Foundations and methods of inquiry* (pp. 181–200). San Francisco: Berrett-Koehler.

Yorks, L., O'Neil, J., & Marsick, V. (Eds.). (1999). *Action learning: Successful strategies for individual, team and organizational development*. San Francisco: Berrett-Koehler.

Zander, R. S., & Zander, B. (2002). *The art of possibility: Transforming professional and personal life*. New York: Penguin.

Zuber-Skerritt, O. (1995). Developing a learning organization through management education by action learning. *Learning Organization, 2*(2), 36–54.

Index

About the Authors

Michael J. Marquardt, EdD, is known throughout the world for his knowledge and expertise regarding Action Learning and learning organizations. In addition to authoring 20 books, 4 on Action Learning, Dr. Marquardt has introduced Action Learning to thousands of leaders and hundreds of organizations around the world since 1995, including Marriott, DuPont, Alcoa, Boeing, Caterpillar, United Nations Development Program, the U.S. Department of Agriculture, IBM, Nokia, Constellation, Samsung, Hong Kong Transit, and Siemens as well as government agencies in Singapore, Mauritius, Japan, Canada, Qatar, China, Korea, and Brazil.

Currently a professor of human resource development and international affairs at George Washington University, Dr. Marquardt has held a number of senior management, training, and marketing positions with organizations such as Grolier, Association Management Inc., Overseas Education Fund, TradeTec, and the U.S. Office of Personnel Management. His achievements and leadership have been recognized though numerous awards, including the International Practitioner of the Year Award from the American Society for Training and Development.

H. Skipton Leonard, PhD, trained as a social and organizational psychologist. Dr. Leonard has devoted his career to helping individuals, teams, and organizations achieve their goals and accomplish their missions by learning how to be more adaptive, creative, and innovative. A noted authority on leadership and team development, he has coached and trained thousands of executives, managers, and professionals and their teams.

Dr. Leonard's consulting clients have included Microsoft, Dell, HP, Boeing, Chrysler, Bechtel, AllState, United Services Automobile Association, American Express, Bank of America, Shell, AstraZenica, the International Monetary Fund, the World Bank, and U.S. government organizations such as the Army, the Postal Service, the General Services Administration, the Department of Agriculture, and the Government Accountability Office. A leader in his field, he is the author of 3 books and over 50 articles in refereed journals, is a fellow of the American Psychological Association (APA), and past president of the Society of Consulting Psychology. He was also the founding editor of an APA-published journal, *Consulting Psychology Journal.*

In addition to his role as executive director for the World Institute for Action Learning, Dr. Leonard is currently on the faculties of the Carey School of Business at Johns Hopkins University and the School of Human and Organizational Learning at George Washington University.

Arthur M. Freedman, MBA, PhD, is a principal in Freedman, Leonard & Marquardt Consultancy and chair of the research committee for the nonprofit World Institute for Action Learning. He earned both his BS and his MBA at Boston University's College of Business Administration and his PhD in personality and clinical psychology at the University of Chicago. He has been a member of the NTL Institute since 1969.

Dr. Freedman is a visiting scholar at the University of Pennsylvania. He has consulted throughout North America as well as Estonia, Latvia, Lithuania, Serbia, Sweden, Germany, Russia (and the former Soviet Union), Vietnam, Singapore, and Zimbabwe. He is a fellow of the American Psychological Association's (APA's) Division 13 (Society of Consulting Psychology) and a fellow of APA's Division 52 (International Psychology). He is a past president of the Society of Psychologists in Management. Dr. Freedman is a member of the Board of Advisors for the National Hispanic Institute and cofounder of the Nieto–Freedman Center for Organization and Community Development. He is a member of the editorial boards of the *Journal of Applied Behavioral Science* and the *Consulting Psychology Journal.*

Dr. Freedman received the RHR International Award for Excellence in Consulting Psychology from APA's Division 13 in 1994. He received the Most Outstanding Article award from the editorial board of the *Consulting Psychology Journal* in 1998, for his article "Pathways and Crossroads to Institutional Leadership." In 2007, he received the Harry and Miriam Levinson Award for Exceptional Contributions to Consulting Organizational Psychology.

Claudia C. Hill is an executive consultant and the director of Action Learning at Personnel Decisions International (PDI), where she is responsible for design, development, and global delivery of a variety of leadership development learning systems. Ms. Hill's area of special expertise is experiential learning. She has led and designed Action Learning or simulation-based programs for organizations around the globe. She has 28 years of experience in the design, delivery, and evaluation of strategic performance improvement interventions to her client interactions. Ms. Hill is the author of PDI's Active Leader Workshop, which features a unique large-scale business simulation. In her leadership role, she has delivered the program in 20 countries and trained delivery teams who offer the workshop globally. An active researcher in the world of Action Learning, Ms. Hill is currently a board member for the World Institute of Action Learning. Her publications explore theory building for global virtual teams, simulation-enhanced learning, and Action Learning–leadership development systems. She was the lead author of *A Consultant's Guide to Action Learning* (2006, PDI). Ms. Hill has served as a keynote speaker at international conferences focusing on Action Learning. She has a BA in economics and statistical analysis, and is a PhD candidate in the University of Minnesota program for human resource development.